500 MORE
LITTLE-KNOWN FACTS
in
MORMON HISTORY

500 MORE
LITTLE-KNOWN FACTS
in
MORMON HISTORY

GEORGE W.
GIVENS

BONNEVILLE BOOKS
Springville, Utah

ISBN: 1-55517-791-3
e.1

Published by Bonneville Books
Imprint of Cedar Fort Inc.
www.cedarfort.com

Distributed by:

Cover design by Nicole Shaffer
Cover design © 2004 by Lyle Mortimer

Printed in the United States of America
10 9 8 7 6 5 4 3 2 1
Printed on acid-free paper

Library of Congress Control Number: 2004110356

Dedication

Published posthumously and dedicated with deep love and gratitude to our much adored husband and father.

Thank you for your constant devotion to your family and for instilling in us your own passion for learning. We miss you and look forward to our eventual reunion.

Acknowledgments

While acknowledging that the volume you hold in your hands is not a scholarly tome, reaction to the first volume suggests that it fulfills a need for lay lovers of Church history. It is to such members, including my wife and children, who were always "interested" in the facts I uncovered, that I must acknowledge a gratitude for keeping me enthused even after I was diagnosed with cancer. Now they are encouraging me to continue work on one of the many other projects I have started, aware of not only the testimony-building aspects of delving into Church history but of the curative powers of the gospel.

Oh yes—another acknowledgement. My daughter Bobbie should probably be listed as a coauthor. Not only has she edited each of my works, but when I run into dead ends in my research, her expert use of the Internet either sets me straight or tells me when it is time to "give up" on some facts.

And finally, my deepest gratitude to all of you who were so complimentary about my first book, which led to this one. My greatest pleasure has been in hearing teachers of Church history tell me they have been using my book in their classes. Such humbling experiences cause me to remember to acknowledge the hand of our Heavenly Father in all things and thank Him for giving me the "extra" time to finish what I have always considered to be for His glory and honor.

Table of Contents

Introduction

As may be deduced by the word "More," this is actually volume 2, following *500 Little-known Facts in Mormon History*, published by Cedar Fort in 2002. This second volume of facts was compiled as a result of the enthusiastic reception of the first book and requests that I try to find another 500 facts. Although compiling these facts was enjoyable, it was not always easy. As I pointed out in the first book, "facts" can certainly be disputable and subject not only to changing interpretations, but to the accuracy of the sources. Researching the latter can become very frustrating and time-consuming. Let me offer three examples of such "facts."

One well-known author mentioned, without any reference, that Sidney Rigdon applied to be a territorial governor of Utah. I could find such information in no other source. Most of Sidney's life is well documented and it seems obvious he would have had neither the time nor inclination to fill such a position.

Another "fact," again listed without a reference, concerned a wagon train of "fifteen hundred disillusioned" Saints who left Utah for the East in 1860. Such a remarkable "fact" obviously tempted me to spend considerable time trying to run down the source of this information. Certainly such a wagon train of "disillusioned" Mormons would be well-known in Church history, but I could find no other evidence that it ever existed.

The third "fact" concerned Mt. Palomar in California. One of my sources factually mentioned it was named after the "Mormon prophet, Joseph Smith," until a petition in 1901 restored the original Spanish name. Some time-consuming research revealed that the mountain was indeed once named Smith Mountain, but it was for a former sailor named Smith who was the first to build a home on the mountain.

These are only three of many other examples of such fiction I encountered. It is my prayerful wish that none slipped through the research crack to become a little more imbedded in Mormon History.

1

The Beginning
(1801-1831)

More Than Courage! (1801)

Whitingham, Vermont is known for little more than being the birthplace of Brigham Young. Perhaps that is why it was felt necessary to put up two markers indicating that fact. One marker, erected by the Church and Young's descendants, consists of nearly ninety words and succinctly lays out the pertinent facts of Brigham's life. The second marker, however, is the one that attracts attention, although it consists of only fifteen words and does not indicate who paid for its erection. It was put in place sometime before the twentieth century and reads, "Brigham Young, Born on this spot 1801, A man of much courage and superb equipment."

Should Have Smothered Him! (1805)

It may or may not be a fact, but that the story exists is certain. When the Prophet Joseph was born in 1805, the attending doctor was supposedly Dr. Joseph Adam Denison, who kept a diary. Many years later a descendant mentioned a story his aunt told him of cleaning out Dr. Denison's home after his death and finding that diary. Unfortunately, she disposed of the diary but read it first and noted the birth of the Mormon prophet. Under a later date, after the Prophet Joseph became known and anti-Mormonism had developed, the doctor appended an entry saying, "If I had known how he was going to turn out I'd have smothered the little cuss."

1

Who Was Aagaat Bakka? (1823)

Most Latter-day Saints would recognize her by her adopted name—Ellen Saunders. She was one of the three women accompanying the pioneers to Utah in 1847 as a wife of Heber C. Kimball. Ellen was born in Norway in 1823 and given the name of Aagaat Ysteinsdatter Bakka, after which her parents migrated to America. When her mother died, her father scattered his several children among relatives. Ellen received her Americanized name from her adopted family. Embracing the gospel after hearing it from traveling missionaries, she moved to Nauvoo where she met and married Heber with whom she eventually had five children. Her daughter Rosalia was the last of Heber's sixty-five children to die—in 1950.

The Autopsy (1823)

The Prophet Joseph often spoke against the dangerous practices of what were termed "heroic" medical procedures common in the early nineteenth century. One of the earliest events that convinced Joseph to encourage the use of herbal or natural healing was undoubtedly the death and autopsy of his brother Alvin when Joseph was almost eighteen. A quack doctor had given Alvin a dose of calomel (mercurous chloride, one of the most deadly medical treatments) for a simple case of colic. The calomel was found still lodged in Alvin's intestines, having caused gangrene. A Dr. Robinson who performed the autopsy gave a lecture to some younger physicians about the case, referring to Joseph's beloved brother as "murdered" by a "careless quack." Joseph would not forget that.

The Forgotten Affidavit (1825)

In 1834, E. D. Howe, a Painesville, Ohio editor, published *Mormonism Unvailed*, a vicious anti-Mormon book that to a large degree formed the basis for most of the anti-Mormon books that followed. Much of the book was taken up with affidavits supplied by D. P. Hurlbut, who had previously been excommunicated from the LDS Church for immorality. He was then hired by anti-Mormons to destroy the reputation of the Smith family and attempted to do so with very questionable "affidavits." He asked some of the residents in the Palmyra area to sign papers denouncing the family's reputation. Quite forgotten is an affidavit composed nine years earlier in 1825 by Dr. Gain Robinson, an uncle of the Smith family physician. In an attempt to aid the Smiths in preventing the loss of their farm, he gathered within an hour sixty signatures attesting to the Smith family's good character.

"Thrash the Stumps with Him!" (1827)

After years of preparation, the Prophet Joseph was informed that he would be able to obtain the plates on September 22, 1827. As he prepared to recover the plates, he was aware of Samuel Lawrence, "a neighbor who had pretensions to seership and knew about the plates and the annual visits." Lawrence was one of the local "money-diggers," and had associated with Joseph on such occasions. According to Joseph Knight, Joseph feared Lawrence might cause trouble in his recovery of the plates. He "therefore sent his father up to Sam's as he Called him near night to see if there was any signs of his going away that night. He told his father to stay till near Dark and if he saw any signs of his going you tell him if I find him there I will thrash the stumps with him." Lawrence did not show up.

It Wasn't that Easy! (1827)

In spite of a general belief that Joseph had little difficulty translating by using the Urim and Thummim found with the plates, such was not the case. Eyewitnesses reveal that Joseph simply didn't know how. On the day he received the plates he told Joseph Knight, "Now they are written in characters and I want them translated." Three months after Joseph received them his father wrote, "Not being able to read the characters, (Joseph) made a copy of some of them which he showed to some of the most learned men." Both Joseph Knight and Lucy said that the characters that Martin Harris took to Professor Anthon in New York City were "to see if he could get them translated." Joseph later admitted that on the sheet Martin took he had only translated "some of them." It was true the trip fulfilled an Isaiah prophecy, but seemingly Joseph wanted some verification by known experts.

Two Sacred Interpreters or Three? (1827)

The Urim and Thummim assigned to Joseph were the same interpreters received by the Brother of Jared on Mount Simeon. Abraham received a different Urim and Thummim while he was in Ur, of the Caldees. Martin Harris said that the prophet also possessed a seer stone by which he was able to translate, as well as with the Urim and Thummin. Whereas the Urim and Thummim were composed of two crystal stones set in the rims of a bow (and detachable), the seer stone was a small, oval, kidney-shaped stone. This was separate and distinct from the Urim and Thummim that were delivered to the angel after the translation. The seer stone is still in the possession of the Church President.

Who Was the First Missionary? (1829)

One of those bits of common knowledge in Church history is that Samuel Smith was the first missionary in this dispensation—but was he? According to the employees at Grandin's print shop, the printing of 5,000 copies of the Book of Mormon extended over several months from late 1829 to early 1830. Before the copies of the Book of Mormon were bound and available to the general public, "interested parties" were taking extracts to share the contents with others. According to his own reminiscences, one of those parties was Solomon Chamberlain. Taking sixty-four pages from the Grandin press, he traveled 800 miles across Western New York and into upper Canada, preaching the Book of Mormon in probably the first missionary trek of the Restoration. He was about forty years of age at the time, and he lived and died in the faith.

Not Translated in Sequence (1829)

It is commonly assumed that when Martin Harris lost the manuscript containing the first 400 years of Book of Mormon history, Joseph proceeded to translate the plates of Nephi that covered the same time period and went on to translate the rest of the records. Such is not the case. After the tragic loss and in the winter of 1829, Joseph and Emma took up the translation around the first part of the Book of Mosiah where Martin had left off. When Oliver became Joseph's scribe, they continued to the end of the Book of Mormon before returning to begin work on 1 Nephi around June. It apparently took some time before the Lord revealed what Joseph should do about the gap left by the loss of the manuscript.

Lucy's Losses (1829)

When Joseph's oldest brother, Alvin, died in 1829, the entire family felt the loss keenly, especially his mother Lucy. Most Latter-day Saints are painfully aware of the losses Lucy later suffered in the deaths of her son Don Carlos and her husband in the early days of Nauvoo, and then her sons Joseph, Hyrum, and Samuel in 1844, leaving only one son, William, and three daughters. Actually, Lucy lost two other sons, making a total of seven sons lost out of eight. Her first-born son died at birth in 1797 without even being given a name. She lost another son, Ephraim, in 1810 when the infant was only eleven days old. Lucy's consolation in the survival of one son was tempered by the fact that it was he who had caused both Lucy and Joseph the greatest amount of grief because of his selfishness and quick temper.

An Appropriate Name (1830)

July 19, 1830 is a date with little significance to most Latter-day Saints, but it is quite significant to a family named Harris. On that day, Parna Chapelle Harris gave birth to the first Latter-day Saint born after the organization of the Church in April. The father was Emer Harris, brother to Martin, who was one of the three witnesses. Emer was one of the first converts, having received from his brother the first bound Book of Mormon after it came from the press in Palmyra (that copy is now owned by the Deseret Book Company). Although the parents were not baptized until a few months later, they were converted enough to name the child a most appropriate name, which he carried until his death in Salt Lake City in 1909—Joseph Mormon Harris.

The First Woman Suffrage (1830)

When the organization of the Church of Jesus Christ of Latter-day Saints took place in that cabin in Fayette, New York in April 1830, the questions Joseph Smith posed were whether the forty to fifty people present were willing to accept him as their spiritual leader and to be organized as a religious body under the laws of the State of New York. Breaking with the tradition of such organizations being established by men only, the minutes of that historic meeting recorded that "unanimous consent being given, the purpose of the meeting was effected." That "unanimous" consent in the first body of Latter-day Saint voters included several women.

Does It Really Matter? (1830)

Occasionally an individual will question the credibility of the Church by attempting to demonstrate alleged cover-ups in its history, even though the "cover-up" has no rationalization. Such is the case in the charge that the organization of the Church was not at Fayette but in the Smith family home in Manchester. Michael Marquardt points to the sections in the Doctrine and Covenants that, without a date other than April 1830, name Manchester as the location. A little more compelling is the argument that references in the *Evening and the Morning Star* before 1834 refer to Manchester as the location. Less convincing is the reason given for the change—somehow it would confuse creditors and thus the new church could escape some of its debts. This charge, however, lacks credibility when there is no explanation as to what difference this should make or why the Church would still be interested in a cover-up of such information as the place of organization.

No Celibacy for Sidney (1830)

Most Saints are familiar with the story of the mission of Sidney Rigdon, Parley P. Pratt, and Leman Copley to a Shaker community not far from Kirtland in 1830, but know little more about it than is found in Pratt's autobiography: "They utterly refused to hear or obey the gospel." The pocket journal of Ashbel Kitchell, "First Elder" of the Shaker community, gives us a little more insight into the mission and its failure. Kitchell recorded that the doctrines of Mormonism were investigated but "we found that the life of self-denial [celibacy] corresponded better with the life of Christ, than Mormonism." When Sidney Rigdon said he did not bear the "cross" and did not expect to, Kitchell "set him without the paling of the Church, and told him I could not look on him as a Christian."

Mrs. Hubble and the Peep Stone (1831)

Section 28 of the Doctrine and Covenants, which states that only the Prophet Joseph was to receive revelations for the Church, came as a result of Hiram Page claiming to receive revelation through a peep stone in his possession. A few months later in February 1831, a woman by the name of Hubble began to make similar claims of revelations through a peep stone in her possession. Because some members were still deceived, the Lord gave another revelation in which He stated that Joseph Smith was the only person "appointed unto you to receive commandments and revelations until he be taken, if he abide in me." Unfortunately, Mrs. Hubble was not the last to deceive members, but she did become one of the least known.

2

Seeking Sanctuary
(1832-1838)

Sealed Up to Eternal Damnation! (1832)

George A. Smith joined the Latter-day Saints in 1832 and within seven years was ordained one of the Twelve Apostles. Before his conversion he was active in the Presbyterian Church. During a revival, at the age of fourteen, he witnessed his friends sitting on the "anxious" bench, waiting to be led away to be preached to by an assistant minister until they were "anxious" enough to publicly renounce the world, the flesh, and the devil. When George repeatedly refused to take the "anxious" bench, the Reverend Mr. Cannon pointed his finger at George as he now sat alone in the gallery. "O sinner, I seal you up to eternal damnation, in the name of Jesus Christ." This was done nine times—George soon joined the Saints.

The Last Bison in Utah (1832)

When the Saints made their initial journey west in 1847, bison herds on the trail east of the Rocky Mountains were so numerous that the Saints had to send advance parties ahead to clear the trail so the teams could pass. Frank G. Roe, author of *The North American Buffalo*, noted that during the winter of 1848-49, "There are no buffalo among the 1,229 wild species slain by the Mormon hunting companies for the extermination of wild beasts" in the Salt Lake Valley. Ute Chief Walker told the Saints, however, that when he was young the buffalo were "more plentiful than Mormon cattle."

There are many legends about their demise, but the most logical seems to be that they never were plentiful in Utah, and by 1832, with the arrival of trappers and the acquisition of horses and firearms by the natives, they were soon extinct and thus a factor in the starving conditions of the early Mormon pioneers.

Only a Village Carpenter (1832)

Before Brigham Young became a member of the LDS Church in April 1832, he was an uneducated carpenter, known only by a few friends in and around Auburn, New York. Although some of those friends, such as William H. Seward, Isaac Singer, and Henry Wells of Wells-Fargo, would become famous in their own right, for the rest of his life Brigham was convinced that without the gospel of Jesus Christ, he would have remained unknown. Years later he told his daughter that without the gospel he would "have been today, but a carpenter in a country village. I am what Mormonism has made me." Once, while Territorial Governor of Utah, a visitor addressed him with all of his high-sounding titles. Brigham interrupted to say, "Sir, you have omitted my most cherished titles: Carpenter, Painter, and Glazier."

"I Opened My Mouth" (1832)

Thirty-eight years after his baptism, Brigham Young delivered a talk in the Tabernacle in Salt Lake City on the subject of "preaching the gospel." This was only one of more than 800 sermons he had delivered, and yet he noted that he "never felt free from this timidity when rising for that purpose." Nevertheless, he was considered by even visitors as one of the best of all Latter-day Saint speakers. He recalled the very first talk he had given, only a week after his baptism in 1832. In that first public address, like all those that followed, he never prepared nor made notes. Admitting that he was "but a child" in public speaking, he recalled that his first discourse occupied over an hour. He said, "I opened my mouth and the Lord filled it."

A Greater Understanding (1832)

The 1832 revelation specifying the three degrees of glory led to the assumption by early members, including the Prophet Joseph, that the celestial kingdom was reserved only for those who had been baptized into the restored Church. Four years later, while reflecting on the earlier death of his brother Alvin, who had not been baptized, Joseph received a more complete understanding of those who died "without a knowledge of the gospel, but would have received it if they had been permitted to tarry." They, as well as children who had died before the age of accountability, would also inherit the celestial kingdom.

Joseph's Money-Digging (1833)

One of the most "damning" charges critics have been able to level against the young Joseph Smith regards his practice of money digging. This charge stemmed from a series of anti-Mormon affidavits gathered around Palmyra by an apostate, Philastus Hurlbut, who was hired by anti-Mormons to destroy the Prophet's reputation in 1833. Although still used as a criticism by many, most non-members as well as members are not aware that the practice of money digging was common in upstate New York in the early nineteenth century, with as many as 400 teams scouring the Finger Lake hills about that time for gold and silver. This author was raised in that area and well remembers the "Winchell Holes" on his family's farm made by a money-digger from Vermont, a man that one nineteenth-century writer claimed was one source of the "monster—Mormonism."

An Unsound Temple (1833)

Recent publicity about the reconstruction of the Nauvoo Temple and its high-quality original dramatically illustrates the less-than-quality work in the Kirtland Temple. The first temple was originally planned to be of brick, but that plan was abandoned when sufficient bricks could not be produced. A new convert, Artemus Millett, who had more experience in building than most of the brethren, took over and supervised the building of rubble walls covered with stucco to mask the unevenness of the stones. Unfortunately, the extra weight and inadequate foundations have caused the building to settle and the walls to crack. In addition, inadequate and defective girders, possessing only one-sixth of the modern code-required strength, have given way, making necessary the addition of supports.

When the Stars Fell (1833)

Latter-day Saints were not the only ones to witness this event—it was noted with interest throughout the United States. It occurred on the night of November 13, 1833, only nine days after the Saints had been driven from Jackson County, Missouri. Parley P. Pratt described what was witnessed: "Two o'clock the next morning we were called up [by] the cry of signs from the heavens. We arose, and to our great astonishment all the firmament seemed enveloped in splendid fireworks, as if every star in the broad expanse had been hurled from its course . . . thousands of bright meteors were shooting though space in every direction . . . [and] only closed by the dawn of the rising sun." Many gentiles took the unusual meteorite shower as the end of the world, but the Saints interpreted it as a sign of God's displeasure with the human race for driving the Saints from their "New Jerusalem."

A World Constitution? (1833)

After the Saints had been driven from Jackson County and were suffering continuing persecution in Missouri, the Prophet Joseph received a revelation revealing the reasons for their chastisement, but also detailing the purpose of the U.S. Constitution. That revelation, contained in Section 101 of the Doctrine and Covenants, states in verses 77-80 that the Constitution was written and should "be maintained for the rights and protection of all flesh." Convinced that the Lord's use of "all flesh" refers to the entire world, many Latter-day Saint leaders have used this revelation to justify American involvement in foreign wars when "rights" of other nationalities were being infringed. B. H. Roberts was one of the first, when at the age of sixty he joined the military to serve as a chaplain in World War I.

Checking Out Joseph's Character (1834)

In the early days of the Church, anti-Mormons often visited Palmyra to check out the character of the Prophet Joseph as remembered by the Smith family neighbors. Far less known is the fact that even some members of the Quorum of the Twelve did the same thing. In 1834 the two senior members of the original Twelve, Thomas B. Marsh and David W. Patten, did exactly that. After visiting Martin Harris and the Hill Cumorah, they traveled though the town of Palmyra, going "from house to house," inquiring into the character of their prophet as remembered by his old neighbors. Unlike the alleged critical comments recorded by later visitors, Marsh and Patten reported that they were told that as a youth Joseph had been "as good as young men in general."

A Law or a Covenant? (1834)

Although the concept of tithing seems to have been introduced in Kirtland in 1831—"it is a day for the tithing of my people" (D&C 64:23)—scholars and Church authorities normally recognize that the law of tithing was not introduced until July 8, 1838, at Far West (D&C 119). However, on November 29, 1834, Joseph recorded in his journal in Kirtland that he "united in prayer with Brother Oliver" and thanked the Lord for a recent loan from the East of more than $400 and agreed to enter into a covenant with the Lord. If the Lord would continue to prosper the Saints, "we will give a tenth, to be bestowed upon the poor in his Church or as He shall command." Andrew Jenson referred to this covenant as "the first introduction of the law of tithing among the Latter-day Saints." Perhaps it had to be canonized.

Maximilian's Limited Admiration (1834)

Prince Maximilian of Austria was traveling in the frontier of America in 1834 when he encountered in Clay County, Missouri, the Saints who had recently been expelled from Jackson County. Learning of their situation he commented on the "great disgrace to the administration of justice in this country, which calls itself the only free country in the world." Apparently the Prince's admiration was false or he changed his views on freedom over the next several years. This was the same Prince whom Napoleon established as Emperor of Mexico during the American Civil

War. When Napoleon withdrew his troops at the urging of the victorious Union, Maximilian was deposed and executed by the Mexicans, who wanted the same freedom Maximilian had seemed to admire when he encountered the persecuted Saints thirty-three years earlier.

Joseph's Ordained Successor (1834)

The succession crisis of 1844, in which Brigham Young prevailed, might have turned out differently if David Whitmer had not been excommunicated in 1838. Only a month before Whitmer's excommunication in April, the Prophet Joseph, in a meeting of the High Council at Far West, related the history of the ordination of David Whitmer "to be a leader, or prophet to this Church, which (ordination) was on conditions that he (J. Smith Jr.) did not live to God himself." That ordination, Joseph mentioned, had taken place in July 1834, but had been made known to only a few and had not been published for the entire Church membership. It is unlikely that David Whitmer himself really understood the significance of the ordination or he might have conducted himself in a manner that would not have brought about his excommunication only a month after Joseph had affirmed his ordination.

"Grieving Away the Spirit" (1834)

Physical manifestations such as swooning, fits, spasms, and so forth normally associated with camp meetings were a problem for early Mormon Church leaders. The first permanent High Council in the Church was organized at Kirtland on February 17, 1834, and its first case was that of Elder Curtis Hodge, Sr., who, while speaking in a meeting, had gone into a Methodist spasm, shouting and screaming in such a manner that one of the elders felt compelled to rebuke him. The High

Council determined that good witnesses had sustained the charges in the case, that Elder Hodge should have confessed when rebuked by Elder Ezra Thayer, and "if he had the spirit of the Lord . . . he must have abused it and grieved it away."

A Prestigious Missouri Friend (1834)

The violence and extent of the Missouri persecutions project an image of universal hatred of the Saints by all residents of the State. Such was not the case, and a classic example was Col. Michael Arthur who lived in Clay County where many of the Saints found temporary refuge after their expulsion from Jackson County. He employed several of the refugees in building a home, and for the next four years he was their defender, writing to the State Legislature to request protection for the Saints from the "demons" persecuting them. After their surrender at Far West, he made a futile demand that the Mormons have their arms returned so they could defend themselves. Most of his efforts were in vain, but they assured him what should be a place of honor in Mormon memory.

Recently Lost Scripture (1835)

It should be in the Pearl of Great Price, but Joseph never completed the translation and it was consequently never published. It is called the Book of Joseph and was on one of the rolls of papyrus purchased from Michael Chandler in Kirtland, Ohio in 1835. One roll that was translated and published was the Book of Abraham, now in the Pearl of Great Price. The only thing we know about the Book of Joseph, the author or which was a great-grandson of Abraham, comes to us from Oliver Cowdery, who was one of the scribes for the Prophet Joseph. He said it contained information on the Creation, the Fall, the nature of the Godhead, and the final judgment. The original roll ended up in the hands of apostates and was possibly destroyed in the Chicago fire in 1871.

Bonds for Faithful Performance! (1835)

The first Quorum of the Twelve was organized in February 1835 and one of their first duties, as is commonly known, was to perform missionary work. Although they were called by inspiration, the Prophet Joseph knew that even apostles might fall (as several did) and take advantage of their fellow men. Less known to members today is what Joseph did to protect members and investigators from being wronged out of their property. According to John Taylor, not then a member of the first Quorum but soon to be called, Joseph required the Twelve "to give $2,000 bonds for the faithful performance of their duty." This, according to Taylor, was a "precautionary measure to keep the Saints from being imposed upon."

Not the First Time (1836)

When President Spencer W. Kimball received the revelation in 1978 granting the privilege of holding the priesthood to all worthy male members, it was assumed by most Saints that this would be a "first" for Blacks. It wasn't. In September 1832, Ezekiel Roberts was baptized a member of the Church and on March 3, 1836, he was ordained an elder. Laboring as an undertaker in Nauvoo in 1841, he was ordained a Seventy on April 4. As a faithful Saint in Salt Lake City, he and his wife managed the Farnham Hotel (later called the Denver House). In 1883 he was a member of the Third Quorum of Seventy and at the age of 73 was called on a mission to Canada. Two weeks after his return from Canada he was performing missionary work in Ohio when he died on Christmas Day in 1884.

Four More Brighams (1836)

When a twin boy was born to Mary Ann Angell, Brigham Young's second wife, in Kirtland in 1836, he was named Brigham, Jr. Without doubt, Brigham never thought he would have another son named after him. Actually he had three more! In Nauvoo he married his first plural wife, Lucy Ann Decker, and their first son, Brigham Heber, born in 1845, was one of the first children born into polygamy, if not the first. The following year, only weeks before leaving Nauvoo, another wife, Margaret Pierce Young, gave birth to Brigham Morris. Eight years later in Salt Lake City, the fourth little Brigham, Brigham Oscar, was born to Harriett Cook Young. All four "Brighams" lived into the twentieth century, dying firm in the gospel.

Hardly a Coincidence (1836)

When Elijah appeared in the Kirtland Temple on April 3, 1836, to turn the hearts of the children to the fathers, inspiring the Saints to search out the records of the dead, few apparently asked themselves how that would be done. But the Lord made provisions. As though anticipating that momentous event, in July of the following year, England began the civil registration of births, marriages, and deaths. Seeing this, American States began keeping vital records, starting with Massachusetts in 1841. Four years later the first genealogical society in the Western Hemisphere was organized in Boston. Today there are over 2,000 such societies in North America alone.

The Prayer Was a Trial of Faith (1836)

Most Saints are familiar with Section 109 of the Doctrine and Covenants—the Dedicatory Prayer for the Kirtland

Temple. Most assume it was recorded during or after the prayer was given. It wasn't! The day before the dedication, March 26, 1836, the Prophet Joseph met with Oliver Cowdery, Sidney Rigdon, W. A. Cowdery, and Warren Parrish, when he apparently received the revelation, after which it was put in print. It was from this printed copy that Joseph "read" the prayer the following day. Speaking nearly 30 years later in Ogden City, George A. Smith said the "reading" of the prayer "was a trial of faith to many. 'How can it be that the prophet should read a prayer?' What an awful trial it was, for the Prophet to read a prayer!"

Never Again! (1836)

In 1836 the Quorum of the Twelve Apostles met at the home of Heber C. Kimball in Kirtland, Ohio. This was the worst of times for the Church in Kirtland as there was a great deal of contention, with several of the authorities soon to apostatize. Brigham Young prayed that the entire Quorum would not meet again until it could meet in peace and union. This turned out to be the last time the entire Quorum would meet for thirty-two years. At the October General Conference in the Salt Lake Tabernacle in 1868, the entire Quorum met for the first time since Brigham's prayer in Kirtland.

But They Kept the Name (1836)

To solve the "Mormon Problem," the Missouri legislature decided in 1836 to form two new counties in northern Missouri for the exclusive use of the Saints—Daviess and Caldwell. It was primarily from Caldwell County that the Saints were driven in 1838 when Far West was besieged and forced to surrender. General Doniphan, a lawyer friend of the Saints, was given the job of drawing up the bill for the creation of the new counties so it was he who selected the names. One was for the renowned Indian fighter, Matthew Caldwell, a friend of Doniphan's father and whose grandson (also Matthew Caldwell) was a faithful Latter-day Saint. It is difficult to believe the Missourians never connected the names— but they still kept the name after the expulsion of the Saints.

Oldest Continuous Unit (1837)

It's at least ten years older than any Church unit in the Salt Lake Valley. Seven missionaries from Kirtland arrived in Preston, England, in June 1937 and within nine months had baptized 1,000 members. On August 6, a branch was organized—the first overseas—and is now the oldest continuous unit in the Church. So many Saints in England migrated to Utah that when Gordon B. Hinckley arrived in Preston as a young missionary in 1933, the Preston Branch was "a weak outpost" with about ten members meeting in a rented room. Sixty-five years later, President Hinckley presided over the dedication of the Preston Temple.

Removing Social Dangers (1837)

When the authorities of Nauvoo destroyed the *Expositor* press in 1844 because it was considered a danger to the civil peace of the populace, they immediately raised the wrath of Illinois citizens because the destruction was a serious violation of press freedom. It was the event that resulted in the imprisonment and death of Mayor Smith, who had presided at the city council meeting that legally approved the action. However, when an anti-abolition mob destroyed a press and killed its publisher, Elijah Lovejoy, in Alton, Illinois, in 1837, only seven years previously, it was considered justice "within the bonds of society" in removing a social danger. There were over three dozen such riots in the nation during the 1830s, and none of them resulted in the same righteous indignation as the *Expositor* affair.

Record Number of Signatures! (1837)

The New York firm of Halstead and Haines believed they were taking no chances on default by the Mormon Church in Kirtland in 1837 when they made a loan of $2,250.77 for merchandise. Although it was the peak year for land values before the nationwide depression hit the Kirtland area late in the year, some decision-makers within the firm apparently believed that the promissory note for that loan should require more than just the signatures of the Kirtland Temple Building Committee. Four years later the defaulted note was put in the hands of the Browning and Bushnell law firm in Quincy, Illinois for collection. The Prophet Joseph's signature, along with those of his brother Hyrum, Brigham Young, Oliver Cowdery, Sidney Rigdon, and twenty-eight other Church leaders, totaling thirty-three, were not enough to draw blood from Mormon stone at that time.

Some Kind of Record! (1837)

It's not the kind of record most would desire to establish for a Guinness record, but there seems little doubt Joseph Smith would have held it—for lawsuits against him. In 1837 alone the Prophet endured seventeen such suits in Geauga County, Ohio, for claims involving more than thirty thousand dollars. Speaking in the Ogden Tabernacle in 1871, Brigham Young reminded the congregation that Joseph "was hunted and driven, arrested and persecuted, and although no law was ever made in these Untied States that would bear against him, for he never broke a law, yet to my certain knowledge he was defendant in forty-six lawsuits." Such time-consuming legalities dramatically illustrate his talent for accomplishing so much in his short life.

First Convert to America (1837)

William Garner was the English heavyweight champion pugilist when he met the first Mormon missionaries to the British Isles in 1837. Having accepted the gospel and having sufficient means to migrate at once, he crossed the Atlantic to the United States before the first boatload of converts who later came on the ship *Britannia*. William became the father-in-law of another record holder, Mary Field Garner, who, when she died in 1942, was the last living witness of the Palmyra martyr.

First Published Reply (1838)

What is most surprising about the pamphlet by Parley P. Pratt is that it took so long—eight years after the Church was established—for the Church to publish a reply to the published anti-Mormon attacks. Parley P. Pratt's *Mormonism Unveiled: Zion's Watchman Unmasked* was a milestone, a first of a vast number of pamphlets by Pratt and other Saints, written in reply to anti-Mormon attacks. In this tract Parley responded to an eight-part article in the *New York Zion's Watchman*, edited by La Roy Sunderland, which appeared between January 13 and March 3, 1838, in the *New York Zion's Watchman*. In 1835 Parley had published an account of the rough treatment he received at the hands of an anti-Mormon mob in the Town of Mentor, but it was not a reply to any anti-Mormon publication.

A Strange Resolution (1838)

The High Council of Zion, meeting in Far West on June 23, 1838, passed several resolutions, but one of them is most strange because of its wording. The sixth of eight resolutions voted on established a committee "to labor with John Burke, Adam Lightner, and Joseph Smith, Jr., keeper of publick houses, that they keep good orderly houses, and have no drinking, swearing, gambling, or debauchery carried on therein." It was not necessarily strange that the leader of a church in the nineteenth century kept a public house (a place where travelers could find rooms and meals), it was only strange that it was considered necessary to labor with him to keep an orderly house. Perhaps it was to appear impartial to Burke and Lightner, who it was recorded five days later, "manifested a perfect willingness to comply."

The Time Will Come! (1838)

After the Saints surrendered at Far West in 1838, an officer of the mob-militia, Colonel Sterling Price, was given the pleasure of transporting the hated Mormon leaders to await their trials in Richmond, Missouri. The vulgar, foul-mouthed, and abusive militia under Price made life unbearable for the Saints as they awaited their trials. The Saints could only pray that the time would come when the mob commander would be rewarded for such treatment. It came. Eight years later, as an officer in the Mexican War, Price entered Santa Fe with his cavalry command and received no public demonstration from its commander, General Doniphan. Especially galling was learning that Doniphan, an old friend of the Saints in Missouri in 1838, had ordered a two-gun salute to the Mormon Battalion that entered Santa Fe a few days later.

Don't Prophesy Evil! (1838)

Brigham Young's second wife, Mary Ann Angell, shared many of her husband's most difficult early years, demonstrating a faith and fortitude similar to that of her famous husband. An example of this occurred as she was being forced from Missouri after the Extermination Order of 1838. Seated on a loaded wagon with an infant twin in each arm, the vehicle struck a rut and her baby girl was thrown under a wheel, her head being crushed. The driver picked up the badly injured infant, saying, "The poor little thing will surely die." Calmly Mary Ann responded, "Don't prophesy evil, brother," and skillfully, with fervent prayer, reshaped the baby's head. The baby recovered but died later at the age of seven.

How Will They Be Judged? (1838)

When the Missouri mob-militia surrounded Far West in 1838, members of the militia demanded that Adam Lightner, not a member of the Church (his wife was a loyal member), and John Cleminson and his wife, who had lost the faith, be brought to them and offered safe passage out of the doomed city. Cleminson replied that he knew the Saints to be an innocent people, "and if," said he, "you are determined to destroy them, and lay the city in ashes, you must destroy me also, for I will die with them." Adam Lightner agreed and the four (Adam's wife accompanied the other three and told her husband he could leave and take their child) returned to their friends in the city. Mary Lightner, having remained faithful, died in Utah in 1913 at the age of 95.

A Benevolent Legislature (1838)

The Missouri Legislature of 1838 is not remembered for its sympathy for the persecuted Saints driven from their State, but the height of hypocrisy was reached in its appropriations for that year. The same legislature that appropriated $200,000 for the mob-militia that dispossessed the Mormons of their homes, their farms, their animals, and personal possessions, then proceeded in a gesture of "benevolence" to appropriate $2,000 for the destitute Saints now forced to flee their former homes. Their generosity, amounting to less than 20 cents per refugee, was paid to a few selected anti-Mormon merchants who claimed the appropriation by charging so much per pound for Mormon hogs they killed and remnants of cloth and other sundries from ransacked stores. A history of Caldwell County published in the late nineteenth century noted, "Gentiles were the sole beneficiaries."

Always Listen to Your Wife! (1838)

Although they gained the field at the Battle of Crooked River against the Missouri mobs in 1838, three Saints were killed, including David W. Patten, the leader of the Quorum of the Twelve. A number were wounded, all of them eventually recovering fully except James Hendricks, who was so incapacitated by his wound that he needed help dressing for the last thirty years of his life, although he was able to serve as Bishop of the Nineteenth Ward in Salt Lake City. On the night before the battle, a number of Saints stopped at the Hendricks' home and asked him to join them. While he prepared, his wife, Drusilla, got his gun down from the fireplace and handed it to him. As he left she said, "Don't get shot in the back." James was shot in the back of the neck.

The Meaning of a Word! (1838)

Latter-day Saints have universally condemned the notorious Haun's Mill Massacre by a mob-militia shortly after Missouri Governor Boggs issued the infamous extermination order as the result of actions of a Hitler-like official. A second look at the definition of the word "exterminate" as it was used in 1838, however, might cause us to take a second look at Governor Boggs as well. *An American Dictionary of the English Language,* published in 1828, defines "exterminate" as "literally, to drive from within the limits or borders." Is this all the Governor intended? Actually the order said the Mormons "must be exterminated or driven from the state." This apparent order to kill or drive away could be interpreted as "exterminated or [in other words] driven from the state." This is not proof that Boggs was justified in his order—only that we must always consider how word meanings change in time.

3
The Nauvoo Era
(1839-1845)

The First Photo – a Latter-day Saint (1839)

The birth of photography in 1839 by the French inventor Daguerre is well known. Far less known, however, is his connection with the Latter-day Saints. Gustave Henriod, a French convert and pioneer to Utah in 1853, became known for his connection with L.J.M. Daguerre in LeHavre, France, where his father ran a boarding house. Daguerre, who conceived the idea that images could be fixed on a plate, asked Gustave, who was only a child at that time, to sit for him as he experimented with capturing his image in a camera noire. Henriod later recalled that "seven months after I began to sit for him he produced a very fair likeness and he was the happiest man you ever saw."

Nauvoo's First Prophet of Doom (1839)

Latter-day Saints normally associate Isaac as the gentile who sold the Saints most of the land on which they established their settlements at Commerce and across the river in Iowa. Offering generous terms to the Mormons, he watched as the Saints flocked to their new lands in the spring and summer of 1839, but he had apprehensions. In July 1839 he wrote a letter now in possession of the Community of Christ Church, in which he prophesied that Nauvoo would flourish "until they again acquire a sufficient quantity of 'Honey-comb' to induce the surrounding [people] to rob them again, at which time they will no doubt have to renounce their religion; or submit to a repetition of similar acts of violence and outrages as have already been."

What Happened to Adam-Ondi-Ahman? (1839)

The town didn't die when the Saints were expelled by the Missouri mob-militia in 1838 and forced to move to Far West until they could leave the state. In 1839 the Federal Government sold the site, and mob members who had forced the Saints to leave purchased it at bargain prices. A Dr. John Craven bought the entire center of the town, renamed it Cravensville, and was able to sell or rent the homes formerly built and owned by the Saints. For some time the newly named but declining town vied with Gallatin for county seat of Daviess County before it was totally abandoned in 1871. The Church of Jesus Christ of Latter-day Saints now owns over 3,000 acres of the site.

Turning a Deaf Ear (1839)

The Hibbard family was firmly ensconced on their farm when the Saints arrived in 1839 at what was to become Nauvoo. According to Helen Mar Whitney, the family accepted the gospel but soon lost the faith. She liked the father but thought his wife was a shrew. Joseph Smith III recalled years later how the old gentleman, who was called "Deaf" Hibbard, asked young Joseph if there was anyone nearby. When the boy shouted "No," Hibbard said, "When there is no one near you needn't speak so loud to me." He then confided to the boy that he had been shamming his deafness for years. He explained that his wife was a perpetual scold, but by pretending deafness, he could always pretend he never heard her. Joseph said it was an enlightening experience in hearing only what one wanted to hear.

Skeps (1839)

Of the millions of insect species, only two in the history of man have been domesticated. One is the silkworm that Mormons experimented with in Utah. The other is the honeybee that Nauvoo Saints made use of when the town was first settled. The type of beehive used there was made of coiled straw and became a symbol of Mormonism when the Saints reached Utah. These beehives were called skeps, as they had been called in Europe for hundreds of years, whereas the hives used in the eastern and southeastern United States were made of sections of logs called bee gums. That name comes from the kind of tree used—red gum trees. It is of special interest in recognizing the straw skep on so many Mormon items (even the name Deseret that is found in the Book of Mormon is found throughout Mormondom).

First Vicarious Baptism (1840)

The Prophet Joseph mentioned baptism for the dead for the first time at the funeral of Seymour Brunson in August, 1840 in Nauvoo. After the funeral, a widow by the name of Jane Nyman was baptized in the Mississippi River for her deceased son. In 1891 Wilford Woodruff, referring to the revelation that followed, later said: "Never did I read a revelation with greater joy." In fact, he tells of going into the river later along with Joseph and others and baptizing hundreds. "We were strung up and down the Mississippi," he said, "baptizing for our dead. But there was no recorder." A year later, with fuller understanding of the revelation, Joseph halted the river baptisms until they could be performed in the temple—with complete records of each one.

Who Were the Plunderers? (1840)

Although Mormon missionaries had been in Great Britain for the past three years, on November 8, 1840, the *London Dispatch* carried a critical report on the arrival of "a new religious sect . . . for the purpose of plundering the ignorant people in the neighborhood of the palaces and cathedral" (Gloucester and Bristol). In the same article the editor lamented the failure of the Bishop of Gloucester to prevent converts to Mormonism—in spite of the fact that he was the recipient of 9,000 pounds per year in salary and palace housing. In addition, it was noted that he had more than 80 clergymen to help him and 86 palace workers—all paid out of public funds. Apparently the editor never noted the irony of referring to the nearly impoverished missionaries as "plundering" the people.

That Brewster Boy (1840)

It was not unusual for would-be leaders to challenge Brigham Young's leadership in 1844, but one of those had also challenged Joseph's prophetic calling years earlier. James C. Brewster was only sixteen or seventeen in Kirtland when he claimed visions in connection with the Book of Esdras. Later in Nauvoo Joseph severely rebuked him for claiming that the gathering place for the Saints, according to the Book of Esdras, was to be in the valleys of the Colorado and Gila rivers. In 1848 Brewster and Hazen Aldrich challenged Brigham's leadership by organizing a church at Kirtland. They then proceeded to carry out the boy Brewster's "revelations" by leading a small colony west and establishing "Colonia" on the Rio Grande. By 1852, internal disputes had broken up the entire settlement.

A Sensible Archbishop (1840)

All professional churchmen were not unreasonable anti-Mormons in 1840, including the Archbishop of Canterbury. The missionary success of the Twelve in the British Isles at that time prompted the ministers in southern England to call a convention and send a petition to the Archbishop. They asked him to request Parliament to pass a law prohibiting the Mormons from preaching in the British dominions, noting that one Mormon missionary had baptized 1,500 (undoubtedly a reference to Wilford Woodruff). The Archbishop, however, familiar with the laws of England guaranteeing toleration to all religions, sent word that if the ministers "had the worth of souls at heart as much as they valued ground where hares, foxes, and hounds ran, they would not lose so many of their flock."

Immigration Fatalities (1840)

The first convert immigrants from the British Isles arrived in the United States in 1840. For the next twenty-eight years, until the advent of steam ships, over 47,000 Saints from the Isles crossed the Atlantic, a voyage that averaged 35 days. For only 12,000 of those immigrants do we have fatality statistics, which were undoubtedly higher than most other immigrants because of the larger number of children and the elderly. From such things as measles, small pox, and consumption, fatalities were .36% for adults, 2.92% for children, and 7.7% for infants. According to Professor Ronald Goettler of the Tepper School of Business at Carnegie Mellon University, the infant mortality rate, mathematically, would equal 55.1% for the year. Such a high rate was not a result of mismanagement but of disease and sailing ship conditions in the nineteenth century.

A Profitable Decade (1840)

Latter-day Saints are familiar with the success of such early missionaries to the British Isles as Wilford Woodruff. During a period of only eight months, according to his own journal, he was able "to bring into the Church, through the blessings of God, over eighteen hundred souls." Often overlooked is the success of the other missionaries to the British Isles. During the decade of the forties, 64 missionaries were assigned to Great Britain and during that same decade there were 34,299 baptisms in the British mission. That averages out to approximately 535 baptisms per missionary. It must be assumed that a number of those baptisms were the work of previous converts, but the overall success of so few missionaries cannot be overestimated.

Ocean Insurance? (1841)

In 1841 the *Millennial Star* carried an article about a Latter-day Saint whose conversion saved his life—he crossed the Atlantic in a Mormon-chartered ship rather than the one he had originally planned on before his conversion. The original ship was lost at sea, taking with it 122 lives. This may have been prophetic. In only six years, from 1847 to 1853, fifty-nine immigrant vessels sank, with none of them carrying Mormon immigrants. In contrast, in the fifty-year period from 1840 to 1890, over 500 ships crossed the Atlantic with companies of Latter-day Saints. There were fatalities on these ships from disease, but none of those ships were lost.

It Seems Brigham Was Right! (1841)

Although Orson Hyde dedicated the Holy Land in 1841 for the return of the Jews, no serious attempt was made to proselytize among the Jewish people for over a century. Brigham Young did not believe that mortal missionaries would convert them. He was certainly in favor of dedicating the land for their return; in fact, Brigham sent George A. Smith to rededicate Palestine for the Jewish return in 1872, but God himself would do the converting. Apparently forgetting Brigham's words about converting the Jewish people, several Jewish Missions were established in the early 1950s in California, New York, and Utah, but they were all closed very shortly due to lack of success. It seems Brigham was right after all.

Even the Replacement Left (1841)

The events of Orson Hyde dedicating Palestine in 1841 for the return of the Jewish people and his companion, John Page, abandoning him are well-known. Less known is that there was a replacement, George J. Adams, who accompanied Hyde as far as England. Apparently, in his association with Hyde, Adams became a fervent proponent of the gathering of the Jews—so much so that he returned to the United States to prepare for the Second Coming. He stayed with the Church for another three years before his complete apostasy. He briefly joined with those who were against Brigham Young and then formed his own Church of the Messiah and became head of the Palestine Emigration Association, expecting to witness firsthand the glorious return of Christ. In 1866 Adams led a group of such believers to Palestine, establishing them in Jaffa before running off with their money.

The Mormon Mutiny (1842)

At least that is the official charge placed in the log of the ship *Henry* by its notorious Captain Pierce against the leaders of a company of immigrating Saints. Contention between the Mormon passengers and the abusive captain as they crossed from Liverpool to New Orleans resulted in Captain Pierce keeping the passengers prisoners on his ship for six days when it reached its destination in December 1842. When Pierce informed a boarding officer that "the passengers were then, and had been, in a state of mutiny, from the time they were three days out from Liverpool," leaders John Snyder and James Morgan were taken ashore as prisoners. The American authorities did not pursue charges and the Saints continued their journey to Nauvoo.

Joseph Didn't Know! (1842)

Nine years after the Book of Mormon appeared, the first published account of the ruins of Mesoamerica, *Incidents of Travel in Central America, Chiapas and Yucatan,* by John Lloyd Stephens, appeared in print. Church leaders in Nauvoo received a copy in 1842 and published excerpts in the *Times and Seasons.* Shortly thereafter they noted that in reading the book they discovered that the main homeland of the Nephites must have been Central America, not South America. This was a significant admission, when we note that the Prophet Joseph never specifically identified the Hill Cumorah near his home as the site of the last battle of the Nephites—his followers just assumed that was the site. Most scholars now believe the original Cumorah is in Mesoamerica.

Only the Worthy (1842)

With membership in the Relief Society open today to any adult female member, it is assumed that membership in the Church means worthiness for membership in the Society—but such was not always the case. When the Prophet Joseph advised an early meeting of the Society in Nauvoo that "none should be received into the society but those who were worthy," the advice was taken seriously. In the first year, 1842, ten women were denied membership or investigated. A committee for reviewing names submitted may have rejected others without even putting them to a vote. It is not difficult to conclude that Mormon sisters were more concerned about worthiness of the Relief Society's members than the brethren were about the worthiness of the general Church members.

"Nonsense, Folly and Trash" (1842)

In 1842 Joseph Smith's printing establishment in Nauvoo published a pamphlet supporting plural marriage entitled *The Peace Maker*, which the Prophet Joseph immediately denounced as "nonsense, folly and trash," stating that it had been published without his approval. John D. Lee later "revealed" that Joseph had actually assigned Udney Jacobs to write the pamphlet, "testing the waters" of Nauvoo for plural marriage, but denied it when the reaction was negative. Another publication called *The Little Known Discourse of Joseph Smith*, also presenting a negative view of marriage, with much identical material as *The Peace Maker*, is even today viewed as Joseph's work. Actually, the author, Udney Jacobs, was an enemy of the Saints in 1842, but joined the Church a year later, influenced by his son, Norton, who was a member. In January 1844 Jacobs wrote to the Prophet Joseph, revealing that they had never met. The facts indicate that like so much anti-Mormon "evidence," the assertion that Joseph had Udney write the pamphlets doesn't stand up to scrutiny.

Improved Conditions? (1842)

The "good old days" would certainly be a misnomer for the weeks spent by passengers on the Atlantic crossings in the nineteenth century. Only two years after the first convert Saints made the journey in 1840, the British Government put into effect the Passenger Act of 1842, designed to improve the traveling conditions of ocean travelers. We must wonder how horrible conditions were before that date. According to the Act, each passenger was "to have at least ten square feet of space between decks." That was an area the size of their bunks that could not be less than six feet by eighteen inches. Children under fourteen had to share that space. Each passenger was allowed three quarts of water per day. Only two to four lifeboats were required for ships that often carried 200-300 passengers.

Bringing Lorenzo Home (1842)

On April 1, 1842, the editor of the *Nauvoo Times and Seasons* announced he had received a letter from Parley P. Pratt informing the Saints of the death of Lorenzo Barnes, the first missionary to die while preaching in a foreign land. Parley wrote that Brother Barnes had died in December at Bradford, England, "the first messenger of this last dispensation" to lay "down his life in a foreign land." In a discourse delivered in April, the Prophet Joseph said, "I should have been more reconciled to the death of Elder Barnes could his body have been laid in the grave in Nauvoo or among the Saints. I have very peculiar feelings in the matter of receiving an honorable burial with my fathers." Following such advice, the Saints removed the body from England to a Salt Lake City cemetery in 1852.

Counterfeiting in Nauvoo (1842)

A common charge anti-Mormons in Illinois made in the 1840s was that Nauvoo was a center of counterfeiting. Although it existed there, most of those involved were non-Mormons intent on placing the blame on the Saints. It must be understood, however, that counterfeiting then was different and viewed differently than it is today. First of all, there was no U.S. currency—only specie—so counterfeiting would be primarily coins. Since "clipping" and filing coins was a common practice, replicas of the entire coins was not considered as serious a "crime" as it is today. It was even justified by many considering the shortage of specie and its demand by many merchants and by local governments in the form of taxes. In 1842, Governor Ford estimated that the half-million residents of Illinois possessed only $200,000-$300,000 in specie, about fifty cents apiece on the average.

Book of the Law of the Lord (1842)

Although it is mentioned in 2 Chronicles 34:14—"And when they brought out the money that was brought into the house of the LORD, Hilkiah the priest found a book of the law of the Lord given by Moses"—few Latter-day Saints recognize this scripture's connection with the restored Church. Joseph mentioned it in his journal on August 22, 1842, however, in a tribute to some members of the Colesville Branch: "I am now recording in the Book of the Law of the Lord, . . . of such as have stood by me in every hour of peril, for these fifteen long years past." The book also contained the names of those who contributed badly needed funds and the amount they gave. The book is today in the vault of the First Presidency. To add to the confusion, James Strang, the Beaver Island apostate, also published a book by the same title containing alleged revelations from the Lord.

Recognizing the True Church (1843)

Perhaps the leaders of the splinter groups that broke from the Church after Joseph's death were not present the day the Prophet spoke on that very subject in Nauvoo shortly before his death. Edward Stevenson, one of the seven presidents of the Seventies, remembered Joseph speaking from a stand in the unfinished temple, telling the Saints, "I will give you a key by which you may never be deceived, if you will observe these facts: Where the true Church is, there will always be a majority of the saints, and the records and history of the Church also." Such a "key" of knowledge of the true church is perhaps a clue as to the reason so many apostates returned to the Church as the splinter groups failed to grow.

It Really Happened (1843)

The details of how it happened are sketchy, but the historical record indicates it really did. A Mrs. Cartwright was drowned while being baptized near Chester, England, on the evening of November 23, 1843. Elder Pugmire, who was performing the ordinance, and Mr. Cartwright, who had been baptized a few weeks previously, were both arrested and jailed for more than six weeks. Both were found blameless at the trial that followed. Reports at the time indicate that Mrs. Cartwright, who was furious when her husband was baptized, had stated, "If she should ever be such a fool as to be baptized, she hoped to God that she would be drowned in the attempt."

Charge for Saving a Prophet (1843)

In June 1843, while visiting Dixon, about 200 miles north of Nauvoo, the Prophet Joseph was taken into custody by two law officers from Missouri. Joseph was able to get a desperate message back to Nauvoo, asking for rescue by the Nauvoo Legion. The soon-to-be apostate Wilson Law, Major General of the Legion, claimed a lack of money made the rescue impossible. Brigham Young said, "In two hours I succeeded in borrowing $700 to defray the expenses of the expedition." After his martyrdom, the Prophet Joseph's estate received a bill from Wilson Law for various forms of help he had provided the Prophet, including $100 for "expenses incurred in going North, with men and Arms, to protect sd. Smith from violence" including "my own servises [sic], and injury of health, in going at that time." Such a bill causes one to question the disposal of the original $700 and to ponder the value of a prophet's life.

Breaking with Tradition (1843)

At a time when most Americans—and the laws they formulated—considered women intellectually and legally inferior, the Latter-day Saints broke with tradition. In an editorial in September 1843, John Taylor, the editor of the *Nauvoo Neighbor*, summed up quite succinctly the Mormon leadership view of the place of women in society. He advised husbands to "make it an established rule to consult your wife on all occasions . . . undertake no plan contrary to her advice and approbation . . . Your wife has an equal right with yourself to all your worldly possessions." Could such alien thinking be a reason the gentiles wanted the Saints removed from their midst?

"A Right Hand Brutus" (1843)

Speaking from the stand in Nauvoo in 1843, the Prophet Joseph shocked his people by saying, "If I were to reveal to this people the doctrines that I know are for their exaltation, these men would spill my blood," referring to such brethren sitting on the stand as President Marks, William and Wilson Law, and Austin Cowles. They would all apostatize, but William Law was so shaken by Joseph's apparent foreknowledge and rumors that his life was in danger that he called the entire police force before the City Council to question each of them as to whether Joseph had given any of them instructions for his murder. Joseph's reaction was to say, "I might live, as Caesar might have lived, were it not for a right hand Brutus." Law, like his fellow conspirators, fulfilled Joseph's prophecy.

Winfield Scott and the Saints (1843)

The Commanding General of the American army, Winfield Scott, opposed the military expedition against the Saints in 1847. Secretary of War John B. Floyd, however, who benefited through kickbacks from the supplier contracts, kept a letter of opposition secret from President Buchanan. This may have been farsighted on the part of Scott, but it may have also resulted from earlier contacts with the Saints and an observation of their military prowess. Several journal keepers noted that during Nauvoo Legion maneuvers east of Nauvoo on April 16, 1843, there were U.S. military officers present, General Winfield Scott being one of them. Levi Richards noted in his diary the "perfect satisfaction with the Legion . . . expressed by the officers."

But They Still Sustained Him (1843)

At a special conference in Nauvoo, Sidney Ridgon was sustained as a counselor to Joseph Smith in spite of the Prophet's objections. What exactly did the Prophet object to? When the Saints were expelled from Missouri in 1839, Rigdon, discouraged and disillusioned, claimed that "he would never follow any revelation again that did not tend to his comfort and interest, let it come from Joseph Smith, God Almighty, or any body else." He was also urging the Saints to scatter after their expulsion, "for the work seems as though it had come to an end." The big question should be not what Joseph objected to, but why the people sustained Rigdon in spite of such statements.

Almost an Idiot (1843)

One of the most popular pseudo-sciences in the nine-teenth century was phrenology, the practice of revealing character and mental capacity by feeling the conformation of the skull. The leading phrenologist in the mid-nineteenth century was O. S. Fowler, whom Brigham Young visited "at the request and expense" of a local elder while on a mission in Boston. Fowler examined Brigham's head and gave him a chart, which the future prophet duly noted in his diary: "After giving me a very good chart for $1, I will give [Fowler] a chart gratis. My opinion of him is, that he is just as nigh being an idiot as a man can be, and have any sense left to pass through the world decently." On May 6, 1844, the Prophet Joseph interviewed a phrenologist visiting Nauvoo and objected to him performing in the city.

Who Was Dennison L. Harris (1844)

There are many little-known persons in LDS history, but Dennison Harris deserves more recognition than most—and for more than one reason. First, he was the nephew of Martin Harris, but unlike his uncle, never wavered in his loyalty to the Church. Such faithfulness resulted in his grandson, Franklin Harris, becoming a president of BYU. More important perhaps was his invitation, along with another boy's in Nauvoo, Robert Scott, to meetings with such apostates as the Laws, Higbees, and Fosters, who were largely responsible for the deaths of Joseph and Hyrum. Unknown to the conspirators, the boys were loyal to Joseph and reported the conspiracy. Their reports were suspected and their lives threatened by the apostates and although their reports did not save the lives of the Prophet and his brother, Dennison was able to partially restore the name of Harris in the community.

Temple Robes at Carthage (1844)

Were Joseph and Hyrum wearing their temple robes at the time of their assassination in the Carthage Jail? The best evidence we have that they were not is found in William Clayton's journal for December 21, 1845. He wrote that on that day he attended a meeting in the east room [of the temple] in which H. C. Kimball presided. During the meeting, according to Clayton, "John Taylor confirmed the belief that Joseph and Hyrum and himself were without their robes in the jail at Carthage, while Doctor Richards had his on." According to W. W. Phelps, Joseph had revealed to him that because of the hot weather, he had removed his on a day previously. Two residents of the Mansion House, Oliver Huntington and Julia Dalton both verified that Joseph removed his garments before going to

Carthage. Oliver said it was because he would be killed and "he did not want his garments to be exposed to the sneers and jeers of his enemies."

When He Won't Come (1844)

On March 11, 1844, the Prophet Joseph wrote that he met with twenty-three brethren in Nauvoo "whom I organized into a special council." This group became known as the Council of Fifty, formed, as believed by most members, for the primary purpose of becoming or at least controlling the political kingdom of God on earth in anticipation of the imminent coming of Christ. Overlooked by these believers is what occurred the day previous to that organizational meeting. Responding to the publicity generated by the Millerites and thousands of others who believed that Christ was destined to return to earth in the next few days, Joseph, on March 10, declared, "I . . . prophesy in the name of the Lord, that Christ will not come this year, as Father Miller has prophesied, and I also prophesy that Christ will not come in forty years." Organized with non-members also, the primary purpose of the Council was to elect Joseph as President of the United States and, if unsuccessful, to take the Saints west.

The First Foreign-Language Mission (1844)

There are few Latter-day Saints who are able to identify the names of the first missionaries to begin a foreign-language mission, much less the site of that mission. On May 1, 1844, Elders Addison Pratt, Noah Rogers, and Benjamin F. Grouard landed on the island of Tubuai in French Polynesia as the first missionaries of the Church to not only the islands of the Pacific but to a foreign language land. This was the same small island where the natives had driven off the bounty mutineers when they attempted a settlement there before they settled on Pitcairn Island. On July 28, Elder Pratt organized the first foreign-language branch of the Church with eleven members. During the first year Pratt baptized a third of the population, about sixty people.

A Test of Faith (1844)

Richard Ainscough, a twenty-nine-year-old Mormon living in Warsaw, Illinois in 1844, fell into the hands of an anti-Mormon mob that falsely accused him of theft. Taking him into some woods, they tied his wrists and drew him up to the limb of a tree. They then proceeded to whip him with a rawhide, pausing only to ask if he believed "old Joe Smith" was a prophet. Each time he affirmed his belief until his flesh was so torn that his ribs were bared. Tiring, the mob cut him down and a stranger rescued him. His employer, D. S. Witter of Warsaw, offered a $500 reward for the apprehension of the mob members but they were never arrested. Ainscough lived in torment for three and a half months before dying in late December. He was buried in Nauvoo.

East or West? (1844)

On the night of June 22, 1844, the Prophet Joseph and his brother Hyrum were rowed across the Mississippi River, leaving the Saints and their families in Nauvoo, in their planned escape westward to flee from their enemies. There is evidence, however, that Joseph still planned to work his way back to Washington to plead for help from President Tyler as had been discussed in a meeting earlier that day. Early on the morning of June 23, before he decided to return to Nauvoo, Joseph had sent a letter back to Emma with Porter

Rockwell in which he wrote, "I do not know where I shall go, or what I shall do, but shall if possible endevor to get to the city Washington." How differently LDS history might have developed if Emma, Reynolds Cahoon, and Hiram Kimball had not urged Joseph to give himself up!

Overcoming the Curse! (1844)

A revealing but fairly well-known incident in Mormon history is the story of Emma's request for a blessing from Joseph before he left for his martyrdom in Carthage, and Joseph's answer that she should write it out and he would sign it on his return—knowing he would not return. Equally revealing is what was in the blessing that Emma composed and called "these desires of my heart." She desired that she "be enabled to overcome that curse which was pronounced upon the daughters of Eve." The "curse," which has been interpreted to mean subjugation to her mate, was apparently strongly enough felt by the better-educated Emma that she found difficulty in always "honoring and respecting" Joseph, which was also a part of the desired blessing.

"It Was No Such Thing" (1844)

A most persistent story in Mormon history is that the soon-to-be-attacked prisoners in Carthage Jail sent out for a bottle of wine. When John Taylor heard an apologist report that it was taken as a sacrament, he said, "It was no such thing; our spirits were generally dull and heavy, and it was sent for to revive us." A lesser-known fact is that Joseph had earlier adjudicated the case of some brethren who had been brought before him for drinking whiskey. He concluded by saying "no evil had been done" and even gave the men some money to "replenish the bottle to stimulate them in the fatigues of their sleepless journey." The interpretation of the Word of Wisdom advice seemed to vary over time.

A Mysterious Wound (1844)

After the assassination of Joseph and Hyrum at Carthage, it was found that the wound that killed Hyrum was sustained in his face while he was apparently holding the door against the mobbers. This was verified by one of the survivors, Willard Richards. Also discovered, however, was a wound in his lower back. The mystery of that wound is hard to explain if he was shot in the face and, falling backward, never moved as the survivors later testified. One report stated that he was shot in the back by a rifleman outside the window, but this is not a credible report since the martyrdom room is on the second floor and the door is some distance from the window. Other wounds found on his body were in front, sustained as he lay on the floor. But that back wound, after 160 years, is still a mystery.

Exposing a False Prophet (1844)

After the Saints in Nauvoo rejected Sidney Rigdon as Joseph Smith's successor, Sidney continued to work against the Twelve and Brigham Young. At a small meeting after his rejection, while prophesying evil against the Church, he predicted that there would not be another stone raised upon the walls of the temple. William W. Player, in charge of the masonry work on the temple, was present at that meeting. Immediately after the meeting adjourned, Brother Player went with Brothers Archibald and John Hill to the partially completed temple on the hill and there proceeded to raise and set another stone upon one of the walls. They were determined that Sidney's prophesy would fail that very day. The effect on the Saints was not recorded but it can certainly be imagined.

Women to the Rescue (1844)

Students of Latter-day Saint history have noted that work on the Nauvoo Temple progressed much faster after the death of Joseph—ascribing part of its progress to the leadership of Brigham Young. Although partly true, much credit should be given to the sisters in the LaHarpe and Macedonia branches of the Church. The women in these settlements proposed to raise funds for the construction of a third crane for the temple. When the Temple Committee agreed, the sisters went to work and within a month of the Prophet's death had raised $194 (approximately $10,000 in 2003 prices), more than enough to allow the temple construction to progress much faster.

Another Set of Plates! (1845)

One of the most serious contenders for Brigham Young's leadership of the Church after the death of Joseph Smith was the apostate James Strang, who claimed to have been visited by an angel who led him to some buried plates on the banks of the White River in Wisconsin. These plates, translated by Strang, told the story of some ancient inhabitants in America descended from Israelite immigrants. Strang later claimed to have received the brass plates of Laban mentioned in the Book of Mormon. He published his translation of these plates as The Book of the Law of the Lord. He even had seven witnesses listed in this publication as a testimonial. The Strangite movement was almost as short-lived as memory of that publication.

"Shall We Finish It?" (1845)

It is a widely held belief that when Joseph was killed, the first concern of his successor, Brigham Young, was to finish the Nauvoo Temple. He eventually did and at a much faster rate than it was progressing under Joseph's leadership. It was apparently not his "first" concern, however. He wasn't even sure that it should be completed. As late as January 24, 1845, seven months after the martyrdom, Brigham mentioned in his diary that while conducting some of the sacred "temple" ceremonies at his home with Heber and Bishop Whitney, he inquired of the Lord whether the Saints should stay in Nauvoo and finish the temple. Fortunately, for all those who would receive their endowments there before abandoning the city, Brigham wrote, "The ansure [sic] was we should."

A Joyful Bit of Work (1845)

After his excommunication in 1844, Robert D. Foster became such an open enemy of the Prophet Joseph that the Saints held him primarily responsible for the martyrdom. He became so reviled in Nauvoo that his very visits after the Carthage killings became a cause of riots between the Saints and Foster's companions, at one time preventing the steamer Foster was on from docking. Hosea Stout recorded in his diary how the Saints volunteered to fill in an excavation Foster had dug previously for a new home: "A large company of other brethren came to assist we worked till 12 o'clock hauling sand and throwing into the cellar . . . and had a joyful time."

Robert Foster's Remorse (1845)

One of the apostates most responsible for the death of the Prophet Joseph was Robert D. Foster, who after his excommunication in 1844 for immorality and apostasy, worked diligently with the Law brothers to destroy Joseph. After the martyrdom, Abraham C. Hodge, a loyal member of the Church, related the following conversation with Dr. Foster: "I am the most miserable wretch that the sun shines upon. If I could recall eighteen months of my life I would be willing to sacrifice everything I have upon earth, my wife and child not excepted." When Hodge pointed out that Foster was an accessory to Joseph's murder, Foster replied, "I know that, and I have not seen one moment's peace since that time. I know that Mormonism is true, and the thought of meeting (Joseph and Hyrum) at the bar of God is more awful to me than anything else."

Keeping Order in Meetings (1845)

Members who are concerned at times about reverence in church meetings might do well to think of meetings in Nauvoo where the city police were given the responsibility of keeping order. Since so many meetings were outdoors in the groves, there were problems with horses in the aisles, boys sitting on the women's side, uninvited youngsters on the stand, and so on. Even "unwelcome" guests had to be occasionally escorted out of the meetings. On September 14, 1845, there was normal intermission between the morning worship service and the afternoon business meeting. Only those in good fellowship were allowed to attend the business meetings, but on that day, according to police chief Hosea Stout, the police "had to flog three who were determined to stay."

"On Top of the Spire Post" (1845)

John Taylor kept meticulous journals but often overlooked the unusual, as on August 24, 1845. He mentions speaking near the Nauvoo Temple and watching the cupola being put on and then ascending to the top of the tower to partake of some melons. He apparently thought it frivolous, however, to include an incident that occurred while he was speaking, but Willard Richards included it in his journals. Brother Richards recorded that he interrupted the proceedings to announce that the dome was raised (the cupola) and a man was standing on top of it. Actually he was doing more than just standing. According to Willard, "Bro. Goddard . . . stood on his head on the top of the spire post."

Disinterring the Dead (1845)

In 1845 the bodies of two brothers, William and Stephen Hodge, were buried in the Pioneer Burial Ground to the dismay of many in Nauvoo. After being hung in Burlington, Iowa, for murder, authorities, believing they were Latter-day Saints, sent the bodies to Nauvoo where they were buried. Actually, there were a brother and father by the name of Hodge who were members, but the murderers were not. At a City Council meeting in July, John Taylor raised an objection to the presence of the brothers in the burial ground and Brigham Young agreed. The Prophet Joseph's brother William Smith defended their burial, saying they might be innocent. A vote was taken, however, and it was decided that the Hodge brothers should be removed. Their final resting place is unknown today.

What William Wanted (1845)

On June 30, 1845, a year after the death of his two brothers, William Smith wrote a letter to Brigham Young. In it William pushed his case not for control of the Church, which had already been ceded to Brigham, but for independence from the Quorum of the Twelve. William claimed the Smith family to be of "royal blood and promised seed." He claimed his right as Patriarch to his "share of the kingdom" and to attend to all ordinances anyplace and anytime, "no man being my head." Brigham responded with a letter explaining that all members must be amenable to the

Twelve. He then took the letter to the Smith family for approval, which William's mother and two sisters, Catherine and Lucy, gave. In October William was excommunicated.

Nine Men with One Gun (1845)

The trial of the assassins of Joseph and Hyrum over a year after the murders was a farce—most noticeably demonstrated by the wording in the indictments. Although sixty names were presented to the grand jury, the jury kept voting off names until only nine remained who were then indicted for the trials—Joseph's and Hyrum's being tried separately. The indictment for Joseph's killing charged that the gun that discharged the bullet responsible for the death of the Prophet was "held" in the hands of all nine defendants. Such wording was unnecessary since the law only provided that anyone indicted only had to "participate" in the crime. It was suggested that claiming all nine held the gun would permit proof of guilt for all of them, but it could be equally suggested that a jury would scornfully dismiss such an absurd charge. It did!

From Cannibals to Saints (1845)

One of the first missionaries to the Islands of the Pacific, Benjamin Grouard established a mission in the Tuamotus Islands in French Polynesia in the Southeastern Pacific. Elder Grouard did not know what to expect since the people—most of whom were no more than a generation removed from such practices—had a reputation for ferocity and cannibalism. Within six weeks, however, Elder Grouard had baptized twenty-four natives and by September, a mere four months after his landing, he had organized five branches with 620 good members. By

September 1846, the first Mormon Conference in the Pacific was held in French Polynesia with a Church membership of 866—a giant leap from cannibalism.

4

The Uprooting
(1846-1847)

The Battle Axe System (1846)

It appears to be common knowledge that an important reason for Sydney Rigdon's break with the Prophet Joseph was his opposition to plural marriage. There is also weighty evidence, however, that Sidney may have taught that same doctrine after he established his own church. One of his followers from Antrim Township reported that during a Rigdonite conference in 1846 held in a barn, "Mr. Rigdon had introduced a System of Wifery or the Battle Axe System or free or common intercourse with the women." Although evidence suggests that Sidney did not personally practice the system, the "Journal History" for April 18, 1859, reveals that Harvey Whitlock, who was a Rigdonite until June 1946, reported that the Rigdonites had engaged in an "arrangement for temporary swapping wives."

Justifying Her Denial (1846)

For 160 years many have wondered how Emma Smith could have denied, with a clear conscience, the evidence of Joseph's involvement in plural marriage. Emma was an intelligent woman and her thoughtful rationalizations gave her a clear conscience. First of all, since polygamy was illegal and thus her husband's plural marriages illegal, she felt truthful in denying that her husband had "other" wives. Second, she easily denied any "improper relations" by

Joseph, as she told her sons, because if they were the result of a revelation they were certainly "not improper." Finally, as she wrote in a letter in 1846, responding to historical events in Nauvoo, she could truthfully feel doubtful about "everything that has not come within my immediate observation."

Conditional Support for Lucy (1846)

When Lucy Mack Smith finally decided to stay in Nauvoo after the exodus, the Church provided her with a home formerly owned by Joseph Noble. Although small, it was comfortable. Because her surviving son, William, whose wife had died, wanted to move in with her, however, Church leaders discovered and objected to the plans. When the Church threatened to withdraw support if Lucy took him in, she wrote to the Church property disposal committee left in Nauvoo, telling them that such an action would "restrict my conscience, put limits to my affections, [and] threaten me with poverty." She defended William, saying, "He is my son and he has rights." There is no evidence that William moved in, and Lucy herself stayed in the home only a short time before moving in with Emma.

When Porter Backed Down! (1846)

Although Porter Rockwell and Sheriff Jacob Backenstos were allies in the conflict against the anti-Mormons in Hancock, the sheriff was forced to arrest Porter as the Saints were exiting Nauvoo in the spring of 1846. The charge? Harassing and threatening Joseph's old enemy, Chauncey Higbee. Taking additional deputies, the sheriff was searching the Mansion House where Rockwell lived when he encountered Porter at the head of the stairs threatening to kill Backenstos if he came any farther. The sheriff told one of his deputies, "When he shoots me, kill him." Rockwell had met his match in courage and gave up. After his arrest the court charged Porter with other crimes, but he was exonerated when the sheriff himself testified on his behalf.

Music Soothes the Soul (1846)

John Taylor, who had soothed the soul of the Prophet with his singing shortly before his martyrdom in the Carthage Jail, knew the power of music. During the exodus two years later, he was called on to settle a dispute between two brethren who would not accept the counsel of the local leaders. When he brought the two together, he asked for their approval for him to sing one of the songs of Zion. He then asked for their indulgence while he sang yet another song and finally ended up singing five hymns. By the time he was ready to listen to their complaints, they were so touched by the Spirit that they were in tears. They then stood, thanked him for the meeting, and left without mentioning a word of their forgotten dispute.

A Murder Mystery (1846)

It seems that most murders have some mystery about them, but it would appear especially so in Nauvoo. Thomas Bullock, a well-known Mormon journal keeper, mentioned such a murder in his 1846 journal. Admitting the details were unclear he relied on an article in the anti-Mormon *Warsaw Signal* that reported on March 4, 1846, "We learn that on Saturday last a man by the name of Gardner, was shot, in Nauvoo by a Mormon named Cotton and instantly killed. The cause of the difficulty was this: Gardner, who is not a Mormon, has a wife belonging to the Church. She wished to emigrate with the Saints, but her husband would not go along. She therefore left him and took up with Cotton. This led to the quarrel which terminated in the death of Gardner." This Gardner might have been a Thomas Gardner who the year previously had been caught with stolen goods in his home.

A Most Unique City (1846)

In my first book, *In Old Nauvoo*, I compiled in the preface a list of seventeen unique traits about Nauvoo, most of them coming as a surprise to non-Mormons who thought they knew American History. For example, "no other city in modern times trained and supported an army for its protection from hostile fellow nationals." Although the Nauvoo Legion was part of the state militia, it was primarily designed for protecting the Saints from such mob-militias as they encountered in Missouri. Nauvoo was also unique in that "no other American city in time of peace has ever been besieged by an army of American citizens." In the same vein, "from no other American city has such a large percentage of the inhabitants [approximately 80%] been forced from their homes and driven into exile."

Rockwell's Gold Watch (1846)

As the Saints exited Nauvoo for their trek west, Brigham Young left a committee in Nauvoo to settle all Church business, taking necessary expenses out of the sale of Church property. Almon Babbitt, an attorney, was one of the committee members. In June Porter Rockwell, still in Nauvoo, was indicted on some bogus counterfeiting charges and asked Babbitt for legal help. After relieving Porter of his gold watch as a fee, Babbitt was able to quickly get the charges dismissed. Later while crossing Iowa, Porter told Brigham of the loss of his gold watch.

Respecting Babbitt's talents but not his integrity, the President fired off a letter to his crafty attorney, demanding he return the watch immediately, saying he was already being paid for such work.

The Invasion of Iowa (1846)

After a brief battle between the remaining Saints in Nauvoo and the large mob surrounding the city in September 1846, the vastly outnumbered Mormons surrendered and, with no time to prepare, about 650 impoverished refugees were driven across the river into what became known as the "poor camp" on the Iowa shore. It was there that the well-known miracle of the quails gave respite to the shelterless and starving Saints. Less known is a small incident involving Daniel Wells, the future mayor of Salt Lake City and member of the First Presidency, who had stayed behind to help defend the nearly defenseless city. When the mobs in Nauvoo fired their cannon across the river into the refugee camp, Wells gathered the cannon balls and sent one to the governor of Iowa informing him of the "invasion" of his state by Illinois.

The Preacher Didn't Show (1846)

When traveling as a group on extended journeys, the Saints often asked different individuals to give sermons in the style of ministers of other denominations. Crossing Iowa in 1846, Brother W. J. Earl was asked to preach a Methodist sermon. Unfortunately, some gentiles in the neighborhood heard about it and, thinking it would be a legitimate sermon, showed up for the preaching. Taken by surprise, the Saints felt the visitors would be offended if they discovered who the "minister" was, so when everyone was assembled, John D. Lee stood up and called for the supposed visiting minister,

saying he understood one was expected. Of course, no one responded, so the visitors went home, disappointed with the "Methodist minister" but not angry with the Saints.

With a Wife and Eight Children (1846)

The name Nelson Higgins is not a common name in Church history but it was at one time. He was an uncommon man—and boy. At the age of eleven, he was living with a married sister in upstate New York when she died. Knowing his father was living someplace in Ohio, he started off alone on foot on a 400-mile journey to find him, which he did. That was not his last unusual journey on foot. Twenty-nine years later he was a member of the Church in Nauvoo, married, with eight children. After crossing Iowa at the time of the Exodus, he enlisted in the Mormon Battalion for their epic march across the continent, accompanied by his wife and eight children—giving a new meaning to the term "military family."

First Impressions (1846)

There are few Saints not familiar with the story of Philip St. George Cooke, an officer in Johnston's Army who, as it marched through Salt Lake City in 1858, removed his hat as a mark of respect for the Mormon Battalion he once commanded. Less known is his first impression of that battalion when he took command of it in Santa Fe in 1846: "Some were too old, some feeble, and some too young; it was embarrassed by too many women; it was undisciplined; it was much worn by travel on foot and marching from Nauvoo, Illinois; clothing was very scant . . . their mules were utterly broken down . . . animals scarce and inferior and deteriorating every hour." Still, he grew to respect the Battalion Saints—their courage, patriotism, and fortitude.

Buttons, Chips, and Sticks (1846)

Most Latter-day Saints identify John E. Page as the Apostle who never fulfilled his assignment to the Holy Land and was excommunicated in 1846. Less known, perhaps, is his love for money, which showed itself immediately when, upon learning of the martyrdom of Joseph and Hyrum, he advertised in a newspaper for a preaching position for anyone who would pay him. In March 1846, as the Saints were beginning their exodus, Page was in Nauvoo trying to win over Saints to James Strang, but still seeking personal gain for his preaching. Thomas Bullock recorded in his journal for March 18, "This p.m. John E. Page, after preaching a begging Sermon opposite Daniel Avery's house, U. C. Nickerson . . . sent the hat round for a collection, which was returned with a few coppers, buttons, chips and bits of stick being so much for the effects of apostasy."

Never Again! (1846)

Chief of police Hosea Stout recorded in his diary that it was discovered in September 1846 that some young men were out with some girls "for fifteen nights in succession until after two o'clock." He was therefore asked to "enforce obedience to the Law of God" and punish the young men for the crime of "having carnal communication with the girls which was well known to many and [for which] the legal punishment was death." With six other men, Brother Stout took the young men, one at a time, into some nearby woods and there gave them "18 hard lashes which stiped [them] well." After several lashes, one of the young men exclaimed, "If you will only stop I'll never touch another girl again."

59

First Mormon Settlement in the West (1846)

Salt Lake City was certainly the first permanent settlement in the West but not the first settlement. Although it existed for only two years as a Mormon settlement, that honor belongs to New Hope, a short-lived agricultural colony (1846-1848) on the Stanislaus River in central California. After Sam Brannan and 238 Saints arrived at Yerba Buena (now San Francisco) on the ship *Brooklyn* on July 31, 1846, Brannan sent about twelve families of the *Brooklyn* Saints to found the first Mormon colony west of the Rockies. William Stout was placed in charge, but when he usurped the first completed farm and dwelling and ousted the brethren, New Hope began its break-up. An added reason, of course, was also the uncertainty of Brigham Young's plans. When he established Salt Lake City, however, at least half of the New Hope pioneers moved to Utah. The rest, including Brannan, apostatized.

The Most Prosperous and Happy Tribe (1846)

As the Mormon Battalion crossed what is now southern Arizona, it encountered a most unusual tribe of Indians—in fact a most unusual society of humans. While the Saints camped on the Gila River, 1,500 to 2,000 Pima Indians visited them. Although the Battalion's personal and military property lay scattered about, there was not a single instance of theft. One of the military guides told the men that the Pima Indians "were so scrupulous that they had been known to follow travelers half a day to restore lost property to the owner." Such honesty, a novelty to the persecuted Mormons, apparently was fully rewarded. The Battalion commander, Colonel Cooke, congratulated the chief "on having the most prosperous and happy tribe he had ever met with" and one of the men, Daniel Tyler, later wrote, "The poison of the civilized asp is unknown among them."

Joseph Didn't Answer (1847)

Presiding over a High Council Meeting at Winter Quarters in February 1847, Brigham Young uncharacteristically described a vision he had recently experienced. He had had a visit with the martyred Prophet Joseph: "I told him that the Latter Day Saints w[ere] very anxious to know about the law of adoption and the sealing powers and desired word of council from him." Joseph did not answer the question but instead gave advice on keeping the spirit of Jesus. The question was important to the Saints at that time and it is mystifying why Joseph didn't respond to the question. But we do know the Saints had to await an answer from another prophet years later—Wilford Woodruff, who informed his people they were to stop adopting other families and to seal only their own.

Not the First (1847)

Many Latter-day Saints commonly believe the odometer that William Clayton designed on the pioneer trek West was a totally unique mileage device. It wasn't! One of the pioneers, Appleton Harmon, noted in his diary on July 10, 1847: "The company altogether bought about $100 worth of goods of Mr. H. Quelling, a Quaker, he had a roadameter on one of his wagons." Although B. H. Roberts gives Orson Pratt credit for perhaps furnishing the scientific principles for the odometer, it is more than likely that Harmon, being a skillful mechanic and having noted the Quaker's "roadameter" in his diary, was a primary catalyst for the famous odometer. Whatever the case, it was not a unique instrument among travelers.

Another Good "Place" (1847)

Few today question Brigham Young's decision to settle the less-than-desirable Salt Lake Valley rather than the West coast. There was, however, another "little-wanted" part of the West that he was advised to settle but decided against. Colonel Cooke, the non-Mormon commander of the Mormon Battalion, was so impressed with the Tucson Valley and the prosperity of the Pima and Maricopa Indians that he suggested that area for settlement by the Saints. Henry Standage, a member of the Battalion, told of the soldiers' holding a meeting on the Gila River south of the present Phoenix, Arizona, and sending a recommendation to Brigham Young to bring the Saints to the Salt River Valley. Obviously their impression of Arizona was better than some of the Pioneers' first impressions of the Salt Lake Valley.

Not Just the Right But the Only Place (1847)

"My mother was heartbroken," wrote Clara Decker Young, one of the women of the pioneer company. Lorenzo Young remembered the first impression of the valley upon other pioneers was equally disheartening. There were certainly other parts of Utah that were less dry and treeless and would have been less "disheartening," but without being aware of it, the Saints ended up in the only part of the territory that averted a serious challenge by the natives. They just happened to make their first settlement in the neutral zone between the Shoshone tribes to the north, the Gosiute to the west and south, and the various Ute tribes south of the valley. As a salt source for the various tribes, the Salt Lake area was not contested by the Indians. As the Saints moved north and south into the contested areas, they encountered opposition, but by then they were firmly established.

The M-Factor in Mormon History (1847)

About forty years ago George W. Pierson published in the *American Quarterly* an article on the "M-Factor in American History." His thesis was that the factor of "migration" or excessive mobility made Americans different from other peoples. Actually, the M-Factor seems to apply even more to the Latter-day Saints in that there are several M-Factors that have made the Saints a different people. This was perhaps more true when the Church was predominantly a Utah church, but those factors are still significant when viewed as a product of our history. The first includes the *mountains* that gave the Saints the isolation they needed. Second, perhaps, was *Mexico*, which owned Utah when the Saints first arrived and was certainly a factor in the early history of the territory. To these we must add *mining*, a profession the Saints at first resisted and then adopted wholeheartedly. Throughout its history the *military* has been an influential factor, from the Buchanan Expedition to the modern military reservations. Perhaps the most important have been the *migrants* that ensured the salvation and growth of the nineteenth-century church.

Whose Idea Was Irrigation? (1847)

Because of his illness Brigham Young was not among the first Saints to enter the Salt Lake Valley, nor was he present when the first plows unsuccessfully attempted to turn the hard sod of the Valley. He was not there either, as is often stated, to suggest by inspiration to ditch the water—the first form of irrigation. So, whose idea was it? Remember that in the pioneer party were some Battalion members who had wintered in Pueblo, Colorado, after being detached from the Battalion in New Mexico. Some of them joined the pioneer party en route and recalled that farms in New Mexico, as one member noted, "are watered by ditches cut to carry it in every direction." Even before Brigham Young entered the Valley, these Pueblo veterans had dug ditches to soften the soil and water the seeds—the beginning of irrigation by the Saints in Utah.

"Cricket Meat" (1847)

Perhaps the most unique sight encountered by the Saints when they entered the Salt Lake Valley was a Rocky Mountain cricket roundup by the natives. Lorenzo Snow described how they constructed corrals twelve-to fifteen-feet square of sagebrush and greasewood. After driving the huge black crickets into the corrals with branches, they set fire to the brush fence and drove the crickets into the fire. They later picked up the insects, rubbed off their wings and legs, and "separated the meat, which was, I should think, an ounce or half an ounce of fat to each cricket." This was the "dried meat" that helped see the Indians through the winter.

"Summer Quarters" (1847)

There are few Latter-day Saints not familiar with the part played by Winter Quarters on the Missouri River as the Saints moved west. However, since most of those stopping there could not make the trip to Utah in 1847, arrangements had to be made to provide provisions for them either for the trip west or an extended stay, which meant establishing farms. Brigham led the example in provisioning his large adopted family, many of whom had to stay in Winter Quarters for some time by establishing a large farm eighteen miles north of the winter encampment. There, with John D. Lee as foreman of "Brother Brigham's Farm," adopted sons such as Isaac Morley and Lee were able to raise thousands of bushels of grain for the later trip west. Other leaders such as Heber C. Kimball followed Brigham's example.

The Emigration Camp (1847)

Zion's Camp and the Pioneer Camp are both well known in Mormon history. Less known is the term "Emigration Camp," which referred to the second wagon train to leave Winter Quarters for the Great Basin. Parley P. Pratt and John Taylor, who were in charge of this train, did not get away until nearly two months after the pioneer party—much later than Brigham had advised. Other advice they did not follow regarded the size of their train. Brigham told them to keep any trains under 100 wagons, but the "Emigration Camp" started west with nearly 600 wagons and close to 1,500 emigrants. (Another source claimed the number included only adults.) Brigham was obviously not pleased when he discovered this disobedience, but when he left Winter Quarters in 1848 for his second and final trip across the Plains, his train was nearly the same size.

Where Was the Trail? (1847)

It is commonly believed that when the pioneer party of Saints trekked to Utah in 1847, they were following a well-established Oregon Trail or paralleling it. This was the case later, but it was not true of the pioneer party. "He [Brigham] and the company arrived on the 24th of July, having sought out and made a new road 650 miles, and followed a trapper's trail nearly 400 miles." Brigham later stated, "As I remember, there was no trail after leaving Laramie, going over the Black Hills, except very rarely. For a short distance before reaching the Sweetwater we saw a wagon track; it was a great surprise and a great curiosity."

The Wilderness Feast (1847)

In September 1847, as Brigham Young and part of the pioneer party were returning to Winter Quarters from their settlement in the Valley, they met a large train under the direction of John Taylor and Parley P. Pratt headed west. Apprehension over settlement problems, provisions, and an early storm that covered their South Pass meeting site with several inches of snow led the leaders to convene a council meeting. When they emerged from the council, a strange sight met the leaders. The sisters had set up makeshift tables covered with white linens and set with gleaming silverware and fine dishes. On the tables were fish, game, veal, fruits, jams, jellies, and so on taken from their precious wagon stores. No other western trail meal would ever compare with the Saints' famed "Feast in the Wilderness."

A Yellow Bandana with Black Spots (1847)

Traditional Mormon history records that on July 26, 1847, Brigham Young ascended the summit of Ensign Peak and raised the American flag, "the Ensign of Liberty to the world." This story has not gone entirely unchallenged. The *Salt Lake Tribune* ran an article in 1908 that described the "ensign" as a "yellow bandanna decorated with black spots," and attached to Willard Richards's walking cane. This description was immediately challenged by Church leaders upholding the traditional story—but not all Church leaders. B. H. Roberts concluded that the traditional account was "unwarranted" and a "pious fiction," whereas LDS historian Andrew Jenson also questioned the accuracy of the pioneer tale. Although Brigham's daughter, Susa Young Gates, came to the defense of the original account, she later was careful to note that the U.S. flag or "its equivalent" was flown on the Peak on the first day or a "little later."

Another Kind of Feast (1847)

The failure of late-planted crops in the Salt Lake Valley caused widespread hunger in the winter of 1847-48, especially for large families such as that of John Taylor. A friendly Indian, Chief Little Face, brought some vegetables and a delicious meal. When two of his pregnant wives indicated a craving for the meal, John, who had also enjoyed the mysterious food, traveled to the Chief's camp to watch a "harvest" of the ingredients and get the recipe. There he watched as the Indian women ground up a "harvest" of crickets and honey. John lost his appetite for the meal but took some back to his pregnant wives, Sophia and Jane. What they didn't know wouldn't hurt them. Apparently it didn't.

A Negative Impact? (1847)

As the Saints in Nauvoo contemplated their move west, they knew the Federal Government was encouraging the settlement of Oregon to counteract British influence in that area. Without settling there themselves, the Mormons never realized that they would be an influence in encouraging others to migrate there. Matthew Caldwell (see But They Kept the Name—1836) recalled encountering Oregon immigrants near Fort Hall in 1847 as he was returning to Utah with the Mormon Battalion. When asked where he was from, he replied, "From California." His questioner responded, "We don't want to go there, because the Mormons are going to CaliforNey." Caldwell noted in his journal that rumors of the Saints migrating to California revealed why in 1847, "with few exceptions, the entire emigration this year is to Oregon."

Crop Success or Failure? (1847)

"The Mormons raised bountiful crops of grain the very first year of their arrival." So wrote a Salt Lake correspondent from Maine several years after the arrival of the Saints in the Valley. Even many Latter-day Saints, remembering the report of plowing and planting of crops the very day of the Pioneers' arrival in July, believe there must have been some success. Actually, from this "experiment," as B. H. Roberts later reported in his *Comprehensive History*, "nothing matured." Parley P. Pratt verifies this failure in his autobiography, describing the difficulties of surviving the following spring and summer: "My family and myself, in common with many in the camp, suffered much for want of food . . . We toiled hard and lived on a few greens and on thistle and other roots."

Not Even a "Dear John" (1847)

In 1847 Elder Ben Grouard, one of the first and most successful missionaries to the South Pacific, decided to remarry. He had written to his wife at Nauvoo many times but had not heard a word from her or about her and was convinced that she had apostatized and returned to her former life in the Eastern States. Elder Grouard was twenty-seven years old and felt that it was not good for man to be alone. Thus, he decided to take a wife and remain in the islands. In April 1846 he married "the prettiest and best girl on the island," Tearo, but she died shortly after, leaving Grouard with an infant daughter. Grouard married again, this time the daughter of a chief on Anaa. She gave birth to three sons. He was one of a very few missionaries to never again hear anything concerning his American wife—not even a "Dear John" letter.

More than Bulls (1847)

It always seems to be mentioned with a touch of amusement that the only "battle" fought by the Mormon Battalion was the battle with the wild bulls near what is now Tombstone, Arizona. Actually, some Battalion members did become involved in combat after they reached California. In May 1847, Lt. Samuel Thompson, a Mormon from New York, received orders from Battalion commander Cooke to take a detachment of Battalion members to California's Central Valley to stop attacks by Tularenos Indians on ranches in that area. Thompson recorded the resulting combat: "Here we found the enemy ambushed. When they were discovered . . . ordered the attack which they returned with a warm and continued shower of arrows." The combat lasted two hours when the Indians retreated, leaving six of their dead. Two Battalion members were wounded.

The Best Thirteen (1847)

After bringing order to California in only ninety days, military governor General Stephen W. Kearney decided it was time to return east. Impressed by what he had seen and heard of the reliability of the men in the Mormon Battalion, he selected thirteen as his "life guard" to accompany him on his trip. A relative of one of the members later recalled that he ordered Battalion captains to select "the very best all around men: men who could ride the longest and hardest, . . . live on scant rations the longest, do without sleep the longest, load pack-mules the most expeditiously and do double guard duty." History does not report any regrets on Kearney's part.

The "Ram" Becomes a "Dude" (1847)

Most Latter-day Saints have established in their minds the image of Lyman Wight, the "Wild ram of the Mountains," as the tough, no-nonsense defender of Mormonism against the Missouri mobs. A different picture appears when he led his apostate group to Texas in 1846 and settled the community of Mount Bonnell on the outskirts of Austin. A Texas acquaintance described him "dressed in black broadcloth with highly polished boots and a black hat. In fact, he was by the frontier standards of the time termed a 'dude.' He was a real spectacle of a man, heavily armed with two navy pistols in silver-mounted holsters, one on each hip, and . . . from two to six heavily armed and mounted bodyguards."

5
Asylum at Last
(1848-1852)

One Indian Brigham Couldn't Save (1848)

Joseph and George Herring, Mohawk Indian brothers, joined the Church in Nauvoo and went west with the Saints—as far as Winter Quarters. Unfortunately they had a propensity for imbibing too much liquor, which disgusted President Young. A "falling out" with the Prophet occurred and Joseph swore vengeance, saying he would have a war-dance over Brigham's scalp in less than three months and there was every reason to take the threat seriously. William Hickman, a bodyguard for the Prophet but later an apostate himself, described in a vicious anti-Mormon book he dictated years later what he did to preserve Brigham's life: "I found him, used him up, scalped him, and took his scalp to Brigham Young, saying: 'Here is the scalp of the man who was going to have a war-dance over your scalp.'"

Oliver's Loyal Defender (1848)

The person most responsible for bringing about Oliver Cowdery's reconciliation to the Church was his brother-in-law, Phineas. He had not only defended Oliver at the time of his excommunication in Missouri in 1838, but also for the next ten years kept up a constant correspondence and regular visits. With extreme patience he convinced Oliver to humble himself and not wait for an apology from those whom he believed had wronged him. He was also able to convince

President Young of Oliver's sincerity, convincing him to also urge Oliver's return. The reinstatement through baptism finally occurred at the Fall Conference at Winter Quarters in 1848. Perhaps it helped that Phineas was also President Young's brother.

Crickets or Grasshoppers? (1848)

There has been much confusion over the type of insects that destroyed the crops of the Utah pioneers and whether the seagulls really saved the pioneers. There are many conflicting accounts but all evidence suggests three facts. First, they were Rocky Mountain Crickets, not locusts or grasshoppers and thus not able to fly, although the latter did do damage in later years. Second, the crickets invaded and did considerable damage in May and June of 1848, 1849, and 1850. And finally, the seagulls, which were common in the Salt Lake area, lessened the impact of the plague in each of those years—enough to justify the gratitude and regard the Saints have for the bird.

Brigham's Greatest Fear (1848)

Shortly after gold was discovered in California in 1848, President Young voiced his concerns about the greatest fear he had for the Saints—a fear that many Church leaders, with some justification, have today: "The worst fear that I have about this people is that they will get rich in this country, forget God and his people, wax fat, and kick themselves out of the Church and go to hell. This people will stand mobbing, robbing, poverty and all manner of persecution, and be true. But my greater fear for them is that they cannot stand wealth; and yet they have to be tried with riches, for they will become the richest people on this earth."

The Unreliable N.Y.Times (1848)

The New York Times did not live up to its reputation of reliability in the nineteenth century when it came to Mormonism. The paper nearly destroyed the amiable feelings the Saints had for their old Battalion commander, Col. Philip St. George Cooke, when it published a purported letter from him in 1858. This "letter" denounced the Saints as "a set of cowards, like all assassins and bullies" and said the army invading Utah would prove "a more devastating swarm of grasshoppers than any that had yet assaulted Utah." The letter turned out to be a hoax that the *Times* had failed to check sufficiently, but for a while it generated a bitterness among the Saints about this betrayal by an old friend. When Battalion historian James Ferguson wrote a strongly worded letter to Cooke, the officer denounced the *Times* and politely thanked Ferguson for bringing it to his attention.

Even with the Help of Indians (1848)

It becomes difficult not to judge the past without reference to the present, especially in dealing with conservation. We must remember, however, that when the Saints entered the Salt Lake Valley, survival depended on successful competition with existing predators. Thus it was that starting on Christmas Day 1848, two teams of hunters began a contest to see which one could count the greatest number of "kills" over the next several weeks. After a couple of extensions ending in March, John D. Lee's team of 37 hunters won with a kill of 516 wolves, 238 foxes, 173 magpies, 439 ravens, and a scattering of hawks, owls, minks, wildcats, and so on. Lee later reported that he beat John Pack's team in spite of Pack enlisting two tribes of Indians.

And Dog Hair Suits (1848)

We have heard much of how scarcity of food forced the earliest Mormon pioneers in the Salt Lake Valley to eat thistle tops and wild sego lilies, but little has been said of the scarcity of cloth. Animal skins were made use of, but for cloth there was little wool and no flax. Since they still had their handlooms and spinning wheels, the Saints turned to other sources for the yarns and threads for weaving cloth—mainly buffalo and cow hair that they wove into blankets for exchange with the Indians. According to Susa Young Gates, one man sheared his dog annually and was dressed entirely in a suit made from his dog's hair.

Sorry I Missed Him (1848)

William Weeks, famed architect of the Nauvoo Temple, was headed east from the Salt Lake Valley in July 1848 and Brigham Young was headed west when they just missed each other. Actually, Weeks turned out of his way to avoid the President because he had apostatized and still had a wagon and team that belonged to Brigham. When Brigham learned of the lost encounter, he sent a message to William that he would have no peace until he returned to the Valley and made restitution for the wickedness he had committed. The prophecy proved accurate: Weeks spent five years in the Midwest before returning to Utah and asking for rebaptism. He got to Utah in time for the groundbreaking on the Salt Lake Temple, but Brigham had by that time selected another temple architect, Truman Angell.

First Language Training Center (1848)

An event that puts into perspective, more than any other historic event, the importance Latter-day Saints place on missionary work was the establishment of a Missionary Language Training Center in Salt Lake City within a year of the arrival of the Saints in the Valley. Addison Pratt, who labored in the Polynesian Islands for almost ten years (called the Society Islands until 1907), established a school in Salt Lake City in 1848 in which he taught Polynesian three nights a week. Such training permitted the missionaries to be extraordinarily successful in their conversions until the French authorities banished them from the Islands in 1853. Missionaries were not allowed to return there for nearly forty years.

The Unofficial Patriarch (1849)

When John Smith was sustained and set apart as Presiding Patriarch to the Church in 1849, his calling finally became official. Six months before his death at Carthage Jail, the Prophet Joseph had ordained John a patriarch, but it was not official that he be the Presiding Patriarch. That honor belonged to John's older brother Asael by right, but he was too ill to function (he died a month after his nephews Joseph and Hyrum). Although both Hyrum and William had served in that position, John took over after William's rejection at the October Conference in 1845. He served unofficially as Presiding Patriarch for the next four years until it was made official in 1849. When he died in 1854, he had administered 5,560 blessings.

A Strange Extortion (1849)

In 1849 the doctors in Salt Lake City formed the Council of Health to promote better methods of healing. One of the founders was the pioneer doctor Priddy Meeks, who like most Latter-day Saint practitioners, believed strongly in botanical healing rather than in the heroic theory of using poisons such as mercury- and arsenic-laced concoctions. Priddy later related how an anti-Mormon "poison" doctor, a Dr. Cannon, offered to give up doctoring if the other doctors would give him all the surgery to do. Believing this a good way to improve the quality of doctoring in Utah, they agreed, and according to Dr. Meeks, Cannon "joined the Council of Health and proved a great benefit to us, being a man of much experience and intelligence. I learned considerable by helping him to dissect the dead."

A Mormon Peace Corps (1849)

In the fall of 1849, Brigham Young sent over 200 colonists to plant a settlement 130 miles south of Salt Lake City. This expedition, however, had been preceded by a conference with the Utah Indian Chief Wakara, who approved the settlement when it was explained. Manti, the first colony in the San Pitch Valley, would be a mission to cultivate peace with the Indians and to help them change a hunting and food-gathering life-style to an agriculturally based one. Both Wakara and Young recognized that Mormon colonization would eventually reduce the Indians' supply of game. Isaac Morley, the leader of the settlement, verified the goal of this early "Peace Corps" when he stated, "We were sent to enrich the Natives and comfort the hearts of the long oppressed. Let us try the experiment and if we fail to accomplish the object, then say, Boys, come away."

Utah's "First Temple" (1849)

Because Addison Pratt was on an extended mission in the Pacific Islands, he was not able to receive his endowments in the Nauvoo Temple before the Exodus. After his arrival in the Valley in 1849 and because of his faithfulness, he was taken to the summit of Ensign Peak and there received his endowments, Brigham Young relating that it had been consecrated for that purpose. Such endowments were in harmony with a talk by the Prophet Joseph in Nauvoo on May 1, 1842. "I preached in the grove on the keys to the kingdom . . . which cannot be revealed to the elders till the temple is completed. The rich can only get them in the temple; the poor may get them on the mountaintop, as did Moses."

Fact and Fancy (1849)

The difference between facts and the myths perpetrated by the anti-Mormon press in the nineteenth century is best illustrated in regard to the Perpetual Emigrating Fund founded by the Church in 1849 to aid in the cost of immigration by Mormon converts. Although it had aided in the immigration of thousands of Saints during its thirty-eight years, the Federal Government disincorporated it under the Edmunds-Tucker Act of 1887, when the U.S. Marshall discovered it to have no collectable assets. A year after it began, it had only $20,000 in assets and yet an anti-Mormon newspaper article, commonly believed by anti-Mormons, reported that "at its start three and a half tons of gold were laid aside, equal to about 376,320 [English] pounds . . . donations and taxations kept up the amount." It was articles such as this that generated gentile fear of Mormon power in the nineteenth century.

Thomas Kane the "Prophet" (1849)

According to Wilford Woodruff, Thomas Kane told him in 1849 that he had applied, "according to the wish of President Young, for a territorial government. . . . I found he did not feel disposed to favor your people, and he had his men of his own stamp picked out to serve as governor and other officers, who would have oppressed you." Kane felt the Saints were "better without any government. I had to use my own discretion, and I withdrew the petition. . . . All the parties, with the whole congress, are a mass of corruption and abomination. . . . I told Mr. Polk we should not present any petition while he dictated matters." The Mormons were not convinced by Kane's prophecy and shortly thereafter Congress, with few objections by the Saints, granted them territorial status. Col. Kane's prophecy would be literally fulfilled over the next four decades.

PSTAPCJCLDSLDAOW (1849)

Brigham Young's daughter, Clarissa, described the shortage of money in Utah in 1849 when "Father and his assistants did practically nothing else but 'make' money. Bullock would write out the bills, after which Father would sign them, and they would be stamped with the seal of the Twelve Apostles." This same seal was used to identify early missionaries before people would trust them with their tithing. Brigham Young and John Taylor had designed the seal in 1845 in Nauvoo. It consisted of an all-seeing eye under a crown encircled with the letters PSTAPCJCLDSLDAOW that stood for "Private Seal of the Twelve Apostles, Priests of the Church of Jesus Christ of Latter-day Saints in the Last Dispensation All Over the World."

Selling Indulgences? (1850)

Brigham Young wasn't really selling indulgences, but it might have sounded like it to critics. Although credited with bringing at least 50,000 Saints to Utah during its span from 1849 until it was abolished by the Edmunds-Tucker Act, the Perpetual Emigrating Fund was always short of funds—largely because those aided were unable or unwilling to reimburse the fund for their own financial help. Fully a third paid only a part of their debt and another third paid nothing. This prompted Brigham to try a little humor at a General Conference in September 1850, when he announced, "Come on [you] tobacco chewers and put your 1000 [thousand dollars] into [the] Poor fund and I will give you liberty to chew anot[he]r year."

The Last Witness (1850)

When Mary Field Garner entered the Salt Lake Valley in 1850, it seemed inconceivable that she would still be alive during World War II. When she died in 1943, at the age of 107 as a result of a fall, she was recorded as the last living witness to have personally known the Prophet Joseph Smith. She was eight years old when he was killed, and lived ninety-nine years after the martyrdom. Of the ten children born to her and William Garner, Jr., she left over 600 lineal descendants. Three sons and a daughter were still living when she died—all of them in their eighties.

But They Came Back (1850)

Although it was their intention to settle outside the United States when they were expelled from Illinois, it is commonly believed that the Saints found themselves back in the Union when they arrived in the Salt Lake Valley. Not so! Since they were not admitted as a state until 1896 or even a Territory until 1850, their only status for the first three years was that of a possession—similar to such one-time possessions as Puerto Rico or the Philippines. In July, 1854, at the July 24th celebration, the first speaker, Leo Hawkin, expressed the sentiments of the average Saint when he thanked President Young for forming "the Provisional Government of Deseret, removing us from the power of an oppressive state [the U.S.], and giving us the power of self legislation."

We May Never Know (1850)

Utah Territorial Militia correspondence during the war against the Indians in Utah Valley in 1850 shows a number of euphemisms that appear to cover up an atrocity against the Indians—namely the execution of Indian prisoners. Lieutenant Gunnison, who wrote a book on the Utah Mormons, took his information from the Saints several years after the event, blaming the deaths of all of the braves on skirmishing or attempted escape of several prisoners. Correspondence by General Wells to Captain George Grant and Brigham Young at the time, however, suggests that several "hostile" Indian prisoners would be dealt with "in the most summary manner" the following morning. A postscript the next day asked for a suggestion as to the "disposal of some 15 or 20 Squaws and children who probably belonged to some 11 warriors who met their fate in a small skirmish this morning."

Whatever Is Effective (1850)

Captain Stansbury's official report on his visit to Utah during the winter of 1849-50 to survey the Great Salt Lake reported at length on the Mormons and their lifestyles. His observation on the sober habits of the Saints did not emphasize the Word of Wisdom as the reason for their abstinence but he mentioned a very practical cause: "All goods brought into the city pay, as the price of a license, a duty of one percent, except spirituous liquors, for which one half of the price at which they are sold is demanded." A 50% tax would certainly discourage consumption of the forbidden drink and it was, with the absence of grog shops, apparently effective. He goes on to record that during his several months in the Valley, he "never saw a man drunk."

FDR Was Not the First (1850)

The idea of public works is not unique to the Saints or even the United States, but perhaps government "make-work" is. It is normally associated with President Roosevelt and such agencies as the Civilian Conservation Corps during the Depression in the early 1930s. Actually, the Latter-day Saints developed make-work projects to aid the poor and unemployed over eighty years earlier. On January 26, 1850, Brigham Young organized a permanent public works and appointed Daniel H. Wells as the first superintendent. In 1853, President Young defended such make-work projects as the adobe wall around the city by saying, "I build walls, dig ditches, make bridges, and do a great amount and variety of labor that is of but little consequence only to provide ways and means for sustaining and preserving the destitute."

Woman Suffrage Revisited (1850)

Although American histories normally give Wyoming the credit for legislation granting woman suffrage, Utah is generally recognized as the territory where women first voted because of the dates of the next elections. (See *500 Little Known Facts*, p. 198.) That historic election was in 1870, but

LDS women were actually voting in "matters relating to government" over twenty years earlier. Between 1847 and 1850, when it was granted Territorial status, Utah was under its own Provisional Government and without Federal jurisdiction; the Saints gave women the right to vote. Ironically, considering the Federal Government's contention that Mormon women were deprived of "rights," Congress withdrew woman suffrage when it granted Utah Territorial status.

Selecting the Prophet as Counselor (1851)

Orson Hyde baptized one of Mormondom's most faithful members on October 8, 1840. Two years later Edward Hunter moved from Pennsylvania to Nauvoo, where he generously gave of his wealth and time to the Church before going west with the Saints during the Exodus. In 1850 his close friend and Presiding Bishop of the Church, Newel K. Whitney, died, and during the General Conference in April 1851, Brother Hunter was chosen to succeed Bishop Whitney as third Presiding Bishop of the Church. His permanent counselors, Leonard Hardy and Jesse Little, were not sustained until 1856 so he selected as his "temporary" counselors Brigham Young, the Prophet, and Heber C. Kimball of the first presidency. Both served him well.

The "King" Arrested (1851)

The story of James Strang and his attempt to establish a rival church to the Latter-day Saints after the death of Joseph is fairly well known. So too is the "kingdom" he established on Beaver Island in Lake Michigan and his assassination by his own people. Less known, however, is the military expedition sent by President Fillmore in 1851 to arrest Strang and charge him with debauchery (plural marriage), thievery, and trespassing on federal land (Beaver Island). Forty soldiers dispatched on the Navy's first iron vessel, the *Michigan*, carried out the arrest. After a sensational trial in Detroit, Strang and his followers were all found innocent.

A Lack of Virtue? (1851)

Associate Federal judge for the Utah Territory, Perry Brocchus, asked permission to speak to the Saints during General Conference in October 1851. During his address, without specifically mentioning plural marriage, he told the assembled sisters that he hoped they "would become virtuous." Furious over this insult to Mormon women, Brigham Young arose to answer, saying: "Judge Brocchus is either profoundly ignorant, or willfully wicked, one of the two." Several days later President Young wrote to the judge, inviting him to attend the following Sunday service and "then and there explain, satisfy, or apologize to the satisfaction of the ladies." The judge declined and fled Utah the following month as one of the well-known "run-away" officials.

Revelations from Beheemy? (1852)

By 1852, the "Beheemy"ites, a new church established by the apostate, Charles B. Thompson, was gathering in some converts at Council Bluffs. Upon hearing Thompson was claiming to be receiving revelations from Beheemy, Orson Pratt, concerned, asked permission to expose Thompson, who "stole" the name from the Doctrine and Covenants. This was one of the many pseudonyms Joseph Smith used for people, places, and things in some revelations received in Kirtland between 1832 and 1834. He used the pseudonyms to prevent Church enemies from using the information in some manner against the Church. With such danger now past, Brigham gave permission for Orson to reprint the Doctrine and Covenants with the actual names. For technical reasons it was not done until 1876. Beheemy, incidentally, apparently unknown to the apostate Thompson, was the pseudonym for Sidney Rigdon, now an apostate himself.

The Lord's Ten Percent? (1852)

Few topics have been the subject of appeals from Church leaders more often than the one of tithing. Brigham Young was noted for making such appeals and for seldom mincing his words about the Saints' habit of not donating their honest tithes, as in the October Conference of 1852. He brought up the subject of the contemplated Salt Lake Temple and the desire to build it of the best material. If so, why not "pure gold; that is here, I know. But if the Conference want us to build a temple of pure gold, they will have to put into the tithing stores something besides old half-dead stinking cows, and old broken-kneed horses."

6

The End of Discretion
(1852-1857)

Driving Away Somber Feelings (1852)

Official restrictions on "inappropriate" music in church services are not in keeping with LDS history. A visitor to Salt Lake City in 1852 described a typical church service: "While the congregation is assembling and departing from the house, it is usual for the large and excellent band of music to perform anthems, marches, and waltzes, which drive away all somber feelings, and prepares the mind for the exciting and often eloquent discourses." Michael Hicks, in his 1989 work, *Mormonism and Music: A History*, noted that such music by bands was common in LDS Church services, and "no evidence suggests that anyone debated this practice. . . . Good Saints would not question their practice in the church."

Was This Public Pressure? (1852)

On March 5, 1852, the names of 106 men were called from the pulpit in Salt Lake City to go on missions around the world, including South Africa, India, Australia, the West Indies, Canada, and Europe. Today we marvel at not only the faith required of such men to be torn from their families to travel thousands of miles to serve lengthy missions but that it was often done without previous warning. Those 106 men called in March had no previous warning, which prompts us to ask ourselves a question seldom dealt with in Church histories: How many refused to go after their calling? History does not really tell us, but we can be sure that such "public" announcements were an inspired factor in discouraging mission refusals when done in a private session.

The Relief Trains (1852)

Most students of the westward movement picture wagon trains wending their way to the Salt Lake Valley being forced to carry all the supplies necessary for the two- or three-month journey on the trail. Actually, relief trains were continually on the way between Utah and the Missouri River. Historians have noted that the remnants of many immigrant trains were "saved" by the opportune arrival of these rescuing parties. In the year 1852 alone, immigrating companies were reprovisioned at midpoint by 200 relief wagons carrying 50,000 pounds of flour and vegetables. It should be noted that such relief came from those who were themselves destitute and nearly starving.

An Ambitious PR Initiative (1852)

In an effort to counteract the powerful backlash that resulted from the public announcement in 1852 that the Church taught and practiced plural marriage, President Brigham Young, beginning in that year, founded several LDS newspapers in major cities. First was *The Seer*, in Washington, D.C., edited by Orson Pratt. Soon after, *The Mormon* was established in New York City, edited by John Taylor. Next Young founded *The St. Louis Luminary*, edited by Erastus Snow, and *The Western Standard* in San Francisco, edited by George Q. Cannon. None of these lasted long but, edited by the most articulate Church leaders, they were effective in influencing public opinion to some extent by presenting another side of Mormonism, which a hostile mainline press failed to do.

Abolishing the Legal Profession (1852)

Because the legal profession had been used so often in the early persecutions of the Saints, the early Mormon leaders' distaste for lawyers is well known. But it is difficult to believe they went as far as they did in 1852—by actually passing a law that was hoped would drive the profession into oblivion. In 1852 the Territorial Legislature passed an act allowing a man or woman to act as his or her own lawyer or for others, hoping that it would thus become unprofitable for attorneys to practice in Utah. There is little evidence that women took advantage of this law, but men did. Still, lawyers continued to practice, so the legislature could only require that they show proof of good moral character. Many undoubtedly believed that even this requirement would limit the number of lawyers.

Parsnips into Molasses! (1852)

An item the Saints in the Salt Lake Valley missed most was sugar, and so great hopes were based on the sugar mill established in Provo in 1852. Unfortunately, it failed and was moved to Salt Lake City where efforts continued to make sugar from sugar beets until it was eventually successful. In the meantime the Saints were forced to utilize molasses, but not made from sugar cane. Instead, they made a type of molasses from almost any vegetable including melon rinds, corn stalks, and squash. One small molasses factory advertised for "all who had a surplus of beets, carrots or parsnips to bring them along, well cleaned for family use and we will make all the molasses we can and return the owners of the vegetables one-half of the molasses made."

Provider of the Yellow Metal (1852)

The biggest shortage faced by the Saints in Utah was of gold and silver coin. Even donations and sending "gold missionaries" to California did not provide the gold that the Church seemed to be spending. The source, apparently, was the Ute chief, Wakara, who was baptized into the church in 1850. In spite of "on again off again" relations with the Saints, Wakara made a secret agreement with Brigham to provide the badly needed gold. He let Brigham choose one man, who, being sworn to secrecy, would be allowed access to Wakara's gold mine in order to furnish the Saints with the badly needed gold. The man was Thomas Rhoades who kept the secret, and after his death, his son Caleb kept it, after whose time the "Lost Rhoades Mines" (there was actually more than one mine) became lost in history. Not lost is the name of Wakara or "Yah-Keera" which means "Keeper of the Yellow Metal."

Revelation or Common Sense? (1853)

When ground was broken for the Salt Lake Temple in February 1853, President Young made some remarks regarding the building of temples. He said, "Some might query whether a revelation had been given to build a house to the Lord. . . . I know a temple is needed and so do you; and when we know a thing, why do we need a revelation to compel us to do that thing? If the Lord and all the people want a revelation, I can give one concerning this temple." He then added, "Brother Joseph often remarked that a revelation was no more necessary to build a temple than a dwelling house; if a man knew he needed a kitchen, a bedroom, a cook room, etc., he needed no revelation to inform him of the fact; and I, and my brethren around me, know what is wanting in a temple."

A Wife and Other Supplies (1853)

The early Saints were often too busy to make much of courting. John Pulsipher related in his journal his matter-of-fact first marriage to Rozilla Huffaker, a girl of only seventeen. When he was ready for marriage, he related, "The Lord sent me one—not a wife—but a good pattern to make one of." Successful, the marriage lasted until Rozilla's death eighteen years later. Thereupon, John traveled from Dixie to Salt Lake City "to get me a [another] wife & some other supplies." He found one but was forced to return home without her. He then sent a few letters, finally saying that "as we live in the days of short prayers, short sermons, & short courtships," he wanted her to tell him in "plain, mountain-English" if it would be proper to be joined in marriage. She agreed.

A Little Wartime Humor (1853)

The well-known Walker War between the Saints and the Ute Indians under Chief Walker (Wakara) was just beginning in 1853 when George A. Smith gave some counsel in the Salt Lake Tabernacle. He concluded his discourse with a humorous suggestion for ending the war. "Walker himself has teased me," he said, "for a white wife; and if any of the sisters will volunteer to marry him, I believe I can close the war forthwith." With tongue in cheek he added, "In conclusion I will say, if any lady wishes to be Mrs. Walker, if she will report herself to me, I will agree to negotiate the match." The war ended the following year with no volunteers.

First "Execution" of Saints (1853)

This "fact" may be debated since there seems to be little verification of the details—even the exact date—but there is sufficient evidence that it happened. French Polynesia was predominantly Catholic and the Mormon intrusion in the 1840s caused conflict and persecution by the authorities. When a drunken gendarme and two priests invaded a Mormon meeting on the island of Anaa, a fight broke out. The native Saints ended up killing the gendarme, and one of the priests was killed by the gendarme's sword, wielded allegedly by one of the native Saints. Government troops from Papeete, responding to the "revolt," hung five Priesthood holders from a beam between two coconut trees and took several of the sisters away in chains to labor on the construction of roads.

A Prophet's Prophet (1853)

It is noted that the Doctrine and Covenants has only one canonized revelation of Brigham Young, prompting many to wonder why. It was partly explained by Brigham at the April General Conference in 1853 when he was addressing the subject of what kind of building the new Salt Lake Temple would be: "I know what it will be. I am not a visionary man, neither am I given much to prophesying. When I want any of that done I call on Brother Heber—he is my prophet, he loves to prophesy, and I love to hear him." Church history is filled with the dramatic, fulfilled prophesies of Heber C. Kimball. Years later, his grandson, Prophet Spencer W. Kimball, described his grandfather as "a prophet perhaps second only to Joseph Smith himself." Heber, of course, was next in line for the Presidency after Brigham, but he died first.

What Scripture Is That? (1853)

Allen Weeks, who had the responsibility in Ogden in 1853 for seeing that settlers moved their houses into the fort for protection, had a problem with Brother Barnes who refused. Weeks, too, might have wondered about the answer from the First Presidency, who, when he asked for advice, quoted an old proverb or scripture that Weeks "probably remembered": "If tufts and grass only will not prevail stones must be used." The meaning was clear but the source was not, which makes us wonder who was responsible for the "counterfeit" scripture or proverb in the letter from the First Presidency: Brigham Young, Heber C. Kimball, or Willard Richards?

Stay away from New Orleans (1854)

There is no record of the number of Black Latter-day Saints emigrating from England to the United States, but in the Thomas Fisher journal in 1854, there is a notation of the rejection of Jane Hunter from the London Conference because she was a "coloured woman." The reason was for her own protection as there was danger that in passing through New Orleans she risked being kidnapped on the charge of being a runaway slave. A few years later even white males immigrating through any of the Confederate States were warned about the risk of being impressed into the Confederate Army by soldiers who were paid a one-dollar bounty for each man so impressed.

A Baby's Face (1854)

When the "pathfinder" John C. Fremont stumbled into Parowan with twenty-one companions, all in an acute state of starvation in February 1854, the Mormon residents gave them shelter and food. One of the party, an artist named Carvalho, after recovering, saw a grieving father outside his home and when asked if he needed aid, the man said, "My baby girl has just died, and her mother is distracted." Inside the adobe home the artist saw "the most angelic face he had ever beheld." Sketching the dead child, he gave the likeness to the child's mother, a Mrs. Richard Harrison. After leaving Parowan, the artist found in his wagon a basket of dressed poultry, vegetables, and fruit, "to one who had brought comfort." The sketch was donated to the Church museum many years later.

Brigham and Madam Pattirini (1854)

Brigham Young was born in 1854, but he was usually called Morris for that was his middle name. He was the thirty-fifth child of President Brigham Young and spent his entire life working for the Church, either as a missionary or an employee. He married Lorenzo Snow's daughter, Armedia, and later, when his large family was on the brink of poverty, his father-in-law offered him a job in the Salt Lake Temple at $60 a month, where he spent the last thirty-eight years of his life. Morris was well known as an entertainer and humorist and often performed for church social functions as "Madam Pattirini," a great female opera singer. Morris was greatly distraught when his father died from a ruptured appendix in 1877. Perhaps it was not inappropriate that Morris would die from the same rare malady at the age of seventy-seven.

Ugly, Stubborn, and Cross (1854)

The Saints had no restrictions against intermarriage with Native Americans, so when James Brown and Thomas Bullock were sent on a peace mission to the Shoshone Indians in 1854, the subject was raised by the Mormons. When they suggested to Chief Washakie that some of the men might want to take some Shoshone women as wives, the chief gave the following response: "I cannot see why a white man wants an Indian girl. They are dirty, ugly, stubborn and cross . . . it is a strange idea for white men to want such wives." However, he added, if they found a willing Indian girl, it would be all right, but the Indians must have the same privilege among the white women. This reply ended the subject of intermarriage.

Because of One Cow! (1854)

In August of 1854 a company of Saints was approaching Fort Laramie when one of their cows wandered into an Indian camp and was killed and eaten. When the owner complained to the Fort commander, a brash and recent graduate of West Point, Lieutenant Grattan, with twenty-eight men, was sent to arrest the Indian responsible for killing the cow. An untactful confrontation escalated into the massacre of the entire troop except one. This incident then escalated into a costly conflict between the U. S. Army and a major portion of the Sioux Nation. A number of immigrants and natives lost their lives, including 85 Brule Sioux in one massacre alone, before the war ended eighteen months later. And all because of one Mormon cow!

Not Enough Mormons (1855)

During the greatest half-century of Mormon immigration, from 1840 to 1890, more than 85,000 Saints assigned to organized companies arrived in the United States. Remarkably, while shipwrecks were a daily occurrence (557 vessels were lost during a 14-month period ending December 1841), only one Mormon vessel, the *Julia Ann* out of Australia, was lost. A variety of reasons have been advanced, especially that Mormon ships were commonly dedicated and blessed before embarking, but observant captains recognized that the facts existed. During one frightening Atlantic storm in 1874, the captain of the British steamship *Idaho* confidently commented "that there were too many Mormons on board [there were 806] for the ship to be harmed; he had carried [Mormon] companies for 18 years and had never heard of a ship carrying 'Mormons' being lost."

Eliza Obeys—Reluctantly (1855)

In 1855 Eliza Snow was asked to bring her Relief Society minutes (which went back to the founding in Nauvoo) to the Historian's Office. There she was informed they would be revised, a thought that caused the perfectionist mind of Eliza unease. The purpose, she was told, was to revise the sermons the Prophet Joseph preached to the sisters at the founding of the society. Church leaders were concerned these sermons might be interpreted as conferring authority and keys to the sisters, permitting them to act and work outside the authority of the priesthood. Emma Smith had used such implications to justify her anti-plural marriage teachings to the sisters, teachings that prompted Brigham to shut down the Relief Society after Joseph's death. With the reestablishment of the Relief Society, the Church leaders could not permit that to happen again.

The Saints Rejected the "Honor" (1855)

Chief Wakara, or Walker, as he was known to the Mormons, had caused much death and suffering among the Saints during the Walker War of 1854 although he had been baptized four years previously. When he died in 1855, however, he was back in the graces of the Saints and seemed to value his Church membership. He had made plans for his funeral, including the deaths of two favorite wives, two Piede children, and several horses. He also thought it would be an honor if representatives of other groups of friends, including two Pahvants and two Mormons, were sacrificed to accompany him. The Utes made efforts to capture some Saints for the "honor," but, being forewarned, the Mormons kept out of the way until the funeral was over. They respectfully declined the "honor."

Brigham Consecrates Own Property (1855)

Critics of Brigham Young have often accused him of using the law of consecration for his own enrichment. Actually, as early as 1855, to encourage other members, he consecrated his own numerous properties to the Church, including a number of homes, numerous lots, livestock, farming equipment, and such personal property as gold watches, clocks, bedding, and other household furniture—with a total evaluation of $199,625. For those who point out that he conveyed such property to himself as Trustee in Trust, it must be noted that the consecration deed specifically assigned all of this property to his successors in office, whomever they might be, acting in behalf of the Church.

Around the World (1855)

Most Saints associate Richard Ballantyne with the founding of the first Latter-day Saint Sunday School in the Salt Lake Valley in 1849. He is, however, noted for another "first." In 1855 Brother Ballantyne crossed the Plains—but not for the first time. He was returning from a mission that began in San Francisco in January 1853 when he left for India with twelve other missionaries. But this was not a first—other Mormon missionaries were already in India, a mission that would soon be closed for lack of success. After his lack of success in India, Richard left for Great Britain and then returned home to the United States. When he finally arrived in the Valley in 1855, he was completing an around-the-world mission without purse or scrip—the first Latter-day Saint missionary to accomplish this feat.

The Grasshopper Solution (1855)

Although the so-called Mormon crickets had been a major problem in earlier years, the drought and grasshopper crisis of 1855 brought the Saints face to face with wholesale famine. The Mormons were not surprised to discover, in spite of the publicity about their dire circumstances, that newspapers around the country seemed to delight in the possibility of mass starvation as the "solution to the Mormon problem." In fact, only one journal raised a sympathetic voice—the *Woman's Advocate*. Its editor wrote of the mass press's "tone of delighted chuckle that chills the blood. There is a spirit of murder in it," she noted, "that is suppressed only because the triumph is not yet sure."

A Communication Breakdown (1856)

It becomes difficult to find any little-known facts about the Willie and Martin Handcart tragedies. Their late start, lack of sufficient clothing, and early winter on the Plains are common knowledge. Less common, however, is knowledge of an admission President Young made in a letter written in October of 1856: "We had no idea there were any more companies upon the Plains." Resupply trains had been sent from the Valley to meet previous incoming handcart companies with food and other supplies. Information that more handcart companies were on the way was either never sent or never arrived, prompting Brigham to shut down the re-supply trains from the Valley until the following year. It was not until Franklin D. Richards, who had passed the late hardcarts on the Plains, arrived in Salt Lake City that Young learned of their plight.

It Was an Emergency! (1856)

Lucy Meserve Smith, a plural wife of George A. Smith, recalled the most memorable test of the Provo Ward Relief Society over which she presided in 1856. While attending the opening session of the October General Conference in Salt Lake City, President Young announced the news of the handcart pioneers trapped in the snow and cold in the Wyoming mountains and the need for immediate aid in the form of food, clothing, and transportation. Brigham dismissed the Conference and told his people to do what had to be done. As the men set out to ready the teams and wagons to carry clothing and food to the suffering Saints, the sisters "stripped off their petticoats, stockings, and everything they could spare, right there in the Tabernacle, and piled them into the wagons to send to the Saints in the Mountains."

Did We Say Amen? (1856)

On December 22, 1856, the Seventies met at their hall in Salt Lake City. Several of the Twelve met with them because of their concern over the failure of the First Presidents of the Seventies to magnify their calling. The Apostles felt that all of the leaders of the Seventies, except Joseph Young, should resign their positions so that other, perhaps younger, men who would "not obstruct the work of the Lord, could be called to the Presidency of the Seventies." Hosea Stout noted in his journal that "all present responded to this with a hearty & heart thrilling Amen."

In spite of their seeming willingness to adopt this suggestion, none of them did. Most of them died in their calling.

Not Politically Correct (1856)

The general reformation that spread throughout the Church in 1856 and was designed to bring about a recommitment to Church principles, doctrines, and standards is not that unknown. Less known perhaps is the part the Territorial Legislature played—an involvement that would be unheard of in today's secular legislatures. On December 30 of that year, a joint session met in committee of the whole and passed a unanimous resolution "to repent of and forsake our sins and be rebaptized for their Remission." After adjourning, the legislators went to dinner and then, according to member Hosea Stout, "repaired to the Font, filled it with water and some fifty-five were Baptized."

Women Survivors (1856)

Church members today are aware of the high death rate in the Willie and Martin handcart companies. Fewer are aware of the fact that far more men and boys died than woman and girls. For example, in the Willie Company the mortality rate among men was three times higher than for women, and for men over forty, it was ten times higher. Those noting this have often attributed it to males bearing the heavier burden of pulling and pushing the handcarts or skimping on the food rations. Although this was true, recent anthropological studies point out two other major factors. The women were protected from the cold by more body fat, and childbearing toughened them.

The Jaded Mule (1856)

Although agreement is not universal among LDS historians, most seem to concur that the "kickoff" of the Mormon Reformation began with Jedediah Grant at a conference held September 13, 1856, at Kaysville, a small community some twenty-five miles north of Salt Lake City. Brigham Young had sent him to tell the people to live their religion, which he did, but he carried it a step further than originally planned, according to T.B.H. Stenhouse, a Mormon leader who later apostatized. Brother Jeddy's anger was aroused when he noted the worn-out nature of a mule he had loaned to a man who rode it to the meeting. Grant later implied that he was prompted to go a little further than Brigham had suggested. When he "got there he felt like baptizing and confirming them anew into the Church."

Feel Free to Speak Up (1856)

Heber J. Grant's father, Jedediah, died within days of Heber's birth, and the family's bishop, Edwin Woolley, performed the christening. Bishop Woolley later remarked, "That boy is entitled [someday] to be one of the Apostles, and I know it." The bishop's spiritual insight could, however, lead the well-meaning leader to make seemingly unfair decisions. During one church meeting he complimented those who accused him of not acting "the part of a father" and urged his critics to air their feelings. When one critic, William Capener, did so, Woolley abruptly cut him off from the Church. The following week the members debated the bishop's action, with half the congregation refusing to sustain the excommunication. Bishop Woolley, however, would not budge. He was determined to cleanse the Church.

Neckties and Aprons (1856)

On October 5, 1856, Brigham Young announced to the assembled congregation in the Bowery the plight of the Willie and Martin handcart companies and asked for volunteer men and teams to go to their rescue. He also asked for donations of food and clothing and the resulting contributions were more than he asked for—including fourteen tons of flour as well as hundreds of quilts, blankets, coats, boots, shoes, and so on. Within three days a relief train was on the way, and by October 31, 250 teams were on the trail, loaded with supplies for the freezing and starving Saints. Among the supplies were some baffling items, however, including four neckties, four handkerchiefs, a rug, and two aprons.

Very Light Infantry (1857)

The well-known pioneer celebration of July 24, 1857, which was interrupted by the news of the approach of the U. S. Army, is often described with the various militia detachments in attendance. One of these is described as a company of light infantry under the command of John W. Young. They were literally very "light," composed of fifty boys ranging from ten to twelve years of age. They wore striking white uniforms furnished by President Young, who had given them the name "Hope of Israel."

A Young Hero Finds a Bride (1857)

Most Latter-day Saints are quite familiar with the story of the three young men who risked and actually did shorten their lives by going to the rescue of the handcart companies in 1856 and carrying the survivors across ice-covered streams. One of them was David P. Kimball, son of Heber C. Kimball.

A less-familiar story is what happened to these boys later. In 1857 eighteen-year-old David fell in love with Caroline Williams and induced her, with the aid of several other young men, including sons of Heber C. and Brigham Young, to elope. Caroline's father, Thomas S. Williams, was furious and threatened to kill David's father, Heber. Caroline was only fourteen. However, the marriage was successful, but David's life was shortened. He died at the age of forty-four in St. David, Arizona, a town named after him.

7
The End of Autonomy
(1857-1862)

Mountain Meadows Revisited (1857)

Although certainly not an excuse for the 1857 massacre, there is an interesting sidenote not normally mentioned in listing the reasons for the attack on the Fancher wagon train. Word had only reached Utah shortly before the massacre of the assassination of Parley P. Pratt in Arkansas. A public furor arose in Utah against citizens of Arkansas, and this anger, combined with the rumor that the assassin was in the Fancher train, news of the approach of Johnston's army, the alleged behavior of the Fanchers as they traveled through the Territory, and so on, only added to the willingness of some of the Saints to participate in the attack on the Arkansas travelers. It is also of interest that it was Parley's southern exploring expedition of 1851 that discovered Mountain Meadows and that Parley had praised it for its beauty.

Basswood and Hickory Mormons (1857)

Saints who were less than strong in the faith in the nineteenth century were given the name "Basswood" Mormons. During the Reformation of 1856, a number of leaders felt it was an appropriate time to cleanse the Church of the less faithful, especially those who refused rebaptism. A typical leader was Asa Calkin, President of the English Mission who did just that, saying it was better "to apostatize here than after they go to the valley." Matthias Cowley agreed saying that "Basswood Mormons are obliged to kick out and none but the hickory Saints stand." Orson Pratt noted that such excommunications, including those who were not tithing as well as those who refused rebaptism, cut the membership in England to less than half of what it was in 1850.

And That Was Journalism! (1857)

It is a little difficult in reading newspapers of the nineteenth century to always identify historical events, especially in such newspapers as the *Oregon Statesman* of June 15, 1857, which told its readers of an event that occurred the previous year: "Of the 2,500 persons who started from the frontier [Iowa], only about 200 frost-bitten, starving, and emaciated beings lived to tell the tale of their suffering. The remaining 2,300 perished on the way, of hunger, cold and fatigue!" It was reporting, of course, the story of the Willie and Martin Handcart companies to Utah that included no more than 900 in the two companies. And tragic as it was, less than one-tenth of the reported deaths actually occurred.

But Not Pacifists! (1857)

Most of the publicity concerning the Mountain Meadows Massacre concerns the involvement of the Mormons but little of the Indians, other than blaming them for the initial attack. Actually, the Saints involved tended to exaggerate the part played by the Indians to lessen their own involvement. During the initial attack several of the Piedes Indians were killed or wounded. (There is confusion among historians as to the Indians involved—some referring to them as Pahvants, others as Piedes, and others as Paiutes). Whatever the case, the attackers were not interested in what looked like a long siege—they were certainly not as warlike as the Comanche or

Apache—but neither were they pacifists, and as John D. Lee later testified, the Saints were concerned about their potential threat to outlying Mormon settlers if they did not respond to requests for help.

The Effects of Apostasy (1857)

The return of the apostate and one-time president of the Quorum of the Twelve, Thomas B. Marsh, to Utah and Church fellowship, is well known. However, his physical condition, specifically mentioned by President Young at the time of his acceptance back into the Church after nineteen years, is less known. Hosea Stout, present at the time, recorded in his journal that Marsh presented "a sad spectacle of the effects of apostasy. His head was entirely silvered over, he has been palsied on one side having to cripple along with a staff—this with his aged emaciated countenance give him the appearance of a very old man [he was 58 at this time]. . . . His intellect presents a still more deplorable spacticle [sic] of apostate degeneracy which seems to be in the last stage of dotage." On many occasions, for the remaining nine years of his life in Utah, he was heard to say, "If any of you want to see the effects of apostasy, look upon me."

Want of Confidence in Joseph (1857)

Saints in the Bowery on March 29, 1857, heard President Young admit he once experienced a want of confidence in Brother Joseph. "Once in my life," Brigham said, "I felt a want of confidence in Brother Joseph Smith, soon after I became acquainted with him. It was not concerning religious matters—but it was in relation to his financiering." The feeling, he went on, lasted perhaps thirty seconds and was the one and only time until the day he died. "I repented about as

quickly as I committed the error . . . It was not my preroga-
tive to call him in question with regard to any act of his life.
He was God's servant, and not mine."

Destroying the Printed Word (1857)

In the spring of 1857 three federal judges, W. W.
Drummund, John F. Kinney, and George P. Stiles returned to
Washington from their posts in Utah to report the burning of
federal court papers by the Mormons. This false report by the
"run-away judges" was largely responsible for President
Buchanan ordering the military expedition to commence the
Utah War of 1857. This history is fairly well known; the past
history of Judge Stiles is not. Although briefly a member of the
Church until he was excommunicated in December 1843 for
immoral conduct, he was still city attorney in Nauvoo, and as
a member of the city council had advocated the destruction of
the *Nauvoo Expositor* in June 1844. One must wonder if he
considered the irony when he falsely claimed the destruction
of the Utah court records by his old friends thirteen years later.

Brigham and Heber Censored (1857)

When we read the sermons and discourses of such
authorities as Brigham Young and Heber C. Kimball, do we
read what they really said? Perhaps they were closer to J.
Golden Kimball than we think. At a talk in the Bowery in
August 1857, President Young explained what happened to
some of his words between being spoken and publication:
"Brother Heber says that the music is taken out of his sermons when Brother Carrington clips out words here and
there; and I have taken out the music from mine. . . . Our
sermons are read by tens of thousands outside of Utah. . . .
In printing my remarks, I often omit the sharp words,

though they are perfectly understood and applicable here; for I do not wish to spoil the good I desire to do."

Suitably Impressed (1858)

Before Johnston's Army was able to enter Salt Lake City during the Utah War, a Peace Commission arrived from Washington. After Johnston promised the commissioners he would remain where he was until they had finished their business with President Young, the commissioners arranged a meeting with Church leaders. During the meeting Brigham received word that Johnston had broken his promise and was on the move. Angrily, Young halted the meeting and in front of the Peace delegation asked Brother Dunbar, a Scotch songster, to sing "O Ye Mountains High." After hearing two of the lines in the song, which have since been changed, the commissioners were impressed with the unyielding spirit of the Saints and a peaceful solution was soon agreed upon. The two lines in the third and fourth stanzas were: "On the necks of thy foes, thou shalt tred," and "The gentiles shall bow 'neath the rod."

"Civilizing Utah" (1858)

The Gentile press made constant reference to the need for "civilizing Utah" through occupation, whereas the Latter-day Saint diary keepers recorded what happened when that took place. One of the diary keepers during the occupation of Utah by Johnston's Army in 1858 was A. J. Allen. As a resident living only five miles from the army camp, he described the returning "exodus" Saints from their move south as well as his occasional visits to Salt Lake City.

Aug. 7th—I was in Salt Lake City. The streets were thronged with gentiles setting up liquor shops—drunken men on the right and on the left.

11th—I was in Salt Lake City, see 400 more soldiers come in with beef cattle. Supply trains still continue to come in. The gentiles selling liquor, getting drunk, fighting with knives and pistols and killing each other.

Prince Madoc in Arizona? (1858)

Brigham Young was familiar with the story of Prince Madoc, son of the King of Wales, who claimed to have discovered a new world to the west in 1160. Four years later the Prince again sailed from Wales with fifteen ships and 3000 men, never to be heard from again. Upon being told in 1858 that the Moqui (Hopi) Indians in northern Arizona had a language that included Welsh words, Brigham sent a linguistic expedition to discover the truth of the rumor. Although the Mormons found the rumor without any foundation, Llewellyn Harris, a missionary to the Zunis in 1878, claimed the Zunis "have a great many words in the language like the Welsh." The following year Wilford Woodruff visited the tribe and reported, "I had a view of the white Indians. . . . I met with many who had been baptized and they were very glad to see me."

Bounty of Beauty and Booty (1858)

Thomas Bullock, Church historian and pioneer, returned to America from a trip to his native home in England in 1858 near the end of the Utah War. During a stopover in Chicago, he encountered government officials who were recruiting men to reinforce the American Army about to enter the Salt Lake Valley. Apparently the thirty dollars per month didn't seem enough to attract enlistees, so, taking advantage of the anti-Mormon sentiment in the country, the recruiters were also offering the men, when they arrived in Utah, "a bounty of beauty and booty," as Bullock noted in his journal. Going even further they promised that if any man killed a "Mormon," the government would not prosecute him for it. Perhaps it was promises such as this that angered so many soldiers in the Expeditionary Force when the conflict ended peaceably.

"Use Up the Soldiers?" (1858)

Although there is some question as to whether anyone connected with Johnston's Army in 1857 was urging the use of Utah Indians against the Saints, there is little question as to where Brigham Young stood on the issue of using Indian tribes in the Utah War. G. W. Mills, writing to Stenhouse on April 5, 1858, said: "The war chiefs of several tribes of Indians, during the time of the excitement last fall and winter, applied personally to Governor Young for his advice and permission to go out with the tribes and 'use up' the soldiers, which they deemed themselves amply capable to do; but he, in every instance, told them to keep away from the army and show no bad feelings whatever, and . . . to avoid killing the white men."

The "Temples" of Texas (1858)

When the "Ram of the Mountains" died in 1858, he left quite a legacy in the State of Texas. In the twelve years previous to his death, Lyman Wight, believing himself commissioned to carry on the work of the Prophet Joseph, had migrated to Texas from the Pineries with a large group of apostate Saints and established a series of small settlements around Austin. Each settlement eventually failed due to floods or other disasters, including Webber's Prairie southeast of Austin, Mount Bonnell just west of Austin, Zodiac four miles south of Fredericksburg, and finally Hamilton Creek south of Burnet. In each settlement, however, Lyman built or started a "temple," if no more than a room over a storehouse, but a "temple" nevertheless, where the "Saints" performed foot washings, body washings, anointings, and baptisms for the dead.

First across the Colorado (1858)

Not since the Escalante Expedition of 1776 had any white men crossed the Colorado River. The few fords were known and used only by Navajos and Utes, and they were difficult and dangerous at all times. In 1858, however, an Indian guide led Jacob Hamblin, a well-known Mormon missionary and Indian guide, to the Ute ford (Crossing of the Fathers). There Jacob and his small party improvised a raft of poles on which the ten-man expedition transported the men and their supplies while the horses were made to swim. Although dangerous, Jacob used this crossing regularly after that. For a number of years, the Mormons were the only persons, other than the Utes and Navajos, to cross the river at any place.

Brigham's Salary (1859)

When Horace Greeley visited Utah in 1859, he asked President Young how much of a salary he received. The Prophet answered, "I do not have the value of a cabbage-head from the Tithing Office, unless I pay for it." He went on to explain that he should "count himself a poor hand to dictate this people and hold the position I occupy . . . unless I was capable of maintaining myself and family without assistance from the church. . . . My salary consists of the providences of God while I live, and eternal life when I faithfully finish this probation." He did admit, however, that he had a great deal given him by a member of the Church. (See also Plenty of Money—1861.)

Forced out by Indians (1859)

The story of western settlement is usually one of white settlers forcing the native Americans from their lands. This pattern was reversed in 1859 when the Mormons were forced to give up a settled community to make way for the Indians. The Latter-day Saints established the settlement of Genoa near the Platte River about 100 miles west of Omaha. Begun as a way station in 1857, it had become a thriving settlement by 1859 when the government made that area a part of the Pawnee Indian Reservation and the Saints were forced to abandon yet another town like the ones they had been forced from in Missouri and Illinois. Mormon Trail immigrants the following year reported the now-Indian town of Genoa as containing about 5,000 inhabitants.

Not Much Changed (1859)

Horace Greeley's visit to Utah in the summer of 1859 encompassed ten days in which he reported on subjects other than just Mormonism. He was sharply critical of the Federal Government for the wasteful and unnecessary stationing of so many troops in Utah and the cost of contracts to supply those troops. He was disgusted, especially, over federal handling of the contract that carried the mail from St. Joseph, Missouri to Salt Lake City. The contractors discovered they could deliver the mail weekly rather than semi-monthly for the same contract price, but the federal authorities informed the postmasters in Missouri and Salt Lake not to accept the faster delivery. Such non-sensible decisions cause us to wonder if things have changed that much in Federal agencies over the past 145 years.

A Trailblazing Journalistic Feat (1859)

One of the earliest and most notable specimens of jour-
nalistic interviews occurred in July 1859 during the confrontation between one of the world's greatest editors and
the most controversial religious leader of the day—Horace
Greeley and Brigham Young. Although James Gordon
Bennett is usually given credit for the very first such journal-
istic event in 1836 when he interviewed the madam of a
house of prostitution in New York where a murder had
occurred, that never matched the renowned confrontation of
1859 in Salt Lake City. Greeley summed up the two-hour
interview by writing that the Mormon leader spoke with "no
appearance of hesitation or reserve, and with no apparent
desire to conceal anything . . . and to be in no particular
hurry to get to heaven."

Love at Home—on the Plantation (1859)

Sentimental minstrel songs became popular in Utah
after the Civil War as various minstrel groups visited the
territory. One of the most popular songs is included in the
LDS hymnbook, entitled "Love at Home." With the
Mormon emphasis on home and family, it becomes difficult to imagine that particular hymn becoming popular in
any way other than the purpose for which it is sung today.
The earliest known imprint of "When There's Love at
Home" is dated 1859, while an undated imprint bears a
subscript "Christy Minstrel's Song." It was the Christy
Minstrels who popularized the song that depicted for the
listener the feelings of plantation slaves bound together by
the family ties that existed among them.

When Excommunications Were in Order (1859)

As the 1850s ended, so did the greatest era of excommunications—especially in the British Isles. Excommunications were due primarily to alcoholism, sexual misconduct, non-attendance at meetings, and just plain insistence by the leaders on genuine conversion. The European Mission records (primarily British) for the five years from 1850 to 1854 inclusive show 15,197 excommunications. Records from Scotland for the entire decade indicate 3,477 baptisms but 2,269 excommunications. The excommunication rate of new converts for that decade was 65%.

When Providence Smiled (1859)

There is no research to support it, but the fact remains that one of the Saints' most widely held beliefs in the nineteenth century dealt with their "peculiar institution." When Horace Greeley visited Utah in 1859, he reported that the "male saints emphasize the fact that a majority of the children born here are girls, holding it a proof that Providence smiles on [plural marriage]." Greeley claimed that this was the case in all polygamous countries due to the "preponderance of vigor on the part of the mothers over that of the fathers." The lack of vigor of husbands was a result, he believed, of their being much older than their wives.

The Non-Massacre (1859)

History is full of distortions and outright falsehoods, but neither the Indians nor the Mormons, who were often blamed for involvement in such incidents, needed this one. In the late summer of 1859, as the story goes, the

Saints in Brigham City were surprised by the arrival of a handful of survivors of a wagon-train attack at Almo across the border in Idaho. A rescue party of Saints rushed to the scene only to find a need to bury the remains of 300 men, women, and children massacred by Bannock Indians, making this one of the greatest disasters in Western history. Citizens in Idaho even erected a monument in Almo in 1936 for the imagined event shortly after the story appeared in print. A more recent search of contemporary papers and histories, however, reveals the event never occurred. It is still being recorded in history books, however, even as recently as 1981 by the Daughters of Utah Pioneers in their series, *An Enduring Legacy*.

An Extraordinary Judicial Speech (1859)

These were the words used by the *New York Herald* in describing the speech by Federal Judge John Cradlebaugh when in 1859 he discharged a grand jury for refusing to present indictments against Church authorities for the responsibility of the Mountain Meadows Massacre and other unsolved crimes: "You are the tools, the dupes, the instruments of a tyrannical church despotism. . . . You are taught to obey their orders and commit these horrid murders. Deprived of your liberty, you have lost your manhood, and become the willing instruments of bad men. . . . It will be my earnest effort, while with you, to knock off your ecclesiastical shackles and set you free." At least the judge was no hypocrite—he didn't pretend to be impartial.

Without Joseph's Consent (1859)

Brigham Young revealed one of the least-known facts about the final judgment in General Conference in October 1859. He revealed that he could tell "the priests who have thanked God in their prayers and thanksgiving from the pulpit that we have been plundered, driven, and slain, and [those] who have thanked God, thinking that the Latter-day Saints were wasted away, something that no doubt will mortify them—something that, to say the least, is a matter of deep regret to them—namely, that no man or woman in this dispensation will ever enter into the celestial kingdom of God without the consent of Joseph Smith."

John Stuart Mill on Mormonism (1859)

The English philosopher John Stuart Mill is known and quoted by most Americans for his well-received book, *On Liberty*. A part not normally quoted, however, deals with his defense of Mormon polygamy. On that subject he condemned "the language of downright persecution which breaks out from the press of this country whenever it feels called on to notice the remarkable phenomenon of Mormonism." Such persecution revolved around the principle of plural marriage. He went on to defend plural marriage by saying that "the only purpose for which power can be rightfully exercised over any member of a civilized community, against his will, is to prevent harm to others." This well-reasoned philosophy made little headway on either side of the Atlantic.

Rescuing a Gentile (1860)

Two years after the U. S. Army established Camp Floyd to end the so-called "Mormon War," a merchant from Missouri arrived at the base with a wagon train carrying merchandise valued at $200,000. Because they had not been ordered, army officials refused to accept the goods. Solomon Young, the owner, faced bankruptcy until Brigham Young (not related) heard about the situation and invited Solomon to bring his goods to Salt Lake City and open a store where he was able to dispose of the merchandise at a fair profit. Obviously pleased by his reception and Brigham's friendship, Mr. Young made Utah his home, dying there in 1914. This story was related in the U.S. Senate in 1944 by Solomon's grandson and soon-to-be-President, Harry S Truman.

Homesick Horses (1860)

The largest island in the Great Salt Lake was Antelope Island, used by the Church for its cattle and horses. By 1860, according to Solomon Kimball, there were nearly 1,000 horses being raised on that island—all descendants of the best stallions and brood mares available, purchased by Brigham Young a few years earlier. Being raised on the large and rocky island, they became fast, sure-footed, and long-winded, and once broken as so many were every year, they became ideal mounts in every way except one. They became homesick for their island and many Saints were embarrassed at their inability to keep their favorite horses from "returning home" (the waters were shallow and the horses would swim) whenever the opportunity arose. Lot Smith's favorite mount did this several times, even taking the saddle with him on one occasion.

They Were Given an Opportunity (1861)

Louis Bertrand was one of those missionaries who was never intimidated by a potential convert's title or status. Serving in his native France in 1861, Bertrand sent a letter to Emperor Napoleon III requesting a personal interview to "answer any inquiries the emperor might make on the subject of Mormonism." The bold missionary later learned that the Emperor had indeed read his request but had laughed and torn the letter up. Bertrand, a close friend of Brigham Young, had eight years earlier taught Mormonism to Victor Hugo on the Island of Jersey where he was a refugee. Hugo, according to the 45-year-old missionary had "listened with attention at the time, but their heads were too full of revolution to think much about the gospel of Jesus Christ."

Is This in the Gospel? (1861)

Brigham Young's source of personal wealth has often been a question of controversy. He answered that question in a discourse in the Tabernacle in 1861: "I have plenty of money for my private use. You may wish to know how I get it." Since sealing husbands and wives is a religious ordinance, he said, he could not possibly charge for doing it, "but when you ask for a bill of divorce, I intend that you shall pay for it. That keeps me in spending money, besides enabling me to give hundreds of dollars to the poor. . . . You may think this is a singular feature in the gospel, but I cannot exactly say that it is in the gospel."

Not an Ideal Assignment (1861)

Few of the soldiers stationed at Camp Floyd, which was established by Col. Johnston forty miles south of Salt Lake City in 1858, were disappointed when it was closed three years later. It did, however, typify a traditional military outpost in the nineteenth century—unhealthy and boring. In three short years the camp cemetery held eighty-four officers and men who would be left behind, a dramatic inducement to desert, which many did. In 1853 the secretary of war reported that for every 10,000 men, 1,500 would desert every year. The letters of one soldier at Camp Floyd reported that "desertions are quite frequent. . . . No pursuit is made, and the fellows who are dissatisfied walk off in open day without the least fear of being retaken."

A Testimony Is a Testimony (1861)

There are few Latter-day Saints who have not heard of the famous Pitt's Brass Band, which converted as a group in England. They were the most noted musical group in Nauvoo and crossed the Plains to become prominent in the Salt Lake Valley. Nineteenth-century Mormons, however, would have put Pitt's Band second to Ballo's Brass Band. Ballo, a convert from Sicily, once headed the West Point Band before joining the Church and moving west to establish the most popular band in the Valley. A talented clarinetist but shy Church member, he was once asked why he never bore his testimony or expressed himself in meetings. He lovingly fingered his clarinet and said, "I bear my testimony with this."

No Word from the Lord (1862)

Southwest of St. George is a small reservation of Shivwit (or Shebit) Indians, that was reestablished in 1982. A remnant of the Piute nation, they have an interesting connection with Mormonism. In 1862 James H. Pearce brought the entire tribe into St. George from across the Arizona border, and there they were baptized. The number is disputed but is variously recorded as between 130 and

300. Thirteen years later Pearce again visited them but they had a complaint. They "had not heard from the Lord since he left." Perhaps he could take them to St. George again for rebaptism and also write to the Lord and tell Him that they had been good Indians. They also wanted more shirts. Nearly the entire tribe was rebaptized.

Brigham as a Father (1862)

A common impression of Brigham Young is that of a stern taskmaster—but not according to some remarks he made in the Tabernacle in February 1862. In some advice on child rearing, he said, "Let the child have a mild training until it has judgment and sense to guide it. I differ with Solomon's recorded saying as to spoiling the child by sparing the rod . . . It is necessary to try the faith of children as well as of grown people, but there are ways of doing so besides taking a club and knocking them down with it." He felt it sufficient that if they loved him they would keep his commandments: "There is nothing consistent," he pointed out, "in abusing your wives and children." The memories of his grown children seem to bear out such advice. He was a gentle and loving father.

8
Striving for Integration
(1862-1870)

The Ghost Government (1862)

When the Saints were denied for the third time their petition for Statehood and instead granted territorial status, they did not give up. Still hoping to one day see the State of Deseret realized and anticipating a collapse of federal authority because of the Civil War, a ghost government, with a full slate of elected officers, was formed in 1862 and continued throughout the decade to meet each year and enact the same laws passed by the territorial legislature. This body was actually the Council of Fifty first organized in Nauvoo. On January 17, 1863, Brigham Young told the legislature, "We are called the State Legislature but when the time comes, we shall be called the Kingdom of God." This ghost government, including a few non-Mormons, faded out in 1870, although the Council of Fifty continued to exist for another few years.

New Every Week! (1862)

The Salt Lake Theatre, one of the largest and most modern theatres in the nation, was dedicated in 1862, largely due to the efforts of the drama-loving prophet, Brigham Young. Performances were a little different in Utah, however, with a new play every week. The first season saw only two performances per week—on Tuesday and Saturday. The other nights had to be used for rehearsals since the amateur actors had day jobs. Another unique aspect of the theatre was paying for this expensive edifice, which Brigham in his practical way figured out. The cast would not be paid, their "salaries" instead going to pay for the construction. No one grumbled, however. It was considered an honor to play the theatre, especially with the prophet so often in attendance.

At Least He Was Impartial (1862)

As a result of his 1862 trip to Salt Lake City, Mark Twain was able to fill several chapters in his well-known book *Roughing It* with some humorous observations on Mormonism. One of his best-known jabs in this book was taken at the Book of Mormon, which he refers to as "chloroform in print." Critics of the Book of Mormon, many of them Christians, take delight in quoting this "analysis," without knowing the author's feelings about the Bible. A few years later we find Twain making even more cutting comments on the Bible: he refers to a "God, so atrocious in the Old Testament and attractive in the New—the Jekyl and Hyde of sacred romance," and "the Bible absurdity of the Almighty's only six days building the Universe and then fooling away twenty-five years building a tow head on the Mississippi."

A Pestiferous Cesspool (1862)

After a trial of defendants involved in an armed insurrection in 1862 (Morrisites) in which two members of the Marshal's posse were killed, seven defendants were found guilty of murder. Federal Governor Stephen Harding, however, over the objections of Federal Judge Kinney, pardoned all the convicted. Whereupon, the grand jury, composed of several prominent Mormons sent a protest to Washington saying the Saints considered the Governor as they would "an unsafe bridge over a dangerous stream—jeopardizing the lives of all who pass over it, or, as we would a pestiferous cesspool in our district, breeding disease and death . . . unworthy [of] the confidence and respect of a free and enlightened people." Harding was removed from office.

A "Friendly Complaint" (1863)

Relations between the commander of Fort Douglas, Colonel Connor, and the Saints reached a boiling point in 1863. The Mormons resented the presence of a military fort looking down over Salt Lake City, and Connor believed the Saints were guilty of anti-Union sentiment. When rumors reached the Church authorities that Connor had plans to arrest Brigham Young and take him back east before the Saints could protect him, a "friendly complaint" was filed with Chief Justice Kinney, charging Brigham with violation of the Morrill Anti-Bigamy Act. He was arrested, bail was set at $2,000, and he was bound over to await the action of the grand jury at the next term. The grand jury found no indictment against him, and he was discharged, by which time the excitement was over. Question—was the "friendly complaint" by Brigham himself?

Don't Tell My Followers! (1863)

When the Saints left Iowa for the Salt Lake Valley in 1847, they left behind a well-known apostate who had founded his own church—Alpheus Cutler. Also left behind with him were two daughters and two sons fathered by Heber C. Kimball. Before he left them, Kimball blessed his sons that they would someday join the Saints in Utah. In 1862 a fearful Abraham Cutler (Kimball) did exactly that, partly believing the lies his grandfather Cutler had fed him about the Utah Mormons.

After converting to the Church, Abraham was sent on a mission back to Iowa to bring his brother west, which he did in 1863. While in Iowa, however, his grandfather Cutler made a remarkable confession: "I know that Brigham Young is [Joseph's] legal successor, and I always did know, but the trouble with me was that I wanted to lead. . . . One favor I wish to ask you, namely, that you will not divulge this confession to those whom I lead, while I live."

Two Spared Brothers (1863)

On January 29, 1863, one of the largest Indian massacres in the west occurred on the banks of the Bear River in northern Utah Territory by soldiers under the command of Colonel Patrick Connor, stationed at Fort Douglas in Salt Lake City. Over 250 men, women, and children were massacred by the troops with no chance given to surrender, leaving few survivors. One of those survivors was a six-year-old found in a frozen condition wandering the battlefield after the massacre. He was later raised by a Mormon family, given the name Frank Timbimboo Warner, and educated at Brigham Young College in Logan. He went on to teach penmanship and reading to whites throughout Cache Valley and served two missions to Vermont. His twelve-year-old brother, Yeager Timbimboo, who survived the massacre by playing dead, encountered Mormon missionaries years later, converted, and joined his brother in faithfully serving in the work the Lord had spared them to do.

A Bit of Advice to a Gentile (1863)

In 1863 John Wickersham Woolley was captain of a Church train sent to bring immigrants to Salt Lake Valley. In a letter written to his father from a camp near Fort Laramie, he describes a meeting with a gentile train on the way west. When the captain of that train complained that "it was damned strange that these Mormons could travel all over the country without being molested (by Indians) in any way, I told him it was easy enough accounted for and if he would keep the secret I would tell him. That the Mormons always feed instead of fighting them and that they did not make a practice of sleeping with the squaws." The gentile didn't buy this. According to him, "They all say that the Indians are all Mormons."

Behind the Dickens' Visit (1863)

Most Latter-day Saints are fond of quoting the complimentary comments Charles Dickens made in his *Uncommercial Traveler* about his visit to a Mormon emigrant ship in 1863. Less known is the reason he made that visit. The ship *Amazon* was the first Mormon emigrant ship ever to depart from London, and the local newspapers considered it an event worthy of reporting, as did Dickens. The great majority of Mormon emigrant ships departed from Liverpool. Actually Dickens followed up the article, which first appeared as an essay in *All the Year Round*, by later reporting that he had learned of a dispatch received from the Captain of the *Amazon,* "highly praising the behaviour of these emigrants, and the perfect order and propriety of all their social arrangements."

No Filthy Lucre for Brigham (1864)

A principle of Mormonism that Brigham took pride in was that no Church leaders were supported from tithing money but earned their own livelihood. This included the Prophet. In 1864 the employees of his personally owned businesses numbered 183, making a total of 1,079 Saints, counting the families, supported by Brigham. A few of his businesses included a dairy in Hampton, Utah, a ranch with over 600 head of cattle north of Salt Lake City, a carding factory and grist mill on City Creek, a tannery in St. George, a shoe factory, a cotton and woolen factory at the entrance to Parley's Canyon, a saddle-manufacturing shop, and a wagon and repair shop in the city.

No More Singing that Song (1864)

It has taken a good many years for Latter-day Saints to laugh at themselves—and if they did, they might be told to stop. That was the case with a song composed by a St. George settler by the name of Hicks, who had been sent from his farm in Cottonwood, near Salt Lake City, to be a pioneer in raising cotton in Utah's Dixie region. The harsh life in St. George prompted him to write a humorous song about troubles in Dixie, called "Once I Lived in Cottonwood." This popular song included such lines as "I feel so weak and hungry now. I think I'm almost dead. Tis seven weeks next Sunday since I have tasted bread." Erastus Snow was not amused when he heard it and he ordered it sung no more. It was still sung, however, even by those who loved Dixie.

If Polygamy Is Wrong, Then Why ...? (1864)

Nils Bourkersson, who reluctantly migrated to Utah with his convert wife in 1864, returned alone to Sweden in 1867 to write a book about his three years in Utah. In spite of anti-Mormon feelings he wondered, if polygamy was wrong, as he concluded it most certainly must be, why is the moral standard so high among the Mormons? And why could he not find any evidence of illegitimacy or prostitution in Zion or "fallen women plying the prostitute's trade?" He wrote that he heard of no young girls "ruined—as in Sweden." He also found, contrary to critics, that children from Mormon polygamous unions were equal with each other with each child enjoying his father's "good" name. And also, contrary to what he had heard, there was peace in most polygamous homes and never had he seen any physical strife between wives, nor among children.

Deseret's Seaport (1864)

Brigham's dream for the Deseret Territory was a seaport exporting cotton and iron from Southern Utah and importing goods and immigrants, saving the high cost of overland transportation. It seemed to come true in 1864 when Anson Call founded Call's Landing on the Colorado River about fifteen miles above the present Boulder Dam. Only 125 miles from St. George, this river port was accessible to steamers as large as twenty-five tons. Its success was fairly sure except for one thing—the completion of the transcontinental railroad within the next five years. Some freight did arrive at Call's Landing but its promise was never fulfilled and today the site is under the waters of Lake Mead.

An Indian Scout Loses His Way (1864)

Lewis Dana (also spelled Denna), a member of the Oneida nation, was made an elder in Nauvoo, the first Lamanite admitted a member of any Quorum of the Church. He had even received his temple endowments in Nauvoo, and Brigham Young had sealed Brother Dana and Mary Goat "under the New and Everlasting Covenant for time and all eternity" in the Nauvoo Temple. He was also the only Lamanite to be selected a member of the prestigious Council of the Fifty—but, unfortunately, he was to lose his way. In 1864 he was selected to act as scout for a group of Alpheus

Cutler's apostate group headed north to settle in Minnesota. This splinter group, like most others, soon lost its way.

The Fall of a "God" (1864)

A shrewd newly baptized self-promoter by the name of Walter Gibson was commissioned by President Young to go on a mission to Japan in 1860. Arriving in the Hawaiian Islands when all Mormon elders were absent, he settled in, convincing the native members he was their new leader with absolute power greater than the Prophet. He started charging for offices in the priesthood, and buying considerable property with the proceeds. He appointed his own apostles and confiscated all property of members. He set up a "shrine" on the Island of Lanai, covered it with brush, and threatened a resulting death to any superstitious native who tampered with it. Hearing of these problems, a delegation from Utah including Ezra T. Benson, Lorenzo Snow, and Joseph F. Smith traveled to Hawaii where they confronted the unyielding "God" to whom the natives prostrated themselves.

Gibson lost his standing in a single moment when the elders entered the "holy place," removed the brush and exited with no harm. Gibson was excommunicated and left his "kingdom" in disgrace.

Never Heard from Again (1865)

There are many sad and unfinished stories in Mormon history. One of the most heartbreaking accounts concerns a pioneer couple on their way to Zion. While crossing Wyoming west of Fort Laramie, the Miner G. Atwood wagon train of 200 Saints was attacked by Indians. Seven members of the train were wounded, and although the Indians were undoubtedly more interested in stealing livestock, they took advantage of the situation to kidnap the wife of one of the immigrants, F. C. Grundwig [Grundtvig]. The story of Jesine Grundwig, who was never heard from again, is one of few documented kidnappings of Mormon women by Indians while crossing the Plains.

Was This Tough Love? (1865)

Captain Charles Sisson's treatment of his Mormon passengers aboard his ship *Bridgewater* when he crossed the Atlantic with a shipload of Saints in 1865 is not well known, but we might gain a little insight by noting a story concerning discipline in his own family. Before departing on one of his long voyages, his young daughter had misbehaved and he warned her not to leave their yard or she would be punished. When he left she could not be found but he obviously did not forget his threat. Upon his return he put his daughter over his knee and spanked her. We can imagine the lack of mercy among ship captains who transported the hated Mormons.

Maladjusted Immigrants (1865)

In spite of appearances, all Mormon immigrants did not fit the desired pattern of hard-working and self-sufficient Saints. A fifty-year-old British-born convert from India immigrated to Utah in 1865, but warned the Church leaders that she was "not used to any outdoor or indoor work" as she was from a country "where there are many servants to work for us." She found the Utah climate unfavorable to her rheumatism and asked for a job in which she would not have to "stir from the fireside much less do outdoor work." Brigham tried to be patient but told her frankly, "I really do not know what to do with you. . . . My own folks have to work, carry water, wash, build their own fires, cook, etc., and mostly wait upon themselves." In spite of a number of attempts by various Saints to help, she left Utah after three years of maladjustment.

A Wayward Saint (1866)

Twenty years after arriving in Utah as a handcart pioneer, Robert Parker stood in a priesthood circle in the log church in Beaver, Utah, to give his first grandchild the name of Robert LeRoy Parker and a blessing. Few in that Mormon chapel in 1866 could imagine the time would come when that baby boy would voluntarily give up that name. His younger brothers and a sister would proudly bear the name Parker in Mormon history. The sister Lulu Parker Betenson would even become a Utah Legislator, but the baby Robert would cast off the name to become one of the West's most famous outlaws, Butch Cassidy. There is some irony in the fact that his birth date has generally been listed as April 6, considered by Latter-day revelation as the date of the birth of Christ. Family records, however, give the birth date as a week later—on Friday the Thirteenth.

The Last Pioneer (1866)

Among the Utah pioneers (those who crossed the Plains between 1847 and the "joining of the rails" in 1869) was a six-year-old girl, who unknowingly would set an historic record when she entered the Valley in 1866. Hilda Anderson Erickson would spend her life as an obstetrician, dentist, veterinarian, teacher, a Relief Society president for twenty-five years, and a missionary to the Indians for twelve years with her husband. In 1997 a life-sized statue of Hilda was unveiled at Grantsville, commemorating the last living pioneer who had crossed the Plains by wagon train. She died in 1968 at age 108.

Appearance of the Mormon Capital (1867)

One of the most objective tourists to visit Salt Lake City in the nineteenth century was a German travel writer, Theodor Kirchhoff, who spent two days in the city in May of 1867. On his first day he described the city as "a true oasis in the endless alkali desert!" with "wide and clean streets . . . rows of green acacias, and Canadian poplars alternated in shading the 20-foot-wide sidewalk. Running water murmured beside it." The flowers and orchards especially impressed him. "In every direction countless peach trees, in full bloom . . . cherry, apple, pear, and other fruit trees . . . this idyllic city looked to me like an enchanting paradise. The houses, mostly of adobe, were almost all painted in bright colors. The gardens were enclosed with high walls of mortared fieldstone, above which those fruit trees rose in that full-bloom splendor."

School of the "Profits" (1867)

A School of the Prophets had first been established in Kirtland to prepare the priesthood for missionary work and church leadership by teaching them not only gospel principles but also all branches of learning. In December 1867, another such school was organized in Salt Lake City with branches throughout the Territory—but it was not quite the same. The Utah school was more concerned with creating cooperative enterprises, determining prices and setting hours of labor, discussing and settling economic problems, and in general working for community betterment. Although theology was not totally absent, the reestablishment of the school seemed to be to counter the expected influx of gentile influence associated with the coming of the railroad. Whether highly successful in this or totally unnecessary, there seemed to be a close connection since the Salt Lake school was dissolved only three years after the railroad reached Utah.

A Shrinking Trail (1868)

Most Latter-day Saints, with a minimum knowledge of their history, are familiar with the Mormon Trail and its assumed length and the time it took to travel it. The pioneer party took 111 days to travel from Winter Quarters to the Great Salt Lake Valley. The time was shortened as the trail became improved and better marked, and as organization improved, but became much more so as the railroad was extended westward. By 1868, the last year before the Transcontinental Railroad reached Utah and brought an end to the Mormon Trail, it had reached Benton, Wyoming, approximately 250 miles east of Salt Lake City. The last wagon train to leave for the Valley in 1868 left Benton, Wyoming, on September 1 and arrived in the Valley twenty-three days later.

A Tragic Ending (1868)

The last group of Latter-day Saint immigrants to cross the Atlantic in a sailing vessel and arrive in Utah by ox team sailed from Liverpool in the Emerald Isle on June 20, 1868. Most of the 877 Saints were Scandinavian and few immigrants suffered as much from bad supplies and unpleasant treatment from their ship's crew as did those members. Their fifty-two days at sea would not be repeated as future Saints traveled primarily by steam. Although most of the Emerald Isle immigrants' journey across the United States was by train, many died even on that portion of their journey. By the time this group arrived in Utah, it had lost sixty-seven by death, a record for non-handcart pioneers.

The Marks on the Doorposts (1868)

By 1868 much of the anti-Mormon agitation in Utah was centered in the gentile merchant community. To combat this, Brigham organized the Zion's Cooperative Mercantile Institution (ZCMI). This Church enterprise was designed to not only import and retail goods at lower prices than the gentile merchants, but to wholesale the goods to Mormon retailers around the Territory. To encourage Latter-day Saint retailers to join, and to discourage the Mormons from buying from other stores, every retailer joining the Cooperative had a sign placed over their entrance reading, "Holiness to the Lord: Zion's Cooperative Mercantile Institution." The tactic was successful. By 1873 ZCMI showed dividends of $500,000 on an original investment of $280,000.

The Oldest Department Store (1868)

This claim has often been debated, but the ZCMI claim is not "oldest store" but "oldest department store." In 1868, when Zion's Cooperative Mercantile Institution was organized, there were many general stores selling the same kinds of merchandise it did, but the difference was that, from the first, the merchandise at Zion's Cooperative Mercantile Institution was segregated into related groups called departments, and over each of these departments was a manager who in turn was responsible to a general superintendent. It is this distinctive type of organization that justifies the designation "America's First Department Store."

What Happened to the Great?(1868)

A month after the arrival of the Saints in the Salt Lake Valley, the new city was officially named "The City of the Great Salt Lake" and then in common usage, it became Great Salt Lake City. Why was it called "Great" and why was that adjective later dropped? Originally, it was used to distinguish it from Little Salt Lake, a term applied to a smaller body of salt water located near Parowan, 200 miles to the south. This small lake has since dried up, making a distinction unimportant. By legislative enactment, in January 1868 the adjective "Great" was dropped from the city's name after several years of usage.

Days of Sorrow for Heber (1868)

Before he died in 1868, Heber C. Kimball, Brigham Young's first counselor in the Presidency, was becoming an anachronism in the Church hierarchy. A major complaint by some Church leaders and even the editor of the official Church newspaper, the *Deseret News*, criticized Heber for his uncouth language at a time when the Church was trying to present a more polished image to the public. Even his close friend Brigham, who refused to remove his long-time counselor, was making appointments without consulting Heber. One of Heber's sons later wrote, "Those were days of sorrow for father and he became so heartbroken towards the last that he prayed to the Lord to shorten his days." The Lord did—nine years before Brigham who was the same age.

Best-Governed City (1869)

At the height of anti-Mormonism in the nineteenth century, there were a few visitors to Utah whose judgments were not influenced by their religious opinions. In 1869 the *American Presbyterian*, in Philadelphia, printed the following words of Rev. A. M. Stewart, who had spoken a few months before in the Tabernacle:

"Whatever purposes the Almighty has to subserve with this strange mass of people hereafter, he has already effected purposes the most wise and beneficent, and for which no other agents seemed fitted. Salt Lake City is the most quiet, orderly, and best-governed city in the world. Among the 'Mormons' there is no disorder or outbreak, no profanity or intemperance. The city on the Sabbath is as quiet and orderly as a rural parish in Scotland or New England. Whatever disorder there may be is created by gentile intruders."

Properly Observing Sunday (1869)

The gentile town of Corinne was laid off as a town-site north of Ogden in 1869. It immediately became a boomtown totally different from the Mormon towns around it. J. H. Beadle, a young newspaper man and anti-Mormon, who would attack the Saints a year later with his book, *Life in Utah; or the Mysteries and Crimes of Mormonism*, was apparently more impressed with Corinne than with the more sedate Mormon towns. He described it as having nineteen saloons and "eighty nymphs du pave, popularly known in Mountain English as 'soiled doves.'" But he described this gentile town as observing the Sabbath—"most of the men went hunting or fishing, and the 'girls' had a dance or got drunk."

Will Brigham Young Fight? (1869)

Schuyler Colfax, vice president in the Grant Administration, was an aggressive anti-Mormon, determined to force the United States into another "war" against the Saints. He was able to bring President Grant to the brink of such a military confrontation. During a visit to Utah in 1869, Colfax was riding through the city with T.B.H. Stenhouse, who was disfellowshipped from the Church that very year. During their private conversation Colfax asked Stenhouse if Brigham Young would fight. Stenhouse later reported that Colfax noted that if the Saints would fight, the Grant administration, unlike the Buchanan administration, would make "short shift" of the "Mormon" question. The idea of a second "Mormon War" was not that unthinkable. When Grant had appointed Judge McKean as Chief Justice of Utah, he had promised the reluctant appointee that "if civil process will not restrain lawlessness, I will support you with the army of the United States."

Raising the Cultural Standards? (1869)

Only seven years after the dedication of the Salt Lake Theater, the managers took it upon themselves to temporarily close the theater because, according to their reason, the Saints had become "satiated" with drama and there was a need for a new type of attraction. Since patrons have never become "satiated" with good drama, it appears there was either a lack of good drama or it was not being properly marketed. Whatever the case, the managers contracted with a company in San Francisco to travel to Utah for a ten-day engagement, provided they did not violate local morals or mingle too freely with the public. The new entertainment was a twenty-eight-member minstrel troupe, which was successful and began a love affair between the public and blackface entertainment throughout the rest of the century.

Rescuing a Lost Sheep (1869)

Few Saints are familiar with the name William Homer, who returned from a mission to England in 1869. He decided on his return to Utah to stop at Kirtland to visit his sister's father-in-law, who was once a member of the Church but had become disaffected and stayed in Ohio. When William asked the old man if he would not like to visit his son and family in Utah, the apostate said yes but he was too impoverished to afford the trip. Arriving in Utah, Elder Homer went to visit President Young and told him of the former member in Ohio. On hearing this Brigham authorized Edward Stevenson to raise money for transportation for the "lost sheep." It was done, and in 1870 Martin Harris arrived in Utah to visit his family, was reconciled with Brigham, was rebaptized, and lived faithfully in Zion for the remainder of his life.

Read or Leave! (1869)

It is perhaps significant that Brigham Young, one of our least formally educated authorities, surrounded himself with articulate and educated aides. Such is the mark of a leader dedicated to learning. This was evident in his public addresses such as the one he gave in the new tabernacle in Salt Lake City in April 1869. He couldn't have been more frank about the importance of reading: "All who do not want to sustain co-operations and fall into the ranks of improvement, and endeavour to improve themselves by every good book and then by every principle that has been received from heaven, had better go back to England, Ireland, France, Scandinavia, or the Eastern States; we do not care where you go, if you will only go."

Spitting in the Tabernacle (1870)

The April General Conference of 1870 was postponed until May 7 to permit the completion of the new Tabernacle. It had been used for a Sabbath day meeting the week previously and the consequences must have distressed President Young. In his opening address on the seventh, he spoke to the doorkeepers about the condition of the gentleman's gallery (the men and women sat separately): "Here and there were great quids of tobacco, and places one or two feet square smeared with tobacco juice. . . . When you see gentlemen who cannot omit chewing and spitting while in this house, request them to leave. . . . We therefore request all gentlemen attending Conference to omit tobacco chewing while here."

It Took Ninety-One Years (1870)

Seven years before he was executed at the site of the Mountain Meadows massacre in 1877, John Doyle Lee was excommunicated from the Church. Although no cause was specified and he was not given advance notice, the action was obviously taken for Lee's participation in the infamous massacre in 1857. Few, including Lee, have ever denied his participation in the tragedy, but many have felt he was a scapegoat for an event in which many others were equally involved. To partially rectify this apparent injustice, it became necessary to either excommunicate others or reinstate Lee's membership. The latter was finally done when Lee was rebaptized by proxy on May 8, 1961. All other priesthood blessings were restored the following day by the laying on of hands by Ezra Taft Benson.

9
Striving for Respect
(1870-1877)

Will They Fight? (1870)

Before the anti-polygamy Cullom Bill was finally defeated in 1870, the House of Representatives removed the special military features it included—provisions to enforce the bill with a military force of up to 40,000 troops. Such war-like provisions and President Grant's willingness to use such power was denounced in a number of influential newspapers, including the *New York World*: "If we force them into a hostile attitude, the Mormons can give us a very disagreeable, a very wearisome, and tremendously expensive war. . . .The Mormons can give such a force (40,000 U.S. troops) two or three years fighting, at an annual expense to us of not less than two hundred millions of dollars." Such public pressure did not prevent other anti-polygamy legislation, but it did discourage the sending of another army of occupation as in the 1857 "Mormon War."

Seeking Forgiveness (1870)

One of the most devastating Indian conflicts in Mormon history was the "Black Hawk War," which began in 1865 and for the next three years resulted in the abandonment of at least twenty-seven settlements in southern Utah, the deaths of seventy-five Saints, and more than one million dollars in losses. After the restoration of peace in 1868, the Ute chief responsible, Black Hawk, seemed tormented by his several years of pillage and killings. He was reminded of Brigham Young's foreboding prophecy that those who opposed the Saints would inevitably wither. With this seemingly happening to himself (he was dying of TB) and his people, the Ute chief toured a number of settlements in central and southern Utah in 1870, speaking to Mormon congregations, trying to explain his motives for the war (his people were starving), and asking for the forgiveness of the Saints.

Something They Were Good At (1870)

In 1870 Corinne, the self-proclaimed Gentile capital of Utah and only non-Mormon town in the Territory, just couldn't seem to win. It had lost in its bid to be a rail center, to be the seat of Territorial government or even much of a voice in politics. But it finally found something it was good at—base ball (it was two words back then). As the first town in Utah to field a base ball team, it soon proclaimed itself Territorial champion, only to be challenged to a three-game championship by an upstart club in Salt Lake called the Enneas. Corinne won the first game 42-31 and the last one, but was humiliated in the second game, losing 74-23. This one Gentile loss to the hated Mormons resulted in the erection of a tombstone in the center of Corinne, draped with a flag of mourning.

Ready to Compare Notes (1870)

Shortly after the passage of the Edmunds Act in 1882, President John Taylor gave a talk about anti-Mormon untruths being circulated regarding the alleged ignorance and depravity of the Latter-day Saints. He had his secretary read excerpts from the last census available (1870), which compared Utah with "cultural" Massachusetts and the District of Columbia, which was governed by Congress. It was admitted that Utah was outshone in three categories: paupers (Massachusetts, 9 to 1; District of Columbia, 4 to 1); convicts (Massachusetts, 4 to 1; District of Columbia 3 to 1); and insane and idiotic (Massachusetts, 4 to 1; District of Columbia, 7 to 1). Taylor concluded by saying, "We are ready, as I said before, to compare notes."

What Are We Here For? (1871)

There was a reason visitors to Salt Lake City consistently referred to President Young as the most interesting Mormon speaker in spite of their criticisms of his crude expressions. They seldom commented, however, on the doctrines he expressed, such as he did at the funeral services of Miss Aurelia Spencer in the 13th Ward assembly rooms on September 16, 1871, when he asked one of life's most important questions: "What are we here for? To learn to enjoy more, and to increase in knowledge and experience." Speaking on the same subject fifteen years earlier in the Tabernacle, he had asked, "When shall we cease to learn? We shall never cease to learn, unless we apostatize."

Saints Aid the Afflicted (1871)

One of the greatest calamities to strike an American city was the Chicago fire that burned from October 8-10, 1871. Over 250 lives were lost and 98,500 made homeless. While the city was still burning, a mass meeting was called in the "Old Tabernacle" in Salt Lake City to raise funds for the sufferers, although the Saints themselves were the victims of anti-Mormon propaganda throughout the nation, including Chicago. Another fund-raising event was held in the Salt Lake Theater that same week. President Young himself donated $1,000, while several businessmen donated $500 each and the Mormon City Council voted $1,500. Over $20,000 was raised, comparable to at least $500,000 in 2004 prices.

"What a Good Man Should Be" (1871)

Mormonism was always good for news articles in the last half of the nineteenth century, as was the very name of Brigham Young. Thus one can imagine the newsworthiness of such events as one of Brigham's sons, Willard, being appointed the first Mormon cadet at West Point in 1871. How refreshing it must have been to the Saints, therefore, when an interviewing columnist from the *New York Herald* described the young product of Mormonism at such a prestigious institution: "My opinion of him . . . is that he would make a splendid officer. Some of the cadets laugh at him because he won't smoke, and he complains of having heard more hard swearing since he came to West Point than he ever heard in his life before. But he has such extraordinary notions—extraordinary in a West Point view—of what a good man should be, that I think he would make . . . a capital officer."

"–But Producing No Water" (1871)

In June 1871, the Methodist-Episcopal Church sponsored the first non-Mormon religious revival held in Utah. After the Prophet encouraged members to attend, several thousand did—Brigham among them. When one of the ministers (there were seven) asked permission to address the Sunday School, Church leaders made the arrangements for a Reverend Dole to address 4,000 young Saints, although Saints at the previous meetings had been accused of various sins and crimes. The Prophet described one of those meetings: "Mr. Dole put me in mind of an old, dried up wooden pump, laboring and creaking in a dry well, working very hard but producing no water." After five such meetings, the anti-Mormon local paper, the *Salt Lake Tribune*, reported that as a result of five days of meetings, there had been "one professed conversion."

New York Was Different (1871)

Few American women in the nineteenth century believed anything good came out of Utah—except suffrage. In 1871, only a year after the first woman to vote in a political contest in the United States proved to be a Latter-day Saint (see *Little-known Facts . . .*, p. 197), two renowned American suffragists attended a Latter-day Saint celebration in the Tabernacle in Salt Lake City. Perhaps their association with Mormon women on that Independence Day occasion inspired Elizabeth Cady Stanton and Susan B. Anthony to be more aggressive in their fight for women's independence. Only a year later Susan B. Anthony was arrested in New York for attempting to register and vote, something she learned her "sisters" in Utah had been doing for two years. More than twenty years later, in 1895, Susan demonstrated her feeling about Latter-day Saint women by agreeing to preside over the Intermountain Woman Suffrage convention convened in Salt Lake City.

Will There Be Lawyers? (1872)

There were few subjects on which Brigham wasn't able and willing to offer advice—especially favorite subjects such as the United Orders. At the semi-annual conference in Salt Lake City in September 1872, he offered advice on the need for lawyers in such enterprises. "I cannot see the least use on the face of the earth for these wicked lawyers who stir up strife. If they would turn merchants, cattle breeders, farmers or mechanics . . . they would be useful; but to stir up strife and quarrels . . . seems to be their only business." Instead, Brigham suggested laymen to arbitrate problems. "They are not lawyers, but they understand truth and justice . . . and we will have no lawsuit, and no difficulty with our neighbor, to alienate our feelings one from another? This is the way we should do as a community."

A Fifteen-Minute Bar Exam (1872)

When Georgie Snow was admitted to the bar as the first qualified Utah female lawyer, her training had consisted of "reading law" in her father's law office for three years. This was not unusual training, but her bar examination was. It consisted of a fifteen-minute impromptu interrogation conducted by an ad hoc committee. Even this would probably have been bypassed were it not for the examining court's fear that if she were admitted without an exam of some kind, a precedent would be set for future lawyers. It is of interest to note that on that same date in September 1872, another woman, Phoebe Couzins, was also admitted to the Utah Bar. One must wonder if the fact that Georgie's father was a judge (Zarubbabel Snow) had anything to do with her ease of admission or whether it was the Saints' desire to show the rest of the nation the advancement of women's rights in Utah.

Trampling the Laws (1872)

Were the Federal judges appointed to the Utah Territory really that biased? Perhaps the most striking example of an affirmative answer was voiced by Judge McKean when he was first appointed in 1872 as federal judge, according to Edward Tullidge, a prominent Utah historian, who by this time had himself apostatized. Tullidge quoted McKean as telling Judge Louis Dent, brother-in-law to President Grant, "The mission which God has called upon me to perform in Utah, is as much above the duties of other courts and judges as the heavens are above the earth, and whatever or wherever I may find the local or federal laws obstructing or interfering therewith, by God's blessing I shall trample them under my feet." During his tenure in Utah, he did this most effectively.

The Purpose of Conferences? (1872)

President George A. Smith, in a General Conference talk in April 1872, appeared to suggest a change in the purpose of such conferences. He told the brethren to "leave their business out of doors." He then proceeded to suggest the purpose of conference was to "call upon God in mighty prayer . . . to bless the efforts of his servants for the advancement of his work, . . . to bless the missionaries and to open the way for the gathering of the poor." Such advice was certainly a change from that made rather clear in a General Conference address by President Young in 1857 when the Prophet advised the speakers to use the items of business as subjects for their talks. He gave them permission to exhort the brethren if they wished to stray, "but our Conferences are more particularly for the transaction of business."

Smoke and Fire (1872)

In 1872 Colonel Thomas Fitch, Senator-Elect of the "State of Deseret," called upon President Ulysses Grant to encourage him to support the admission of Utah as a state. Grant's repeated response was, "I am unalterably opposed to the admission of Utah." Further pleas by Fitch elicited only the typical propaganda of polygamy and Mormon murders. Fitch asked, "You surely don't believe everything you hear against the Mormons?" "Where there is so much smoke there must be some fire," Grant replied. "Suppose we should say the same about all the lies told about you?" Fitch responded. Silence. Fitch then asked if more of his arguments asking for support would be useless? Grant's final response: "I am unalterably opposed to the admission of Utah."

No Career Closed, But . . . (1872)

Elizabeth, wife of the long-time friend of the Saints, Thomas L. Kane, was impressed with the freedom granted Mormon women as opposed to other American women: "They close no career on a woman in Utah by which she can earn a living." However, there must have been a reason that over sixty years later there were 598 male lawyers but only 8 females. There was! Women were free to enter law as a profession, but after receiving their license they encountered major legal restraints. The common law of Utah prevented women from acting as independent legal entities and therefore they were unable to make contracts, sue, write wills, and own or convey property. They were thus unable to enter into contracts with clients or act on their behalf. There was little consolation in knowing other states were equally restrictive.

Entering the Sacred Edifice of Marriage (1873)

One of the most important qualifications for entering LDS temples is the declaration that one pays his or her tithing. One of the lesser-known facts in Mormon history is that this was at one time also a qualification for entering the sacred institution of marriage. In a discourse delivered at Logan, Utah, on June 28, 1873, Franklin D. Richards spoke on the subject of tithing. To indicate the importance of such a practice, he asked his audience, "If there is any man amongst you who wants to take a wife, does he not have to obtain a certificate from his bishop that he pays his tithing?" Like tithing itself, however, this requirement was perhaps more evident in the law than in the practice.

"The Worst Places" (1873)

Being driven from the fertile lands of Ohio, Missouri, and Illinois seemed to have taught the Saints not to settle fertile territory but to make bad land good. That is a major reason Brigham and his people were willing to settle in Utah rather than on the California coast in exchange for the religious freedom they anticipated with isolation on normally unwanted lands. George Q. Cannon voiced such a belief in a discourse in the Tabernacle in 1873 when he said, "Good countries are not for us," but "the worst places in the land we can probably get and we must develop them." He went on to warn the Saints that if the Saints took the "good country," it would not be long "before the wicked would want it." We can only wonder if such words were any consolation to the settlers in the Muddy or the San Juan Missions in the extreme southwest and southeast portion of the territory, two of the most difficult missions in Church history.

"Moste Desert Lukking Plase" (1873)

Mormon colonists were a hardy people who seldom surrendered to harsh pioneering conditions—but they did in 1873 in one of their first attempts to settle Arizona. Considering the future possibility of colonizing Sonora, Church leaders needed a chain of colonies south through Arizona and thus in 1873 sent a party of colonizing missionaries across the Colorado

River at Lee's Ferry and south to settle along the Little Colorado River. Within two months the discouraged settlers were headed home, beaten by the desolate conditions, described by one of the missionaries as "the moste desert lukking plase that I ever saw, Amen." In 1876 the second attempt to colonize Arizona in the same general area was more successful.

How It Will Be Done (1873)

It is not just a coincidence that the LDS doctrine of work for the dead and American interest in genealogy coincide. In October 1844, only four months after the death of the Prophet Joseph in Carthage, the New England Historic Genealogical Society was formed. Since that date interest in genealogy has boomed, and work for the dead in the LDS Church has increased many fold. And yet members and non-members alike ask, "How can information on all the dead ever be recovered so that none will be missed"? Apostle Orson Pratt gave the answer in a discourse in 1873, noting that when the Lord promised to "reveal unto you hidden things," that will include genealogical records. Any missing information will be revealed "by the Urim and Thummim, which the Lord God has ordained to be used in the midst of His holy house in His Temple."

Orson Questions a Revelation (1873)

Speaking in the First Ward schoolhouse in Salt Lake City in 1873, Orson Pratt questioned a revelation to Joseph years earlier that resurrected infants will forever remain infants. Aware that this was not true doctrine, he suggested two possible reasons for it being reported that way; either the longhand reporters had misinterpreted the remarks or Joseph had not been fully instructed by the Lord. As evidence for his explanation, he noted that the latter reason explained the later changes in baptism for the dead when it became known that members could not be baptized for the opposite sex as had been done in Joseph's day. He explained further that no revelation gives us full knowledge upon the point being presented.

"I Visited His Grave" (1873)

Thomas Kane's wife, Elizabeth, wrote of her family's visit with Brigham Young in St. George in the winter of 1872-73. While there she observed the visit to Brigham Young of Chief Wovoka (See Wounded Knee—1890), whose religious convictions led to the tragic Wounded Knee Massacre. Mrs. Kane mentioned a close friend of Wovoka, who also felt divinely inspired, as an example of the tragic consequences at times of Native American religious enthusiasm. Wovoka's friend was so convinced of his resurrection, although obviously not understanding the time element, that he ordered his friends to kill him and he would instantly receive a new body. He then laid his head down and his friends chopped it off. Mrs. Kane visited his grave.

When Brother Brigham Joins (1874)

Brigham Young established most of the United Orders throughout Utah in 1873 and 1874, and there was some opposition, especially among the more affluent members. When Brigham asked one prominent Saint near Salt Lake City why he was holding out, the objector answered, "Brother Brigham, when I see you join the Order, then I'll go in." Brigham's response was, "Whenever I can find a man or set of men who can manage my business better than I can, then I'll join the

Order." As clever as that response was, there is logic in suggesting that many of the Saints, although of less financial worth than Brigham, might have used the same excuse.

The Goshute Runners (1874)

In 1874, 100 Goshute Indians were baptized in Deep Creek, Tooele Co., Utah, during a general religious movement among Native Americans in the Great Basin. In 1998 an unusual monument was dedicated in Ibapah, Utah, honoring, among others, that particular tribe. This was an unusual tribe, often disdaining the use of horses (except for meat), preferring to run, at which they became proficient. Pioneer Saints often saw these Goshute (Ghost Utes) runners keeping pace with the stage coaches over the road between Canyon and Willow stations in Snake valley. Young Goshute runners would run beside the stages the entire ten miles, "charging" for the exhibition packages of powder and lead that unthinking but delighted passengers would toss to them. As they neared the station, the Goshutes would put on a burst of speed and leave the stages far behind as they headed for their camps, newly supplied for their next violent encounter with settlers or travelers.

Was It a Test Case? (1875)

The sentencing to prison in 1875 of George Reynolds, private secretary of Brigham Young, for violation of the Morrill Anti-Bigamy law of 1862, has usually been referred to as the result of a "trial case," desired by both sides. Actually there were two trials, and the dismissal by the Territorial Supreme Court of a conviction in the first trial resulted in a second trial. In the second trial Reynolds did not willingly submit to test the constitutionality of the law, but fought it because of the changed attitude of the prosecution. He lost, and evidence of the now-vindictive attitude of the federal prosecutors was reflected in the sentence imposed. The imprisonment was doubled to two years and the term "at hard labor" (eliminated by the Territorial Supreme Court as being excessive) was added.

Fulfilling His Own Prophesy (1875)

When President Grant needed a new Chief Justice for the Utah Territory, he turned to James B. McKean, a New Yorker. Although decidedly anti-Mormon, McKean was reluctant to accept the position, but Grant, equally anti-Mormon, urged McKean to accept the position and enforce the federal laws against the Saints. The judge argued, "In my endeavors to perform my duty in Utah I may become embroiled with the Mormons. No means exist there to execute my decrees, and thus I may stir up trouble to no purpose, and bring humiliation upon myself." Promised military help if necessary, McKean accepted, but in his position made a series of absurd decisions. Finally, only five days after tacitly ruling in favor of polygamy by granting one of Brigham's divorced plural wives alimony and sentencing Brigham to twenty-four hours of incarceration for refusal to pay, McKean was removed in disgrace.

Changing Religions—Not Testimony (1875)

When Martin Harris was rebaptized into the Church in Utah in 1875, he had probably set a record for the religions with which an individual had associated. Before becoming a Latter-day Saint in Palmyra he had been a Quaker, a Universalist, a Restorationer, a Baptist, and a Presbyterian. After becoming disaffected from the Saints, he allied himself with eight different faiths while living in Kirtland. He rejoined the Saints briefly in Nauvoo before joining the Shakers, and then worked as a missionary for Strang's apostate group, and then associated with William McLellin's splinter group. After his rebaptism, he stayed faithful until his death in 1875. In spite of his seeking a religious "home," he never denied his testimony of the Book of Mormon.

Something Had to Be Done! (1875)

It is commonly known that Brigham assigned Junius Wells the task of organizing the first Young Men's Mutual Improvement Association in 1875. Even such inspired ideas sometimes require a nudge, and in this case there is evidence it was the popular Wasatch Literary Association that was organized the year previously. Unsupervised, the sons and daughters of prominent leaders were active in the secular youth group that refused to open its meetings with prayer and openly rejected polygamy. One of those members was young Heber J. Grant, who was then called as Junius Well's counselor at its initial meeting of the YMMIA. Such defections from the Wasatch Association as well as the popularity of the MIA quickly led to the demise of the popular Literary Association. It had served its purpose.

Timpanogos University (1876)

Brigham Young Academy (later BYU), founded in 1876, is normally considered the first such institution of higher learning in Provo. Actually, started six years previously, Timpanogos University was a private school that became the predecessor of the Academy. In that year Chancellor Daniel Wells wrote a letter to Walter Dusenberry, co-owner of the private school, who along with his brother was having financial problems. Wells informed Dusenberry of the Prophet's counsel that his school become a branch of Deseret University, called the Provo Branch. Instead, it became Brigham Young Academy as arrangements were made to manage financial affairs. Warren Dusenberry was then selected to fill the post of President of the Academy for a few months before Karl Maeser was called.

Zina's Terror (1876)

There are few Latter-day Saints not familiar with the attempted silk industry in early Utah. Nothing remains now of that once promising industry except a few rare pieces of "Utah" silk and some scattered mulberry trees. In 1876 the Deseret Silk Association was formally organized on June 15, with Zina D. Young as president. We don't know if her husband, Brigham, was aware of Zina's feelings about silkworms, but they were abhorrent to Zina—in her words, a "terror." She claimed she was terrorized with nightmares of feeding the worms, but like any worthy Saint she silently endured, fed millions of them herself, and watched the industry enjoy a short period of success before it was abandoned.

We're Not That Green, Brigham! (1876)

Self-sufficiency for the Saints in Utah was always a goal of their President, Brigham Young. With this in mind, in 1876 he advised the Relief Society sisters to form an association to sell the "Home-made articles such as are manufactured among ourselves." Within a month the sisters opened the Woman's Commission Store and without "a competent man" to help them as Brigham offered. Brigham's plural wife Eliza Snow took over the management and when Brigham attempted to dictate the terms of commission from his own woolen mill, Eliza wrote to him,

"Although we are novices in the mercantile business, we are not green enough for that kind of management."

Reckoning Time (1876)

The Deseret News Weekly predicted that time would henceforth be reckoned from the event that happened at 5 P.M. on April 5, 1876. Four powder magazines on Arsenal Hill on the heights north of the city exploded, an explosion heard and felt as far as twenty miles away. An estimated forty-five tons of explosives (stored for retail businesses) sent 500 tons of rock and other material into the air, bringing damage throughout much of the city. A Civil War veteran observed, "Fredericksburg after being bombarded for a month did not show so much sign of wreck as Salt Lake did." The loss of life was light considering that boulders weighing up to 115 pounds were hurled over a mile. The most obvious damage was windows throughout the city, with over a thousand panes of glass destroyed in the Tabernacle alone.

Mentally Confused? (1876)

When Sidney Rigdon died in 1876, most of his flock had already deserted him. Sidney had periodically demonstrated mental confusion for the past four decades, ever since the mobbing at Johnson's farm in Ohio in 1832. His flirting with wife swapping, if true, would certainly be evidence of it. Even more so was the report of an event that occurred during a conference of his church in 1846. He continued the conference for six months, and according to a member, one night Sidney and his few remaining followers knelt in the field in back of the church barn from sunset until dawn, awaiting the return of Christ. If the report is true, the Savior's failure to appear likely caused most of Rigdon's last supporters to abandon him.

Apostle Without a Quorum (1876)

Over Jacob Hamblin's grave in Alpine, Arizona, the Church erected a monument that includes these words: "Peace-maker in the Camp of the Lamanites; Herald of Truth to the House of Israel." It was said that this Mormon pioneer did more to ensure peace with the Indians in southern Utah, Arizona, and New Mexico than any body of troops ever sent against them and yet he never killed one. He was so respected by the natives and by Brigham Young that in December 1876 the Prophet ordained Jacob as "Apostle to the Lamanites" but never called him to the Quorum of Twelve Apostles. He compiled a list of rules for dealing with the natives, with the first one perhaps illustrating the reason for his success: "I never talk anything but the truth to them."

The Real Reason (1876)

There seems to be little question that plural marriage was a cause of much of the hostility directed against the Saints in the nineteenth century. However, that did not seem to be the underlying reason for the negative reports of federal judges assigned to office in Utah. Edward W. Tullidge, author of the book, *Life of Brigham Young or Utah and Her Founders* (1876), was able as both a Church authority and later apostate to grasp the underlying reason. It was, he wrote, the Mormon practice of settling disputes in Church courts "after the patterns of the New Testament rather than after the patterns of Blackstone. It was this which made Mormon rule so obnoxious to federal judges and Gentile lawyers." Judges couldn't rule and Gentile lawyers could not "reach the pockets of the people."

Now Is the Time to Strike! (1877)

Because of the rival factions that had arisen after the death of Joseph Smith, non-Mormons expected the same confusion to arise after Brigham's demise. Thus we find the well-known Reverend DeWitt Talmadge calling from his pulpit in 1877 for another Mormon War: "Now, my friends . . . is the time for United States Government to strike. Let as much of their lands be confiscated as will pay for their subjugation. . . . Set Phil Sheridan [Union General] after them. Give him enough troops and he will teach all of Utah that 40 wives is 39 too many." However, thirty years of Young's leadership had its effect—there was no confusion in the transfer of power, to the dismay of Church enemies.

Tombstone and the Mormons (1877)

It seems difficult to make a connection between Tombstone, Arizona and the Latter-day Saints, but the town would probably not even exist if not for the Mormons—at least the Mormon Battalion. Five years after the treaty ending the war with Mexico in 1848, the United States felt the need to purchase additional territory from Mexico as a route for a southern railroad. Mexico was reluctant to lose additional territory and certainly not as much as the Gadsden Purchase specified. Actually, the United States didn't need the southern portion of Arizona that includes Tombstone, Sierra Vista, and Benson, but thanks to the march of the Mormon Battalion through that area in 1847 and with Colonel Cooke's Battalion map, the U. S. negotiators felt compelled to insist on that territory. Since Tombstone was not established until 1877 by silver miners, it is extremely unlikely the town would have been established if that area had remained part of Mexico.

10
The Church Survives
(1877-1890)

Brigham's Wealth (1877)

Non-Mormons, especially anti-Mormons, have always contended that Brigham Young enriched himself at the expense of his followers to the tune of several million dollars. In fact, Ann Eliza Young's divorce lawyers, trying for a sizable settlement, estimated his wealth at 8 million dollars. Even Brigham, in reply, overestimated it when he responded with a figure of $600,000. The major problem, of course, which took two years to straighten out after his death, was trying to determine what was in his name and what belonged to the Church. Brigham had never seemed greatly concerned about the distinction, and that's the reason he resigned his position as trustee-in-trust for the Church four years before his death. After two years of paying off creditors, settling on fees, and determining Church ownership of properties and other difficult legalisms, the executors were finally able to arrive at a final figure of $224,242—a fairly small sum when you consider the number of heirs.

And Only Four! (1877)

Some of the first ordinances performed in the St. George Temple in 1877 were those performed by Wilford Woodruff and others for 100 prominent men, including the signers of the Declaration of Independence. A careful perusal of Wilford Woodruff's journal will show four of those men were ordained as High Priests. The interesting thoughts this information prompts is not "why only four?" but "why those particular ones?" George Washington, being one of them, is easily understood, but the other three might pose questions, especially when we note that such a prominent figure as Thomas Jefferson was not one of them. They were Christopher Columbus, John Wesley, and Benjamin Franklin. We can only assume Mr. Franklin had seriously repented of his "womanizing" mortal years.

"A Reasonable Recompense" (1877)

Because of the excessive demands in time and expense of being a General Authority, it is fairly well known that they are allowed a moderate remuneration for their Church duties. Less known is how many years passed before this was done. Neither the first two Church Presidents, their counselors, nor any of the General Authorities were compensated until after the death of Brigham Young. At the October Conference in 1877, John Taylor, President of the Quorum of the Twelve and Trustee-in-Trust (not yet sustained as Prophet), proposed that the Quorum as well as their counselors receive "a reasonable recompense for their services." The motion was carried unanimously and that has been the policy ever since.

The Man Who Didn't Smile (1878)

Encountering Mormonism dramatically changed the lives of many converts, particularly that of Brigham Young's brother, Joseph Young. In 1878, as a Latter-day Saint, he was able to describe man as "an instrument of music" and when the strains "are harmonious, he endorses and enjoys them with supreme delight . . . and [they] absorb his whole being." This was the same man whom Brigham had once described as a "very spiritual man" who neither laughed nor smiled because he had concluded that with no "Bible Christians on the earth . . . all must go to perdition." Brigham said of his brother during this period of religious despair, "I did not know of his smiling during some four or five years."

The Rowdy Boys of Farmington (1878)

They weren't delinquents, but they were rowdy, undisciplined boys that bothered Aurelia Spencer Rogers of Farmington. She expressed her concern about the town's young boys to Eliza Snow, especially the fitness of such youth in making good future husbands. She was especially concerned in the raising of honorable youth in the Church but in preventing such gentile practices as smoking, having given up that habit herself years earlier. Eliza took up the matter with the Quorum of the Twelve, and shortly thereafter Aurelia was set apart to preside over a Primary Organization in Farmington, but it was to include girls also. From this beginning in 1878, the Primary, because of its success, quickly spread throughout the Church.

As a Witness against Them? (1879)

Latter-day Saints have often been advised to ignore or disregard any anti-Mormon literature. This was apparently not the advice of the Prophet Joseph. In 1839, while in Liberty jail, he advised the Saints to gather up and preserve a history of all the facts pertaining to the various persecutions endured by the Saints (1879 Doctrine and Covenants, p. 389). John Taylor and the Quorum of the Twelve in 1879 interpreted this direction to mean the collection of any and all anti-Mormon literature. With this in mind, Taylor assigned A. M. Musser to that specific task. In the March 31, 1879 issue of the *Millennial Star* (pp. 196-198), Musser listed over one hundred anti-Mormon books, pamphlets, and newspapers that he wanted readers to gather and forward to him.

The Judge Didn't Understand (1879)

Daniel Wells, who had been mayor of Salt Lake City for ten years and a member of the First Presidency for thirty, was called as a witness in the John Miles polygamy case in 1879. Attempting to gather evidence as to whom Brother Wells had seen during a marriage ceremony in the Endowment House, the Federal Prosecutor demanded that he describe the sacred clothing worn in those ceremonies. Upon his refusal to reveal such sacred information, Brother Wells was charged with contempt of court and sentenced to two days in the penitentiary and a $100 fine. But again, the Federal officials couldn't seem to win. On his release the prisoner was escorted from the prison by a cheering procession of over 10,000 Saints with banners, flags, and signs waving.

Both Tolerant and Tactful (1879)

When American Secretary of State Evart asked British Prime Minister Gladstone to prevent young women in Great Britain from emigrating to Utah (see *500 Little-known Facts*, p. 222), Gladstone replied, "I presume the young people go there of their own accord." In addition to his tolerance, the "People's William" as the English called him, was tactful. When a naïve but dedicated Mormon missionary in Great Britain sent Premier Gladstone some gospel tracts requesting that he read them, Gladstone immediately responded with a kind and courteous answer, thanking the sender. History does not record whether the Prime Minister actually read the Mormon literature.

A Humorous Contradiction (1879)

It was not unusual for anti-Mormon writers and editors, in their zeal to stigmatize the Saints, to forget what they had written in the early parts of their articles. Such was the case in the London Times on August 12, 1879. Referring to the Saints as "an ugly phenomenon" made up of people of "imperfect intellectual and moral education," the editor then lists the inducements that the faith holds out to converts. These are "a well ordered community" with all the "necessities and comfort of life." Utah, he unconsciously adds, is a place "where poverty is unknown and drunkenness is unknown, and want drives neither man to crime nor woman to vice."

Only $200 and a Mule (1879)

The entire world is not necessarily safe for missionaries today, but it is hard to imagine a time when the United States was not safe either. Elder Joseph Parry describes such a time and place in his correspondence from North Carolina in August 1879.Writing from Cherokee County, he noted that "the judges are ruled by prejudice, and the jury can be bought for a little money. It is said here that $200 and a mule will clear the blackest murders." In the last fourteen years, there had been over thirty murders with no convictions. In a post-script to his letter he added that "last night about fifteen to eighteen young men made a raid upon the house where I was staying, and I had to go out and get a severe whipping with switches and clubs."

Emma's Sense of Humor (1879)

When Emma Smith was laid to rest in 1879, her antagonism to plural marriage was the chief recollection most Utah Saints had of the Prophet Joseph's widow. Other aspects of her personality were often forgotten, such as her keen sense of humor. When a man once teased her about fishing for a compliment, she immediately came back with, "I never fish in shallow water." Another time when she was forced to come up with a quick dessert at the Mansion House for Judge Stephen Douglas and some of Nauvoo's leaders, she fried some apple fritters to a fluffy perfection. When her appreciative guests asked what she called the delicacies she smiled and said "candidates." When the amused guests asked why, she replied, "Isn't it just a puff of wind?"

And Then There Was One (1880)

One of the most brilliant minds ever to be called as a member of the Quorum of the Twelve was Orson Pratt. At the Jubilee (50th) Conference of the Church called in 1880, Orson was called upon to speak. He spoke of being in attendance at the first general conference, consisting of seventy or eighty members in all, assembled in the home of Peter Whitmer in New York. In 1880 there were 160,000 members. Orson was the only surviving member of the original Quorum of the Twelve, organized forty-five years before the Jubilee Conference. Still as active as ever in the Lord's work, Brother Pratt would live only one year more, weakened by the strain of travel in his missionary endeavors, at the age of seventy.

The Only Direct Account (1880)

Perhaps the most widely recognized phrase in Mormon history is that of Brigham Young upon viewing the Salt Lake Valley for the first time. The only direct account of that incident was given thirty-three years after it occurred, by Wilford Woodruff at the Pioneer Day celebration in 1880 when he quoted President Young as saying, "It is enough. This is the right place. Drive on." Wilford Woodruff continued and said, "So I drove to the encampment already formed by those who had come along in advance of us." According to several historians, this quote was merely an affirmation of what the pioneer Saints already had recognized as their destination. Everett L. Cooley noted that when Brigham entered the valley, "several acres of corn, potatoes, and beans were already sown." The pioneers were merely assuring Brigham that they recognized their home.

Didn't Know He Knew It (1880)

Heber J. Grant was thirty-eight years away from being ordained as the President of the Church of Jesus Christ of Latter-day Saints when he was called to be president of the Tooele Utah Stake at the age of twenty-four. After a short talk, Joseph F. Smith reminded him that he did not bear his testimony as to the truthfulness of the gospel. When he answered that he didn't know if it was true, Smith suggested his calling be withdrawn. President John Taylor, who was present, started laughing and said, "Joseph, Joseph, Joseph, he knows it just as well as you do. The only thing that he does not know is that he does know it." Heber was to bear his testimony numerous times after that.

Feeding Anti-Mormonism (1880)

The adopted twin daughter of Joseph and Emma, Julia Murdock, died in 1880, having lived an unhappy life. Historians do not usually note part of the reason for that unhappiness, but it deals with the adoption itself. When the Smiths adopted the Murdock twins (Julia's twin brother died as an infant shortly after the mob attack on the Johnson home in Hiram in 1831) they never anticipated the event would fuel the fires of anti-Mormonism. Unfortunately, as rumors spread of plural marriage, her adoption facts became distorted and Joseph was accused of fathering Julia. As Julia later wrote to one of her biological brothers, "It has been a received opinion that . . . my mother was some unfortunate girl that was betrayed by him [Joseph]. . . . is that not enough to make me miserable?"

A Unique Honor (1880)

When a new county east of Sevier County was formed in 1880, the Saints used the occasion to confer a unique honor on a federally appointed gentile official, Governor Emery. As a Territorial Governor, he criticized the Saints. In fact, the initial drive against plural marriage began during his administration, as well as during the trial and execution of John D. Leek. In his fair-minded way, however, he refused to let his office become involved. It was because of his fairness that the Latter-day Saints awarded him the honor of naming the new county after him. It was Governor Emery who entertained President Grant on his visit to Utah when the president asked, in surprise, about the identity of the neatly dressed children who were cheering him in his trip through the city. When Emery told him they were Mormon children, Grant made his famous confession, "I have been deceived."

No False Sentimentality Here! (1880)

Normally a family would be pleased to have the Church President preach a funeral sermon for a member of their family, but we must wonder in the case of President Taylor preaching the sermon for Joseph McCain in the 14th Ward in Salt Lake on February 8, 1880. As he said on that occasion, "We have not come here to indulge in any kind of false sentimentality. He was a drunkard; that is a truth and you know it. . . . He did not die drunk. No, but that was the cause of it. We may as well talk honestly about him. . . . Did I feel sorry when he died? No. Why? Because I knew it was much better for him to leave the earth than to be in the position he has been." The reaction of McCain's family is not a matter of record.

The "Absent" President (1880)

The meaning of the term "elect lady" in the 1830 revelation received by the Prophet Joseph for his wife was explained in 1842 when she was elected president of the newly formed Relief Society. Joseph explained that Emma was called an elect lady "because [she was] elected to preside," a fulfillment of the revelation given twelve years earlier. Although she had no association with the society after 1844, a mystique apparently developed about her calling and title. Although Brigham authorized Eliza Snow to reactivate the society in 1868, she was not set apart to preside until a year after Emma's death in 1879. Was this because of Brigham's belief that Emma was still considered by the Lord as president of the society, absent though she was?

David Rogers' Hymnal (1881)

Since his baptism in New York's East River by Parley P. Pratt in 1837, David Rogers was involved in most of the important events in Missouri, Nauvoo, and early Utah and sacrificed much. When Church hymnals were in short supply in New York shortly after his baptism, he thought he was doing all he could to help. At his own expense he had printed for the New York Saints a hymnal based to a major extent on Emma Smith's 1835 hymnal—but without getting permission or giving Emma Smith credit—and including several of his own hymns. At a Nauvoo conference in 1839 it was decided to bring charges against David for the unauthorized hymnal and to destroy all copies. He accepted the action readily and showed no resentment for the next forty-two years, dying in Provo in 1881.

May We Help? (1881)

When President Arthur presented his first message to Congress in December 1881, he, like his predecessors, urged legislation to end polygamy in Utah. He was reacting to pressure from those advocating federal intervention, one such group being the Reorganized Church of Jesus Christ of Latter Day Saints. This monogamic splinter group, not entirely selfless, offered their own leader, Joseph Smith, III, as territorial governor of Utah. Such an appointment, they believed, would be the ideal beginning of a missionary campaign for their church in Utah, encouraging an anti-polygamy revolt within the Mormon Church. The offer was rejected just as a similar offer by James J. Strang, the "King of Beaver Island," had been rejected in 1854.

Prophesying a "True Religion" (1881)

The first Mormon missionaries entered New Zealand in 1854, but for nearly thirty years concentrated on converting the Europeans—with little success. And then around 1880 President Joseph F. Smith of the First Presidency instructed the missionaries to concentrate on the Maori (New Zealand Polynesians). Their first baptism was in 1881, and the baptisms among the Maori people exploded for the next two decades—for a reason. Since 1830 five of their native priests or tohunga had been advising the natives to wait for the "true religion," which they would know because they would "travel in pairs . . . come from the rising sun . . . visit us in our homes . . . learn our language . . . and when they pray they will raise their right hands." Today the majority of the 93,000 members in New Zealand are Maori.

Closing an Open Door (1881)

An unjustified criticism of the Mormon Church is that access to historical sources owned by the Church is severely limited because there is much they wish to keep secret. Actually, due to the misuse by anti-Mormons of Church-owned materials, access was limited shortly after the Historian's Office was established in Utah. When historian and author Hubert H. Bancroft requested information in 1862 for a book on Utah, George A. Smith responded to his questions about Territorial Governor Cumming by saying that his administration was remarkable "for the amount of intoxicating drinks used, and their consequent effect in producing blasphemy, riot and bloodshed." He also said Governor Wootton's administration "was marked by no event of importance, saving only that when he left, bad liquor fell in price." Fortunately, greater cooperation was eventually extended, and Bancroft's History of Utah was one of the most objective histories of that century.

Then Why Did He Wait? (1881)

It is a well-known fact that Brigham Young waited over three years before calling for a vote declaring him as President of the Church. John Taylor did the same thing before being sustained as President in 1880, over three years after Brigham's death. However, a year later during the general conference priesthood meeting, Taylor said, "In June, 1875, President Young brought up the subject of seniority, and stated that John Taylor was the man that stood next to him; and that where he was not, John Taylor presided. . . . It placed me in the position of president of the church." We must wonder why he didn't reveal this earlier to the Quorum, or if he did, why the long wait before they sustained him as President of the Church?

A Little Less than Balanced (1882)

Utah Territory was entitled to a delegate in Congress, although that delegate could not vote. With Federal officials overseeing the elections, however, the Saints were at a disadvantage although they outnumbered the gentiles and apostates 120,000 to 21,000. The registrars would determine who would be allowed to vote, and the Saints were allowed only eight votes whereas the gentiles were given seven and the apostates nine. This was grossly unfair but the bias really showed up in the population allotments the registrars could register—the Saints only 12,308, the gentiles over 63,000, and the apostates over 68,000. In spite of the disenfranchisements by the non-Mormon registrars, a Mormon delegate was still elected by a majority of over 17,000 votes, but lost when the Federal Governor [Murray] gave the election to the loser.

Senator Brown Understood (1882)

When anti-Mormon polygamy legislation was introduced in Congress, the Saints were not totally devoid of friends. One such ally was Senator Joseph E. Brown of Georgia, who spoke out against the Edmunds Bill in 1882. With unusual clarity for Congressmen at that time, he warned his colleagues of the danger of future legislation against even believers in the infallibility of the Pope or the doctrine of transubstantiation. How long before "no member of a church who believed in close communion and baptism by immersion as the only mode, should vote or hold office?" Such legislation, he noted, was the result of popular vengeance, and he added, "When we are done with them [the Mormons], I know not who will next be considered the proper subject of it."

"Not the Word of God" (1882)

When Brigham Young established Orderville and similar United Orders, John Taylor was less than enthusiastic. He realized that enterprises such as Orderville were pure communism and not the law of consecration. He made this plain after he became President, when in 1882 he sent an epistle to all authorities of the Church in which he bluntly stated: "We had no example of the 'United Order' in accordance with the word of God on the subject. . . . Our relations with the world and our own imperfections prevent the establishment of this system [i.e. the system of consecration and stewardship spoken of at times as the 'United Order'] at the present time, as was stated by Joseph in an early day, it cannot yet be carried out."

Utah Girls (1882)

Because anti-Mormons had written so much about polygamy and its revolting "results," actual visitors invariably commented on the female Mormons they encountered. One such visitor was Phil Robinson, a British journalist who visited Utah in 1882 and spent three months observing those women and girls. He later wrote, "The demeanor of the women in Utah, as compared with Brighton or Washington, is modesty itself; and the children are just such healthy, vigorous, pretty children as one sees in the country by the sea-side in England. . . . Utah-born girls, the offspring of plural wives, have figures that would make Paris envious; and they carry themselves with almost oriental dignity. . . . robust health seemed the rule."

A Reminder to Forget (1882)

In 1882 the Prophet Joseph's surviving brother, William, began to write his memoirs of his dead brothers. His nephew, Joseph III, felt compelled to remind him that he had "long been engaged in removing from father's memory and from the early church, the stigmas and blame thrown upon him because of polygamy." He then continued by demanding that if his uncle, a member of young Joseph's church, was "the wise man I think you to be, you will fail [to] remember anything [except] referring lofty standard of character at which we esteem those good men." William bowed to those demands by denying his brothers' involvement in plural marriage.

Let's Wait until Warmer Weather (1883)

When Brother G. was brought before the High Council in frontier Utah on charges of drunkenness and adultery, he showed no remorse. He was thus given one month to apologize to his ward or he would be excommunicated. He finally apologized but objected to rebaptism because he had not been excommunicated. When the bishop persisted, Brother G. reluctantly agreed—provided he could wait until warmer weather. This objection was put aside when Brother Empy, the bishop's counselor said, "Cold water will not hurt a repentant man."

No Need for Treaties (1883)

One of the most objective visitors to Utah in the nineteenth century was Phil Robinson, a celebrated author and war correspondent of the *London Telegraph* who visited Utah in the winter of 1882-83 and published a book, *Sinners and Saints*, in 1883. He was especially impressed that the Mormons did not make treaties with the Indians and listed the reasons. One reason was the dislike the Indians had for the United States, which had obviously broken so many of its treaties. He noted especially, however, the "conciliatory policy of the Church towards the Indians (that) obviates all necessity for further measures of alliance." He noted, to the dismay probably of many anti-Mormons, that the Indians realized that with the Saints, "whenever their word was given, that word was kept sacred, even to their loss."

The Success of Mormonism (1883)

One of the most astute observations ever made about Mormonism in the nineteenth century by a non-Mormon was by a member of the British Parliament, James W. Barclay. He visited Utah in 1883 during the height of anti-Mormonism and later wrote of his observations for

Nineteenth Century, a monthly magazine in London: "The success of Mormonism and its steady progress is due to two influences. First, there is no religious caste or class." He was undoubtedly thinking of the distinctive clergy caste in most Christian churches. "And, in the second place, Mormonism interests itself as much in the temporal as in the spiritual concerns of its members."

A Little-Known People (1883)

Most Latter-day Saints who hear of Mormon-Indian relations think of such western tribes as the Utes, Navajos, and so on. The most successful missionary work with Native Americans, however, was with a tribe in York County, South Carolina. Elders Henry Miller and Charles Robinson first delivered the gospel message to the Catawbas in 1883. As a result of their activities, virtually the entire tribe, numbering 200-300, was converted. Located near Rock Hill with a 640-acre reservation, these "River People," as they label themselves, received Federal recognition as a tribe in 1993. Numbering nearly 1,400 today, they are still predominantly Latter-day Saints—the most faithful and proportionately numerous Native American Latter-day Saints in the country.

The Southern Exodus (1884)

The massacre of attendees at a Mormon Church meeting at Cane Creek, Tennessee, in 1884, including two Mormon missionaries, was perhaps the epitome of violence against Saints in the American South in the late nineteenth century. Violence against missionaries and members was so great in such states as Tennessee, Georgia, and Mississippi that the Church sent $15,000 to B. H. Roberts, who was temporarily presiding over the mission, to aid in the removal of frightened Church members from Tennessee and other Southern danger spots to western Colorado and Utah. The first immigrant company itself was so large it occupied ten passenger cars on the Santa Fe Railroad. Other immigrant companies soon followed while missionary activity was suspended.

"Greater Love Hath No Man" (1884)

Two of the most valiant defenders of the Saints in the nineteenth century were two youthful brothers at Cane Creek, Tennessee in 1884—Martin Condor, age nineteen, and John Riley Hudson, age twenty-four. Their parents had befriended Mormon missionaries, and a church service was being held in their crude home on August 10, 1884, when an anti-Mormon mob attacked the home with guns. The young men were in the orchard and ran to the house to defend the missionaries inside. Both young men were killed in the resulting gunfire as well as two of the missionaries—Elders Gibbs and Berry. There were actually a number of friends of the persecuted Saints in the nineteenth century, but the names of these two young men who made the ultimate sacrifice should be remembered in honor by all Latter-day Saints.

A Worthy Request Denied (1884)

Jane Manning James, who had lived with the Prophet Joseph and Emma in Nauvoo, wrote to President Taylor, asking to be sealed to Joseph as a daughter. She revealed that Emma had invited such an adoption while Joseph was alive, but not fully understanding the doctrine of sealing, she had turned down the invitation. Now, President Taylor turned her down because she was black. She later appealed to President Woodruff and later still to Joseph F. Smith, being regretfully rejected each time. She was allowed to enter the temple to be baptized for her ancestors and President Smith would speak at her funeral, but her endowments and sealings have only been done vicariously in recent years.

An Unworthy Request Denied (1884)

Mormon history will remember him for several things—but not for his faithfulness to the end. George Watt is noted for being the first person baptized in Great Britain, for being the founding editor of the *Journal of Discourses*, a traveling companion to Brigham and a recorder of his talks, and for his major contributions in the development of the *Deseret Alphabet*. Unfortunately, as a freethinker he had several conflicts with Church leaders over policy and doctrine and was excommunicated in 1874. Without changing his mind on doctrine, he made application four times to rejoin the Church but was denied. His beliefs just differed too greatly from those of the orthodox Mormon. He did not believe in a personal God, nor could he accept the scriptures as infallible guides. He believed that man had not fallen but had steadily progressed. Insisting on rebaptism with these beliefs, there is little wonder that he was still an outsider when he died in 1884.

"Any and All Sisters" (1884)

At the April 28, 1842 meeting of the Relief Society in Nauvoo, the Prophet Joseph affirmed the rights of the sisters to use spiritual gifts, including that of healing. In 1884 Eliza Snow, echoing what she had learned from Joseph, reminded the sisters that no special setting apart was necessary for such ordinances: "Any and all sisters who honor their holy covenants, not only have the right but should feel it a duty, whenever called upon, to administer to our sisters in these ordinances." In 1914 President Joseph F. Smith, in a letter to stake leaders, substantiated this original counsel of the Prophet Joseph. In fact, the *Woman's Exponent* on February 15, 1873, pointed out that such gifts of faith were given to the faithful, irrespective of gender or even age.

When Friends Were Few (1884)

At the time of the "Tennessee Massacre" at Cane Creek in 1884, the Saints had few friends, especially in the South. One did step forward, however, when B. H. Roberts was seeking help in retrieving and returning the bodies of the martyred missionaries to Utah. His name was Bernard Moses, a Jewish clothier in Chattanooga. He not only paid for the steel caskets for the victims but also loaned Roberts several hundred dollars without a note being signed. This was not the end of this fearless friend's help. When Roberts was fighting for his rightful seat in Congress in 1899, Moses came to Washington and made a statement to the press on behalf of his Mormon friend. "He thinks as little of persecution now as he did then," Roberts said.

What Size Was He? (1885)

The arrests, trials, and imprisonment of hundreds of cohabs (those who practiced polygamy) in the 1880s was a period of sacrifice and suffering for the Saints—only occasionally relieved by incidents of humor. One such occurred at the Bateman home, which authorities had visited repeatedly while searching for polygamist Brother Bateman. Such a surprise visit one day found Bateman not at home, but one of the deputies entered and searched thoroughly, including looking in the kitchen cupboards, flour bin, and even a sugar can. Sister Bateman, who knew the deputy, couldn't resist: "Deputy F., have you no idea of the size of the man you are searching for?" Sister Bateman related that when that particular deputy came alone in his periodic searches, he seldom got beyond the sugar can.

The Prohibited Zone (1885)

As the Saints started streaming into Mexico to escape U. S. Government persecution for plural marriage, the acting governor of Chihuahua, fearing a take-over by the Americans, ordered the Mormons in 1885 to leave that state within fifteen days. Elders Brigham Young, Jr., and Moses Thatcher of the Council of the Twelve appealed to Mexican President Porfirio Diaz, who removed the governor of Chihuahua and welcomed the Mormons to settle on lands of their own choosing in the states of Chihuahua, Sonora, or anywhere else except in that narrow strip of land along the border known as the Zona Prohibida. Obviously, such a zone indicated that Mexico was still fearful of losing more land to the United States.

We Can't Accept That! (1885)

In 1885 a bill was designed to disfranchise all Latter-day Saints in Idaho by requiring an oath before voting that the voter was not a member of any organization that believed in polygamy. When this bill was introduced in the territorial legislature, a more fair-minded member wanted to amend the bill so that only the practitioners, not all believers, would lose the vote. He suggested that the oath in the bill read, "You do solemnly swear that you are not a bigamist or a polygamist or that you do not cohabit with any other woman who is not your wife." Judge Brierley, an older member jumped to the floor and shouted: "My God, Gentlemen. We can't accept Hart's proposal. That would disfranchise all of us." The amendment was rejected.

The Soiled Doves Helped (1885)

Tables were briefly turned on the persecutors who were hounding the Saints in Utah in 1885. The Chief of Detectives in Salt Lake City, a Mormon named Brigham Y. Hampton, with the cooperation of the Madame of a bordello on West Temple Street, had his police bore holes in a number of rooms. These enabled the Mormon police to gather evidence on more than 100 federal appointees, including judges, prosecuting attorneys, and marshals as well as members of the gentile ring who had been so zealous in their prosecution of the Saints for "sexual irregularities." The resulting arrests were a bombshell among the gentiles as Hampton started preparing indictments. Many gentile leaders even went into hiding as they had forced so many Saints to do. Unfortunately, Federal Judge Zane quashed the indictments and Hampton himself was arrested for "conspiracy" and sentenced to a year in prison.

"Make Your Fight in Utah! (1885)

President Young, in remarks made in the Salt Lake Tabernacle in 1884, referred to comments made to Saints visiting the Arizona Territorial capital. There they asked the Mormons not to introduce their obnoxious practice of plural marriage in Arizona: "Make your fight in Utah. . . . Introduce only that which can be tolerated." This was followed up the following year when the Territorial Legislature passed legislation disenfranchising members of organizations who practiced plural marriage. Strangely enough, the same legislature repealed this measure two years later without it ever being challenged—three full years before the Church issued the Manifesto forbidding plural marriage.

Creating New Definitions (1885)

The Saints must have known they would never prevail against federal authorities when the courts started creating new definitions for criminal acts. In 1885 President Lorenzo Snow was arrested for unlawful cohabitation when he was observed walking with a wife down a street in Salt Lake City and charged with "living together." It seemed pretty obvious according to a court ruling. They were both "living" and they were "together." Thus they were "living together" and Lorenzo was therefore guilty of unlawful cohabitation and sent to prison. At first the Supreme Court reversed the lower court decision but then reversed itself and President Snow was returned to prison.

They Almost Lost $20,000 (1885)

In 1885 the Saints were desperate to see their territory become a state, so when an alleged representative of the Cleveland administration offered to make it possible for $20,000, they decided to pursue the matter. They sent Brigham Young, Jr., and Charles W. Penrose, the editor-in-chief of the *Deseret News*, on a mission to New York to meet the "representative," a Mr. L. Miller (who has never been identified) and Cleveland's people. They actually did meet the President-Elect who knew nothing of Mr. Miller and suggested they have Miller arrested. Later, when an accomplice of Miller showed up at the rooms of the two Mormons, he told them everything had been arranged for statehood, and asked for the $20,000, Young and Penrose refused. The frauds quickly left, knowing the game was up. It would be another decade before Utah entered the Union—without any bribery.

The Loyal League of Utah (1886)

It was secret in its membership, but certainly not in its purpose. According to the published constitution of the secret society that was formed in Utah in 1886, its purpose was to use every means within its power for the disintegration and destruction of the Mormon people as a political and religious body. With its membership secret, the Saints had to accept the Loyal League's claimed membership of over 3,000 with branches throughout the towns and cities of Utah. The "siege mentality" with which the Saints were accused is easy to understand with such "secret" organizations of gentiles living among them.

The Bench Prophet (1886)

A number of apostate groups have split from the Church over the past 175 years—most of them short-lived. One of the most interesting was that of John E. Forsgren, a faithful member since 1843 who had served a number of missions for the Church. Unfortunately, by 1886 this former sailor "had evidently become insane over religion." He established a tent home on the bench east of Salt Lake City, now one of the most beautiful residential sections of the city. Claiming to succeed to the divine calling of the Prophet Joseph Smith, the so-called "Bench Prophet" moved into the tent with twelve women, representing the twelve tribes of Israel. Memory of him and his movement is now forgotten by most Saints. Forsgren's grave is in Brigham City where he was buried after his death in 1890.

A Spy at Fort Douglas? (1886)

When Brigham Young's grandson, 2nd Lt. Richard W. Young, a graduate of West Point, managed to be assigned to Fort Douglas in Salt Lake City in 1886, the anti-Mormon newspaper, the *Salt Lake Tribune,* was furious. An editorial questioned his loyalty when he was "in full sympathy with an alien power" and noted that his assignment was "a gross wrong and insult to the soldiers at the camp . . . where he will be looked upon perpetually as a spy." Actually, Lieutenant Young was not the least bit interested in "spying." In 1889 he resigned his commission to open a successful law practice in Salt Lake City.

The Bread Threw Him Off Balance (1886)

With a $500 reward for his arrest for unlawful cohabitation, George Q. Cannon, Counselor to President Taylor, decided in February 1886 to go to Mexico to escape the increased attempts to arrest him. He got as far as Nevada before an informer spotted him and wired ahead to authorities. He was arrested and started on a return trip to Salt Lake City. On the way he jumped or fell from the rear platform of the train. Badly bruised in the fall, he was recaptured and the trip was resumed. Mormons insisted a lurch of the train caused him to fall, but his captors, according to author Samuel Taylor, noted that even though injured, he escaped capture for an hour and when captured he carried a loaded pistol, a flask of water and two loaves of bread. Maybe the extra weight threw him off balance.

A Significant Distinction (1886)

Many individuals, including many Saints, have questioned how the Mormons in Nauvoo could have publicly denied the practice of polygamy while being so deeply involved. John Taylor explained the perceivable contradiction in the *Deseret News* on May 20, 1886, when he pointed out that the lustful doctrine that men like John C. Bennett tried to promulgate "was a counterfeit. The true and divine order is another thing." In a letter to Joseph F. Smith, Eliza Snow said the system of marriage the Saints were denying was that of spiritual wifery as preached by Bennett and which anti-Mormons believed was being practiced among the Saints. "His was prostitution," she noted, and in such anti-Mormon "articles there is no reference to divine plural marriage. We aimed to put down its opposite."

Dixie's Co-Hab Code (1887)

When Brother Frank Farnsworth was released from his duties as Temple Recorder in St. George in 1887, he had helped formulate a code to be used in communication among co-habs the Federal authorities were seeking. He later described how a list of words such as "Canaan, glasses, splendid, rocks, blowed up, hound, heads, pocket" were used to mean something totally different. In telegraphing a warning to a polygamist in hiding, those eight terms would mean, "You be careful. Things lively at Silver Reef, your retreat discovered, move your quarters." It is amusing that in that list, the "good guys"—Wilford Woodruff, Erastus Snow, and George Teasdale—were Peter, James, and John, whereas anti-Mormon judges such as Boreman and Zane were "Herod" and "Nero."

The "Dance of Death" (1887)

The St. George Stake High Council was little different from other Church stakes when it passed rules on dancing in 1887 stating that the stake leadership was "opposed to round dancing." An article in the *Contributor* that same year referred to the waltz as the "dance of death." An article in the Church's *Young Women's Journal* included a story of a young woman who was not married in the temple but "at home in disgrace and sorrow." Because of her habit

of dancing the waltz, she was led into a precipitous marriage and the story concluded with her words: "If I had
never waltzed with him, I never, of necessity should have
become his wife."

Waiting for the Revelation (1887)

He knew the revelation was coming and prepared his people for it—as much as he could. In his last First Presidency
Message in April 1887, John Taylor warned his people when
he wrote: "The Church is now passing through a period of
transition, or evolution, as some might be pleased to term it.
Such periods appear to be necessary in the progress and per-
fecting of all created things." And only weeks before his death
in July, the Prophet had approved the proposed state constitution that contained a provision forbidding the practice of
polygamy. Although approved overwhelmingly by the Utah
electorate, it was rejected by a Congress that didn't trust the
Saints to really abandon the practice if granted statehood
first. Thus John Taylor died waiting for the revelation that
finally came to President Woodruff.

Most Formidable Adversary (1887)

Left alone, plural marriage would have ended without such
Federal intervention as the Edmunds-Tucker Act of 1887. At
least that was the opinion of Phil Robinson, the well-known
English correspondent who visited Utah four years earlier. He
pointed at the "fashionable milliner" as the most formidable
adversary who made expensive store-bought fashions far
more demanding than homemade clothing and thus far too
expensive for men to consider more wives: "That old serpent,
the fashionable milliner, has got over the garden wall, and
Lilith (Adam's plural wife according to Rabbinical tradition)

and Eve are no longer content with primitive garments of home manufacture . . . No. Polygamy will before long be impossible, except to the rich." Robinson noted that during his tour, "the cost of plurality was on several occasions referred to by Mormons."

The Late Erastus Snow (1888)

He did not become the "late" Erastus Snow only after his death in 1888. He was so oblivious to the time of appointments and meetings that he earned the cognomen, "the late Erastus Snow," which he carried throughout his life. This did little to create compatibility with a very punctual Brigham Young, who often chastised Erastus. Mindful of his absentmindedness, Erastus took such reprimands in stride. And at dinners his table companions had to take his absentmindedness in stride also—especially when he removed food from their plates, unaware he wasn't helping himself from the main platter.

Not in Our Town! (1888)

Most students of western history are familiar with the famous Tonto Basin Feud between the Graham and Tewksbury families—but not the Mormon connection. When Thomas Graham was tried for murder in the Mormon town of St. Johns, the Saints found their hamlet filled with well-armed feud members itching for a fight. Author Hoffman Birney claimed that the Mormon bishop of St. Johns prevented the potential blood bath with a few choice words: "We will have peace even if we must fight for it. If the feud between the Tewksburys and the Grahams is opened up here in St. Johns [and] we are compelled to draw our guns we will not replace them until the last feudist is dead."

The feudists waited until they went home and the Mormons kept their peaceful town.

The Seducing of President Woodruff (1888)

The Church-owned Salt Lake Theater often created controversy when the performances didn't live up to the standards that some believed it should. Such was the case with a new type of minstrelsy made up of scantily clad female minstrels whose erotic performances caused the Church leaders to forbid the use of their theater. The most famous troupe was the Rentz-Stanley minstrels who returned to Salt Lake City with a show entitled "Adam and Eve." It was undoubtedly with some trepidation that President Woodruff, seduced by the title of the show, made the decision to attend a performance. He was outraged by the program and the Church-owned newspaper, the *Deseret News*, said "sacrilege" was now added to the criticism of the now permanently banned troupe.

When He's Dead! (1888)

In 1888 B. H. Roberts was called to serve as one of the presidents of the Seventies Quorum, and four years later his friend, J. Golden Kimball, was called to the same quorum. Roberts, known for his lengthy talks, and J. Golden for his dry wit, were often scheduled to speak at the same conference. Their respective characteristics came together once when Roberts spoke for nearly an hour, leaving little time for his junior colleague. When J. Golden arose, all he had to say in his dry falsetto voice was "B. H. Roberts is the senior president of the Seventy and has taken all the time. Someday he will be dead and I will be president. Then I will take all the time," at which point he sat down.

Especially Lawyers! (1889)

One of the many leading Latter-day Saints sentenced to prison for the "crime" of co-habitation was B. H. Roberts. While serving his time in old "Castle Prison" at the mouth of Parley's Canyon from May 1 to September 10, 1889, he was offered responsible trusteeship positions many times by prison officials. One such offer was to act as supervising headwaiter for a July 4th banquet for Utah lawyers. The officials felt they could not trust the non-Mormon prisoners ("toughs") in the role of waiters with such goods as liquor and wine. Roberts replied that he would "rather be a waiter to all the toughs in the prison than to have any part in serving these men who are locked in severe conflict with my people in Utah." Actually 95% of Utah lawyers at this time were gentiles and, like many Latter-day Saints, Roberts saw little distinction in their virtues.

Lorenzo Snow and Lenin (1889)

One of the most famous utopian books ever written was *Looking Backward* by Edward Bellamy, published in 1889. Some scholars believe *Looking Backward* had considerable influence in the making of Lenin's Soviet Russia. If this is true, then Lorenzo Snow and the Latter-day Saints must receive some of the credit—or blame. Hearing of the success of the United Order in Brigham City, Edward Bellamy made a special trip to Utah in 1886 to study its operation. There he spent three days with Lorenzo Snow, Brigham City's founder and forty-year resident. Impressed with the thirty to forty industries run by its 2,000 inhabitants and the vitality at that time of one of the most successful United Orders, Bellamy returned home and wrote his influential book.

"Till Fully Satisfied" (1890)

Doctrines in the Lord's Church don't change but worship practices do—such as the change from a common sacrament cup to individual ones. Such was the case in the partaking of the sacrament itself. As recently as 1890, according to the journal kept by Abraham H. Cannon, wine was still being used at times in the sacrament in Utah. Far more interesting was the amount of wine and bread consumed. He wrote of partaking of the "Lord's supper" in the manner "as Joseph and the brethren did occasionally at Nauvoo; we had several loaves of bread and bottles of wine." When one considers that the "Last Supper" was truly a meal, such a practice made much sense until the meetings reached an impractical size.

Was It Joseph or Brigham? (1890)

Most Latter-day Saints believe this basic question, referring to Blacks in the priesthood, was answered long before it surfaced in the Whitaker collection at the University of Utah in 1900. In response to where the restriction began, President Snow said he did not know whether it began with Joseph or Brigham. Many thought the Book of Abraham answered the question, but Joseph himself never used that book for justification—but only as a contemporary view. We do know Church leaders felt there seemed a need to distance themselves from another hated group in late-nineteenth century America, "abolitionists." We also know that several Blacks were ordained to the priesthood during Joseph's life, and as early as the Kirtland period when members approached Joseph on the subject, he only "advised" them—perhaps waiting for the day it would become a revelation.

Wounded Knee and the Saints (1890)

The Wounded Knee Massacre in South Dakota in 1890 is too well known to recount here—but the Mormon connection is not. When General Miles was asked whom he felt was responsible for the Messiah craze and the Ghost Dance that precipitated the massacre, he responded, "It is my belief that the Mormons are the prime movers in it." Miles was not just spouting anti-Mormonism. A Paiute by the name of Wovoka, living in Mormon country and being familiar with LDS doctrines and beliefs, proclaimed himself a prophet, copying many aspects of that religion, including a shirt (taken from temple garments) that protected its wearer from all harm. The Dance, intended to redeem a "fallen people" (as the Book of Mormon promised), was even joined in at times by Mormons.

11
A New Era Begins
(1890-1921)

Was It a Revelation? (1890)

There are not many Latter-day Saints who question whether the Manifesto of 1890, ending plural marriage, was received from the Lord. The question, however, is whether it was a revelation. On October 19, 1891, Judge Loofbourow, following instructions from the Federal Courts and as a master in chancery, commenced taking testimony with a view toward deciding to what charitable uses the confiscated Church property should be applied. Presidents Woodruff and Cannon were called to testify. As quoted by the *News*, October 24, the following testimony occurred when the Prophet was asked, "Why didn't you declare it to your church as a revelation and not by way of your personal advice?" After an ambiguous answer, Woodruff was asked pointedly, "Did you say it was a revelation?" His answer: "I gave them to understand that we should stop the practice of plural marriage."

In the City of the Insane (1890)

One of the most important of the Lord's manifestations to a prophet was not in the Mormon capital as might be expected, but in "a mad city, inhabited for the most part by perfectly insane people" as Joseph Kipling characterized San Francisco. In contemplating the temporal salvation of the Church in 1890, President Woodruff and his counselors left for San Francisco on September 3 to meet with prominent businessmen and politicians to discuss the chances of legally continuing plural marriage. It was during Woodruff's San Francisco visit that the Lord apparently spoke to him about discontinuing plural marriage. He returned to Salt Lake City on September 21, "determined to obtain divine confirmation," prompting the question as to why the Lord chose one of the world's most wicked cities of the time in which to speak to a prophet on this subject.

Adding Wine to the Word of Wisdom (1890)

By 1890 the Church in St. George realized it had made a big mistake in accepting wine and grapes in its tithing office. In fact, there were so many grapes that the wine office set up its own press and became the chief single producer of wine in the Dixie area. In spite of Brigham's advice to trade the wine out of the community, the St. George brethren drank so much of their wine that drunkenness became a concern among its leaders. The solution was to stop accepting wine as tithing and to abandon its own presses. It took a while, but by 1900 grape growers had gone out of the business and not drinking wine became part of the Word of Wisdom in St. George.

Murder in Orderville (1890)

Murder ballads in the nineteenth century are not uncommon, except for one set in the well-known United Order community of Orderville. The ballad describes a Mary Steavens whose body was discovered near the town with four bullets in the back. Foot tracks led to a "youth" who didn't want to marry the pregnant girl. He confessed and was sent to prison. The mystery surrounds his killer's name, Alvin Heaton, which was the same as the presiding elder in the

Moccasin Branch, which was attached to the Orderville Ward in 1890, some time after the murder. The solution seems to lie in a 1929 *Improvement Era* article about the Heaton family that stated, "All of Brother Heaton's sons and daughters (26) except one are engaged in Church activities." Was that one Alvin, Jr.?

The Day the Church Died (1891)

A day seldom noted in the history of the Church of Jesus Christ of Latter-day Saints is May 25, 1891, when the Church ceased to exist. That was the literal decision of the U.S. Supreme Court in upholding the disincorporation of the Church, permitting its property to be legally disposed of. It stated, "The Church having become by law dissolved, did not exist at its dissolution, and do[es] not now exist." The reason for such an absurd statement was that if the Church no longer existed, then the government was justified in legally disposing of its property. It therefore instructed the Supreme Court of Utah to set up machinery for the disposing of both the real and personal property of the Church.

The Non-Existent Children (1891)

Over the years, there has been controversy over the ownership of the temple lot in Independence, Missouri. In 1891 a suit was started to recover the lot for the LDS Church, but some strange information arose during the trial. A deed showed up that alleged that in 1838, following his excommunication, Oliver Cowdery paid Bishop Edward Partridge $1,000 for the temple lot on behalf of his children, John, Jane, and Joseph Cowdery. Not only did Oliver have no such money or an interest in Jackson County, but the children listed never existed. The deed was an obvious forgery but the court held that the Reorganized Church was entitled to the property in that Marie, the only surviving real child of Oliver, had conveyed the property to the Reorganized Church in 1887.

Accepting Satan's Plan? (1891)

The Gentiles never really understood the extent to which the Saints were willing to go to achieve statehood for Utah. Even the knowledge that the People's Party was dissolved in 1891 in order to bring about a two-party system along national lines doesn't explain the extent of the compromise. Just as there is no such thing as a "two-party system" in the gospel, Church leaders had always believed that in the ideal government the Saints would meet and agree on a single nominee for each office. Brigham taught that the two-party system was inaugurated in the preexistence when Lucifer came out in opposition to God and Christ, which meant that to become a state also meant adopting Satan's plan. This the leaders felt compelled to do in 1891.

Redeeming Qualities (1891)

When Return Jackson Redden died in 1891, he was a long-standing faithful Church member. Few Saints were aware of his early background that put him in the same group with such notorious characters as Bill Hickman, Judson Stoddard, Caleb Ellsworth, and Tom Brown. With desperado reputations as horse thieves or worse, Brigham Young welcomed their memberships in the Church and used them as bodyguards, defending them against such advisors as Orson Hyde, who once complained about the need to do something with such men. He was merely told by Brigham to calm down. Actually, Tom Brown was a fugitive wanted by authorities in Iowa for murder, but the Mormon leader saw redeeming qualities in such men and a use for them. In most cases, his expectations were realized.

"Wheat!" (1891)

Since he died in 1891, few Latter-day Saints are better known within or outside the Church than Orrin Porter Rockwell, bodyguard to both Joseph Smith and Brigham Young and feared "gun-slinging Danite." It's hard to explain the subconscious pleasure Mormons seem to feel about the notorious and largely false stories told about Rockwell. The anti-Rockwell ballad titled "Wheat" is such an example, referring to Porter as "a devil in human shape" who causes women to shrink in terror when they hear him wail "through the night his dread war cry, 'Wheat!'" The only accurate part of the ballad refers to the word he was so fond of using—"wheat"—which was reported to mean the wheat would be saved but the tares would be taken.

"Admit the Bearer" (1891)

A number of things about the early Mormons cause amazement, not the least of which was their attitude about imprisonment for "illegal cohabitation." Abraham Cannon, in his journal on May 1, 1891, noted a classic example. An elderly Saint named John Murdock was sentenced to thirty days in prison. The judge gave the commitment papers to Murdock along with a note to admit "the bearer" when he appeared at the penitentiary. The warden, because he had not been informed, refused admittance, whereupon Murdock went to town for the night. The next day he tried again and was admitted, indicating, according to Cannon, "integrity never found in real criminals."

With Compound Interest! (1891)

He was ordained an elder in the Church in 1891 at the age of forty-six. This was not unusual for converts, but Jesse Knight was no convert. He was the son of one of the earliest and most faithful members of the restored Church—Newel Knight. Unfortunately, he became disaffected after arriving in Utah in 1850 and experiencing the loss of his father in the crossing of the Plains. He recovered his testimony only after the loss of a teenage daughter, which he felt was his fault for not keeping a promise with the Lord for preserving that same daughter's life as a young child. He not only became a faithful member after his ordination but, now wealthy, he was able to become a major benefactor to the impoverished Church. He proceeded to pay all his back tithing with compound interest bringing his lifetime tithing up to $680,000—comparable to several million in today's dollar value.

Darkites and Whistlers (1892)

Forty years after being driven from the first foreign language mission, French Polynesia, as a result of government and Catholic harassment, Mormon missionaries returned in 1892. Their forty-year absence had taken its toll on the hundreds of native Latter-day Saints who, with no direct contact with the Church, had allowed dissensions on doctrine and procedure to break the Church into a number of factions, few of them recognizable to today's Saints as splinter groups. Although there were a few loyal Mormons, there were groups who called themselves Israelites, the Sheep, Abraham's Church, Darkites, and the Whistlers. In 1867 the French government extended religious toleration throughout the protectorate, but it was another 25 years before the Church sent missionaries back, by which time even the Reorganized Church had established a foothold.

Church Buys Historic Press (1892)

$250: It sounds like a real bargain today, but that was the price the Church paid in 1892 for the original press upon which the first edition of the Book of Mormon was printed in Palmyra. A deal was struck by President Joseph F. Smith with Col. Fred W. Clemens of Newark, New Jersey, who furnished an affidavit sworn to by John Gilbert, one of the original type-setters of the Book of Mormon. Gilbert, ninety years of age at the time, signed the affidavit after examining the press and identifying it by plate marks and repairs. Now owned by the Church, it is displayed at times in the Museum of Church History and Art.

No More Gold (1892)

The first temple to be crowned by a statue of the Angel Moroni was in Nauvoo, but unlike those today, it was more a weathervane and showed an angel in a horizontal position. It was destroyed with the burning of the abandoned temple in 1848. The best-known statue is the 12-foot hammered copper statue overlaid with gold leaf that was placed on the Salt Lake Temple on the day the capstone was laid—April 6, 1892. That statue weighs three tons and has a heavy weight suspended from the feet, enclosed in the spire, to allow its slight movement in heavy winds. It was sculpted by a non-Mormon, Cyrus E. Dallin, and represents a mature man. The statues for the new temples (over 90 temples have such statues) have a new design, sculpted by LaVar Wallgren, and depict the ancient prophet in his youth. They are now fiberglass with most standing six-feet tall and are white rather than gold leaf.

Loving a Rival (1892)

George Albert Smith seemed to be no rival for the hand of Lucy Woodruff, the daughter of Wilford Woodruff, Jr. He had a rival who, to Lucy, had everything George didn't have—looks, charm, money, and romantic courting techniques. In spite of having known Lucy for years with an apparent understanding of their future marriage, George seemed on the point of losing his intended bride. Although she felt it was the wrong decision, she finally married George in 1892. Years later, as Lucy recognized the wisdom of her final decision, George discovered his one-time rival, a ne'er-do-well with his own family, was about to lose his home. George co-signed notes and later paid the amount due on the mortgage. Lucy was heard to say again and again to kin, "I nearly made a terrible mistake."

"Most Fished Stream" (1892)

Wilford Woodruff was noted for his hunting and fishing prowess, but it still comes as a surprise to read a letter he sent to *Forest and Stream* magazine in 1892. In it he described one of his fishing experiences: "Some years ago, one warm day in June, I helped to make a haul at the mouth of Provo River, the trout having gathered about the river mouth for cooled water, the fishermen had made several hauls during the day, out in the lake, and took some 500 pounds of fish and when the net was drawn, the draft was judged to be about 4,000 pounds. A great number of the trout weighed 40 pounds each, on the scales." Another magazine, *Field and Stream*, called the Provo River the "most fished stream, per mile, in the world."

Temple Myths (1893)

This author heard such stories when he joined the Church in 1964 and they are still around today. They concern the vertical shafts constructed in the Salt Lake Temple without the builders knowing their purpose. Later these shafts turned out to be just the right size for elevators. There are similar tales about cutting channels in the granite walls of the temple that were later ideal for electrical wiring. Such stories imply that the architects were inspired to prepare for future innovations. Actually, Truman O. Angell, Sr., went on a fact-finding mission to England and France in 1856 to study significant buildings and their innovations. Louis XV of France installed an elevator at the Palace of Versailles in 1743 and electric arc lamp streetlights were installed in Lyons, France, in 1857.

"To Be Found Dead in Utah" (1915)

The early twentieth century in the U. S. was noted for labor unrest and resulting violence by organizations such as the radical Industrial Workers of the World (IWW). Utah, with Church influence, was not especially sympathetic to such radicalism. Therefore, the IWW was never the influence in Utah that it was nationwide, especially after the arrest for murder and the trial and execution of Joe Hill, a famous Wobbly songwriter and poet in 1915. His major defender, to the embarrassment of the Church, was an instructor at the University of Utah—Virginia Snow Stephen, who was also the daughter of former Church Prophet Lorenzo Snow. She was dismissed from her job and left Utah for California, convinced, like other Wobblies, that Mormon Utah was a lost cause. Hill's last words had been: "I don't want to be found dead in Utah," a favorite Wobbly phrase thereafter.

Music Yes, Tolerance No (1893)

The Church met a mixed reception at the Chicago World's Fair in 1893. The Mormons were denied the opportunity to address the Parliament of Religions at the Exposition, a courtesy extended to any other faith, Christian or not. The Latter-day Saints, however, were thought to be a disturbing element. At the same time the Tabernacle Choir, consisting of 250 members, was permitted to enter, without opposition, a musical contest of choirs and even took second place, receiving a prize of $1,000. Following the contest they were invited to give a concert in the Music Hall in Chicago. To top the compliment they were invited by a noted promoter to give concerts in Carnegie Hall in New York, as well as in Boston and Philadelphia. Time constraints prevented accepting the flattering invitations.

A "Dumping-Ground" for Colorado (1894)

In September 1894 about 900 Ute Indians and 200 Navajos, pressured by Colorado land sharks and a collaborating Federal Indian agent, began moving from Colorado into southeastern Utah. As part of the scheme to open up Indian lands in Colorado to white settlement, they had been told that in the San Juan area of Utah, land was abundant and the hunting better. Much of that land belonged to Mormon ranchers, and the hunting was Mormon cattle. Still without power of statehood, the Saints and their Territorial governor vigorously protested, saying that Utah was "adverse and to being treated as a mere dumping-ground for Colorado's surplus." Reluctant federal authorities started removing the "surplus" back to Colorado shortly thereafter.

Opposition to Women Suffrage (1895)

Having granted women the right to vote in 1870, only to have the Federal Government disenfranchise them by the Edmunds-Tucker Act in 1887, it would seem that few Saints would oppose women's right to vote by 1895, but B. H. Roberts did. Utah was close to statehood and Roberts believed such a right would delay that possibility. However, Utah achieved statehood the following year anyway, and even elected the first woman state senator in the country— Martha Hughes Cannon. Martha was not one to hold a grudge, however, and neither was Roberts. In fact, when Martha died in 1932, the main funeral speaker was the very same man who had predicted awesome consequences if women received the vote.

Normally Not Mentioned (1896)

The first woman elected to a state upper house in the United States was Dr. Martha Cannon, elected to the first state senate after Utah became a state. Obviously she was the object of numerous interviews as a result of her election. One such interviewer was from the *San Francisco Examiner* who expected an exposé on plural marriage from the well-known Mormon feminist. He was undoubtedly disappointed to discover that she was not only a defender of women's rights but of her Church's doctrine of plural marriage. She did, however, present an argument not usually mentioned in mixed groups at the time and especially not to the media. Her defense was to the point: "If a husband has four wives, she has three weeks of freedom every single month."

A Mormon Keeps His Word (1896)

Although he was baptized like most Mormons at the accountable age of eight, Robert LeRoy Parker was certainly not very accountable to Church standards as he grew up. In fact, he even changed his name to protect his good family from the disgrace of his outlaw activities. One principle that stayed with him, however, was the importance of keeping one's word. Thus, when Wyoming Governor W. A. Richards pardoned the incarcerated "Butch Cassidy" in 1896, on the promise that he would stop robbing Wyoming banks and rustling Wyoming cattle, Butch agreed. True at least to that part of his moralistic LDS training as a youth, he kept his word. Instead he turned to robbing Wyoming trains and non-Wyoming banks.

They Prayed All Night (1896)

When Utah entered the Union, Church leaders realized the potential problem of Church leaders becoming involved in political office, detracting from their Church callings. When they asked Church authorities to sign a Political Manifesto, requiring that they receive permission from their Church superiors for approval before running for a political office that would interfere with Church duties, all except Moses Thatcher and B. H. Roberts did so. Roberts, who was a president of the Seventies, was given a deadline of March 25, 1896, to accept. When he met with the Presidency on that deadline day, he admitted he had walked the streets all night, praying, but he knew it was right. Joseph F. Smith, with bloodshot eyes, smiled. "Yes, Brother Roberts, we have not slept either. We have stayed in this room all night praying that you would reach this decision."

An Interesting Exception (1896)

When Utah became a state in 1896, Article 15 of the Enabling Act provided for the organization of a National Guard. A later legislative report detailed those subject to military duty, being "every able-bodied male inhabitant of this state, except Mongolians and Indians, between the ages of eighteen and forty-five years." The legal and cultural status of Indians easily explains the exception for Indians but the other exception is more interesting. "Mongolians" at that time was a term referring to the ethnic Chinese who were in Utah in fairly large numbers as a result of their former employment on the transcontinental railroad. Apparently, Utah did not escape the "yellow-peril" phobia.

A Strange Election (1897)

One of the strangest elections involving a Latter-day Saint was held in 1897 at a time when state legislatures still elected members of the U.S. Senate. One of the two front-running candidates for the U.S. Senate from Utah was Joseph Rawlings, a former delegate to Congress from the Territory who had done much good for Utah, but he was a non-Mormon. The other front-runner was Moses Thatcher, a Latter-day Saint who had a falling out with the Twelve and had been dropped from that Quorum in 1896. The strong Democratic majority (also LDS) in the legislature spent two thirds of their entire session in the balloting before finally selecting Rawlings as the Senator on the 53rd ballot. The irony in the entire process was that the Church and the LDS majority in the legislature supported and elected a non-Mormon, whereas the Gentiles in the legislature and in the population were equally determined to elect a Mormon.

Without Purse or Scrip (1897)

In reading stories of the early missionaries, we hear the term "without purse or scrip" so often that we assume it was a requirement. Speaking in the Tabernacle in April 1897, Joseph F. Smith said, "I have always advocated the principle of preaching the gospel 'without purse or scrip.' I recollect making some remarks on this subject several years ago in this house, when . . . they did not meet with favor." Note that he said "advocated." Without purse or scrip was never a requirement, but being found in the New Testament, it was considered so and missionaries took pride in being able to do so. Joseph Fielding Smith wrote, "At no time were the missionaries compelled to travel without purse and scrip, and at no time have they been compelled to travel with funds in their pockets."

The Prophet and the Actress (1897)

A favorite dramatic actress/lecturer of the Latter-day Saints at the turn of the twentieth century was a native of Jerusalem. As a Christian, Madam Lydia Mamreoff Von Finkelstein Mountford appeared before world audiences over 5,000 times in twenty-five years, speaking on Biblical and Palestinian topics. A statuesque six-foot blonde of middle age, we have record of her speaking a number of times in the Salt Lake Tabernacle from 1897 to 1906. Her most dramatic appearance was at President Woodruff's birthday celebration in February 1897 when she referred to the Prophet as "our honorable President." Not only is she reported to have joined the Church, but there is also compelling circumstantial evidence that she became a plural wife of President Woodruff.

First Sister Missionaries (1898)

Many sister Saints served as unofficial missionaries with their husbands prior to 1898, but no single sister proselyting missionaries had been "called" before that date. The first two single sisters to be officially called were Inez Knight and Lucy Jane Brimhall, called in April 1898 and who labored principally in Ashford, Kent, and London until June 1900. Inez would later serve as Dean of Women at the Brigham Young Academy in Provo from 1900 to 1902. As missionaries they did the same kind of work the men did, distributing tracts from house to house, holding street and indoor meetings, visiting the people and explaining the gospel to them. Lucy Jane Brimhall ended up marrying her companion's brother Jessee William Knight.

Nearer Conversion (1898)

The fiery Mormon missionary, Ben E. Rich, became president of the Southern States Mission at a time when anti-Mormonism was a nationwide phenomenon but was especially so in the South. It so happened that Teddy Roosevelt had met and become a good friend of Rich and respected Mormonism as a result. During a parade in a southern capitol, Teddy had stopped the entire parade to talk with President Rich as a demonstration that the Mormons had powerful friends, a fact he would personally prove in subsequent years. Later, Heber J. Grant wrote to Reed Smoot, "I believe that Roosevelt felt that we were right. I think he was nearer converted to the truth than any man who ever occupied the presidential chair."

The Sixth Sense (1898)

Non-believers often find it impossible to comprehend the testimonies of true believers of the Restored Gospel. This spiritual understanding, often referred to by Saints as the "sixth sense," is perhaps most dramatically understood by the words of Rev. Dr. Prentis, a noted physiognomist who met the Mormon Prophet in 1898: "When I was introduced to President Lorenzo Snow, for a second I was startled to see the holiest face but one I had ever been privileged to look upon. His face was a power of peace, his presence a benediction of peace. The tranquil depths of his eyes were not only the 'home of silent prayer,' but the abode of spiritual strength . . . If the Mormon Church can produce such witnesses, it will need but little the pen of the ready writer or the eloquence of the great preacher."

The Integrity of Susan B. Anthony (1898)

Polygamist B. H. Roberts was elected to the House of Representatives from Utah in 1898 but refused a seat because of intense opposition from around the nation, even though the Church had disavowed further plural marriages in 1890. Roberts was therefore especially gratified at the support of the famous woman suffragette, Susan B. Anthony, since she had written a letter the year previously, published by the *Salt Lake Tribune*, urging the women of Utah not to vote for Roberts. After his election however, when a suffragette petition was presented against Roberts, Anthony objected, saying, "I should hate to see this federation going on record as asking Congress to do something unconstitutional. . . . the Constitution does not give Congress the power to throw him out." She then wrote a personal letter of support to Roberts and arranged to have it published in the national press.

Famous Friends of B.H. Roberts (1899)

There are few today who question the unfairness of the Congressional hearings resulting in denying B.H. Roberts his rightfully elected seat in the House of Representatives. Ironically, however, his brilliant but futile defense won many friends for both Roberts and the Mormon Church. One of these was H.G. Wells who viewed some of the hearings while in Washington and later described Roberts as an inspiration to him: "Mr. Roberts stood like a giant and defended himself and his Church. I never heard a more eloquent speaker in all my travels." The famous defense attorney Clarence Darrow was so impressed with Roberts that he offered him a full partnership in his Chicago firm. After refusing the generous offer, Roberts sighed, "I would have earned more in a month than I have ever earned in a year."

Not Necessarily Nepotism (1899)

During the nineteenth century three-fourths of all General Authorities were closely related. Such figures have often been used by critics to demonstrate uninspired favoritism in selecting candidates for high positions in the Church. Actually, there were factors that were far more important. First of all, the limited numbers in the nine-teenth-century church and the amount of intermarriage in their isolated situation (including plural marriage) resulted in numerous, overlapping family relationships. Second, it was discovered very early that such kinships resulted in greater continuity within the presiding quorums. Finally, the survival of the Church under the intense persecutions of the nineteenth century depended on the type of unity most often within family relationships.

More Valued Senator than Saint (1900)

Reed Smoot was called to the Quorum of the Twelve in 1900, but was far more interested in politics than his apostleship. Elected to the U. S. Senate three years later, it took over thirty months of hearings before the Senate seated him. He served his political office faithfully for thirty years, being referred to by President Taft as "the most valuable man in the U. S. Senate." Such was not the case in his Church, where he seemed embarrassed by plural marriage and temple endowments. Even as a member of the Twelve, he remained only semi-active until his political defeat in 1932. Whether because of an expanding testimony or a decreasing work schedule, he thereafter devoted all of his energy to his apostleship.

What Ever Happened to Jerry? (1900)

Early in the twentieth century, Jerry wandered away from Grantsville, Utah and was never seen again. He had frightened horses but was a favorite of Mormon children, even participating in Pioneer Day parades. Jerry was the last pack camel surviving from the camel importation experiment that began with Secretary of War Jefferson Davis's plan before the Civil War to import camels for army use against the Apaches—believing these strange beasts would frighten the natives into surrendering. The army experiment failed but after the war various individuals imported camels for use as pack animals in the mining camps of Nevada and Utah. When legislation was passed prohibiting their use on roads because they frightened horses, mules, and oxen, they were released in the wild— Jerry being the sole survivor.

Releasing a Bishop (1900)

When a bishop is called today, most members understand his calling is for only a period of time (usually five years in 2004). Such was not always the case. On April 19, 1900, the *Journal History* defines the Church policy for the release of a bishop. There were basically only five reasons: moving out of the ward, death, old age, lack of harmony in the ward, or disobedience. Members normally interpreted a release for any other reason as some kind of failure on the part of the bishop. Even more demanding was the office of stake president, which up to this time was more or less considered a lifetime calling.

The Riches of an Author (1900)

It is difficult to praise too highly the contributions of Brigham H. Roberts in Church history. Born in England in 1857 and emigrating to Utah as a youth, he spent his adult life as a missionary, orator, theologian, teacher, soldier-chaplain, husband, father, and General Authority but is remembered today primarily as the author of thirty major books and over a thousand pamphlets. By 1900, finding himself in financial straits, he mortgaged his home, sold part of his land, and sold the copyrights of his books published to that date to Cannon and Sons Company for $5,000. These included such popular books as a biography of John Taylor, a history of the Missouri persecutions, and the history of Nauvoo. He wrote others later, but records indicate the $5,000 was his entire profit for his books to that date.

Burial Day (1900)

May 5, 1900, was known as "Burial Day" throughout Utah for the funerals of 204 miners killed four days earlier at Winter Quarters, near Scofield, Utah. The disaster was caused by an explosion in mine No. 4 of the Pleasant Valley Coal Company. On the fifth of May, two funeral trains carried the victims, including many members of the Church, from Scofield to various parts of the State, where the killed miners had resided. The extent of the horror can be imagined when we consider the lives touched so tragically—105 widows and 207 orphans. Today the town, once populated by 1,800 people, is abandoned, inhabited some say only by the ghosts of the dead miners and the sounds at night of women crying and moaning.

A Boring Life? (1901)

In truth, very little was going on in Watertown, New York, where the daughter of a farmer was born in 1821, which may explain her thoughts as a young girl: "I used to muse . . . why I could not have been born in a day when something was going on in the nations of the earth." One hundred miles away in Palmyra, the Church of Jesus Christ was being restored to the earth after 1800 years by a young future prophet whom that young girl would later be sealed to for eternity. After the Prophet Joseph was killed, that same young woman, Zina Diantha Huntington, then living as a convert in Nauvoo, would be married to another prophet of the Lord, Brigham Young, becoming one of the most influential women of the restored Church by the time of her death in 1901. Hardly an uneventful life!

President Brigham Young, Jr.? (1901)

It is fairly common knowledge among Church members that Joseph F. Smith became President of the Church in 1901. A lesser known fact is how close another member of the Quorum came to being chosen—and would have been if seniority in the Twelve had not been changed the year previously to reflect date of entry into the Quorum rather than ordination as an Apostle. In 1864, Brigham Young Jr. had been ordained an Apostle by his father but not called to the Quorum until 1868. By 1900 he was considered the senior member of the Quorum of the Twelve since Joseph F., although called to the Quorum in 1867, had not been made an Apostle until two years after Joseph F. Smith. If President Snow had not lived until 1901, Brigham Young, Jr. would have been president of the Church.

LeRoi Snow and the Hack Driver (1901)

Standing near the Eagle Gate one day in 1901, LeRoi Snow, son of President Snow, overheard one of the gentile hack drivers relate some typical anti-Mormon spiel to his load of tourists: "This is the Bee Hive House, where Lorenzo Snow, the president of the Church lives. . . . No one is ever permitted to go in there. We do not know what goes on there." LeRoi thereupon introduced himself to the tourists and to the chagrin of the driver, invited them into the Bee Hive House to meet his father. He later related to the Board of the Y.M.M.I.A. this incident, which became the catalyst for the establishment of the Bureau of Information on Temple Square the following year, severely limiting the negative influence of the hack drivers.

A Losing Cause (1901)

Apostle Heber J. Grant was seventeen years away from his Presidency when he spoke in favor of the maintenance of the Church academies, regardless of the cost. These were privately supported community schools, numbering over thirty, scattered throughout the Mormon West, most of them established by 1890 to teach LDS principles as well as secular subjects. He was fighting a losing cause. By the time he became President in 1918, public schools were enrolling more than the Church academies, and before he died in 1945, all those located in the Mountain West had closed two decades earlier, except those that had expanded to include college work. Grant's predecessor, Joseph F. Smith, had also favored the church-oriented academies, but the "free" public schools were too inviting to members.

Was This a Clarification? (1902)

Probably no Church doctrine is more debated than the Word of Wisdom. Is it really a commandment? What does it include? And every so often a General Authority will issue a statement attempting to clarify the doctrine. This happened in 1902 when Joseph F. Smith made the attempt in the *Improvement Era*. The Word of Wisdom "as understood by the authorities of the Church," President Joseph F. Smith said, "is that food and drink are not to be partaken of for 24 hours, 'from even to even,' and that the saints are to refrain from all bodily gratification and indulgences." The last four words, not familiar to most Saints, certainly do little to clarify the law.

Joseph Smith's History (1902)

In 1902 the Church began publication in book form the *History of the Church of Jesus Christ of Latter-day Saints* by Joseph Smith (edited By B. H. Roberts). Since then thousands of readers have received the delightful impression that it was written by the Prophet himself. Actually, he wrote practically none of it, but he was vitally concerned that there be such a history. He received a revelation that "such a record be kept" in 1830, on the day the Church was organized. Various records were kept, but he didn't begin having it compiled in its present form until he began dictating the History to his clerk, James Mulholland, on June 11, 1839. From that point until 1846, either Joseph or Brigham utilized, at one time or another, the services of no fewer than thirty such clerks.

Smoot's Secret Code (1903)

Although a monogamist, when Apostle Reed Smoot was elected to the U. S. Senate in 1903, opposition to the seating of a Mormon was so intense it took thirty months of hearings. He was eventually seated, but during the hearings and even after, as Senator, he found it necessary to use a secret code in his telegraphic messages to and from Salt Lake City. An example of one such telegraphic message sent in 1903 to Smoot from James Clove read, "Senator Reed Smoot, Catena actual trice chariots judicial tangalize polygraph grand justicifiable solicited. Clove." The codebooks are in the Smoot collection at BYU. Smoot once wrote to Joseph F. Smith that "if I did not send my telegrams in the code, that every newspaper in America would have it the next morning.

The Only Father and Son (1903)

George Albert Smith was called to the Quorum of Twelve in 1903 at the age of thirty-three. Although very young compared to the normal age of those in such a calling today, this was not a record. His grandfather, George A. Smith, after whom he was named, had been called to that same Quorum at the age of twenty-one. What was unprecedented about George Albert Smith's calling was that this was the only time a father and a son had served simultaneously in the Council of the Twelve. His father was John Henry Smith, who was an Apostle from 1880 to 1911.

The Fake Manifesto (1903)

Apostle Reed Smoot, who was fighting to be seated to a legitimately elected Senate seat in 1903, faced a great deal of opposition because of his membership in the Church. Much of this opposition came from Utah's other Senator, a non-Mormon by the name of Thomas Kearns. Because of his concern over the possible seating of Smoot, he "invented" a story that he had received a letter from President Teddy Roosevelt "advising against the election of any apostle to the United States Senatorship." Newspapers around the country picked up this prestigious "opposition," and it was eight years after the "message" had been "received" by Kearns that Roosevelt recorded the facts. His advice had always been that if Smoot were an upright and honorable man, "it would be an outrage to turn him out because of his religious belief."

What Is Binding? (1903)

It is not too unusual to hear the question asked in Church meetings, "What is scripture?" And the answer that is invariably given is: "In addition to the standard works, anything said in General Conference or printed in Church publications." This was pretty much the same question put to James Talmage before a Senate Investigating Committee in 1903 considering the seating of Elder Smoot. One of the Committee, Mr. Worthington, asked, "Has anybody in your church the power to put in the *Deseret News* anything which is not in the standard works, that shall bind the people of your church, if it has not first been approved by the people?" Mr. Talmage: "No one, not even the president of the church. . . . No one could make anything binding by simply publishing it in the *Deseret News*, or any other medium, or any other form."

A Monument to Coyotes? (1904)

The seagull monument on Temple Square is a reminder of the "miracle of the seagulls," credited with saving the crops of the early pioneers from infestations of huge crickets (actually more closely related to grasshoppers). Less known are the outbreaks that occurred years later. In 1904 the *Improvement Era* reported such an occurrence when millions appeared in Rush Valley. The report stated, "The pests are headed towards Vernon. The Indians are gathering them to eat, preserving them for winter use, while the coyotes have stopped killing sheep and are feasting on crickets upon which, like the prairie chickens, they are growing sleek and fat."

Sister Lucy's Greatest Work (1905)

When Sister Lucy Bigelow Young died in 1905, she was remembered for not only being the wife of Brigham and the mother of Susa Young Gates, but primarily for her untiring work for the dead. Her crowning work in this category was probably done in the St. George Temple in August 1877, short-ly before her husband's death. Many Saints are familiar with the baptisms Wilford Woodruff did for the signers of the Declaration of Independence at that time, but few are familiar with Sister Young's work two days later on August 23. On that day Lucy "went forth into the font and was baptized for Martha Washington and her family and seventy of the emi-nent women of the world." Few people would recognize those names today—most of them being the maiden names of the wives of eminent men baptized in the temple at that time.

God Not Needed! (1905)

Congressional hearings over the seating of Senator Smoot were still being conducted in 1905 (he was eventually seated). The *Kansas City Times*, opposing the seating, edito-rialized one of the major reasons for such opposition—Smoot's belief in revelation: "This immediate contact with God through personal relations, should disqualify any per-son for the position of senatorship." The *Deseret News* was quick to pick up on this touch of irony in an editorial: "The country had long ago begun to suspect that most senators were exceedingly particular not to receive any revelations from heaven . . . and will exclude [any] member who is sus-pected of consulting the will of heaven." Many citizens today suspect the same principle applies.

The "Law" vs. the "Theory" (1905)

One of the clearest explanations of the Latter-day Saint stand on evolution was explained by Dr. John A. Widtsoe, director of the Department of Agriculture at BYU. In an article in the *Improvement Era* in 1905, Widtsoe wrote, "The law of evolution is the great cementing law of science. Even so, in the philosophy of Joseph Smith, the doctrine is taught that all things advance; that man shall continue to advance, in intelligence, and all pertaining to it, until he shall become as God is now. . . . Joseph Smith taught the law of evolution as an eternal truth, twenty or more years before Darwin published his views." Widtsoe further explained that Joseph taught, "Every class of creation is subject to eternal progression within the sphere [class] in which it has been placed." This, Widtsoe explained, is the difference between the "law of evolution" and the "theory of evolution."

Mormons in School Books (1905)

It is difficult to combat anti-Mormonism when it is being taught to children in schools. It could well be felt that such is still the case but it was even more obvious 100 years ago. Missionaries in South Carolina took note of the schoolbooks being used in that state in 1905. Lee's *New Primer History of the United States*, under the heading, "Trouble With the Mormons," stated, "The Mormons were the followers of the false prophet, Joseph Smith" and that he "taught that a man ought to marry a great number of wives and that an old maid has no soul. . . . When Utah became a territory, the Mormons refused to obey some of the laws of the United States, and President Buchanan had to send troops to compel them to submit."

Brigham the Actor (1905)

A year before his death, John S. Lindsay, the well-known pioneer actor of Utah, published a book on the Mormons and the theatre. Involved in the theatre in Utah his entire life, Lindsay was well qualified to make assessments of it, such as "Salt Lake spends more money per capita in the theatre than any city in our country." He credits the love affair Mormons had with the theatre to Brigham Young, who got the fever in Nauvoo when he played a Peruvian high priest in the play "Pizarro" in the Cultural Hall. The well-known traveling actor Tom Lyne had made the selection and jokingly told Lindsay later that he always regretted that decision. When asked why, he replied with a chuckle, "Why, don't you see John, he's been playing the character with great success ever since."

A King Investigates Mormons (1906)

Heber J. Grant was an Apostle in 1906 when he and a small party of Saints traveling in Sweden decided on the spur of the moment to ask for an audience with King Oscar. Finding the Saints were from Utah, the king granted their request. Grant later reported that the king made this remark: "Mr. Grant, I have sent my personal representatives, unknown to the people, to nearly every state in the Union of the United States, to find out how my former subjects are getting along. . . . In no other state in the Union are the former subjects of Sweden and Norway more contented, more prosperous and happier than in Utah; and, as long as I am king of Norway and Sweden, your people shall have religious liberty, notwith-standing all the priests and religious denominations are against you." Unfortunately, he would not always be king and problems did later arise in missionary proselyting permission.

No More Emigration (1907)

From its beginning in 1830, a major doctrine of Mormonism was that of "gathering." This began to change at the beginning of the twentieth century with statements by George Q. Cannon, a member of the First Presidency. Although he was counseling missionaries as early as 1890 to "dissuade" converts from emigrating, the policy was ambiguous throughout that decade. In 1907 such counsel had become a policy that members stay in their own countries to build up the church there. This meant, of course, a need to build mission headquarters and chapels in those countries as well as temples. In 1913 and 1915 sites were dedicated for temples in Canada and Hawaii, marking the beginning of the emphasis on Mormonism being a world church.

When Percentages Didn't Count (1908)

When we look at Church activity percentages at the beginning of the twentieth century, we are not very impressed. No more than 5% of the wards held priesthood meetings and five years later sacrament attendance averaged little more than 14%. Such statistics are very misleading because they tell you little about the lifestyle of Latter-day Saints. Their entire lives were wrapped up in the Church, so meetings were secondary. This is in contrast to the present, in which Latter-day Saints are more a part of the world so that attendance at Church meetings may be the primary indication of Church involvement, and thus the emphasis on attendance at meetings.

"Putting A Professional in Charge" (1908)

When the Saints had control of Utah's Territorial government, they severely limited such vices as gambling, saloons, prostitution, and so on, but as the federal government disenfranchised and hounded the Mormons in the late nineteenth century, the gentiles assumed more and more control and established such vices. By 1905 the anti-Mormons, uniting under the American Party, captured control of Salt Lake City's government and governed the City through 1911. To "clean up Salt Lake City," which some community groups were urging, they closed scattered houses of ill repute and constructed the "stockade," a closed community of prostitutes. In fact, to do it right they hired a "lady" from Ogden, Belle London, to take charge of the "stockade." With all the prostitutes in one location under Madame London, the rest of Salt Lake became respectable—only gambling houses, opium dens, saloons, and shooting galleries.

The Experts Should Know (1908)

The Mormon Tabernacle Choir finds it difficult to continually work to live up to its many compliments. Ignace Jan Paderewski, the world-renowned pianist, gave one of his concerts in the Tabernacle in February 1908. After hearing the Tabernacle Choir, he said, "The Mormon Tabernacle Choir is a magnificent and imposing chorus. Their singing is wonderful." On November 16 of the following year, John Phillip Sousa, the world's most famous bandmaster, arrived in Salt Lake City with his band and gave a concert that evening in the Tabernacle. He later said, "I have heard most of the choirs and large choruses of the country, and played with them. Certainly the Mormon Choir is the best trained of any in the United States."

Plural Marriage but Not Plural Marriage (1909)

After the Manifesto of 1890, Saints who were convinced of the need to obey the doctrine without violating the Manifesto tried various schemes. The most ingenious was suggested by George F. Richards, who had tried it himself in 1907 when he was sealed to May Gowans, deceased daughter of President E. G. Gowans, who had agreed to the sealing. In 1909 he urged Francis M. Lyman to present to the First

Presidency the suggestion that authorities who had only one wife could be sealed to some "good dead woman . . . to avoid the disappointments which must follow neglect of opportunity." To what extent this was done is not of record, but we know that some post-humus sealings to living authorities continued as late as 1925.

"A Beautiful Flight" (1910)

"Aviators Sail in Beautiful Flight" was the headline in the *Salt Lake Tribune* the day after the first airplane flight in Utah on January 30, 1910. The pilot was a French barnstormer who flew his biplane before an impressed fairground crowd of 10,000—but the pilot was disappointed. He could reach an altitude of no more than 300 feet, about 80 feet higher than the Salt Lake Temple, because of the rarified Utah atmosphere. Little noticed by aviation historians is that an automobile dealer in Salt Lake City that same year was marketing a personal biplane and predicted that within a year, individuals would be flying such planes "over and around the city."

The Church vs. I.N.S. (1910)

Many people believed the nineteenth-century stories of the Mormons luring young foreign girls to Utah to recruit them into plural marriage, but one would expect government agencies to be better informed or at least less prejudiced. In 1910, however, it was discovered that the Immigration and Naturalization Service in Portland, Maine, believing such stories, was detaining a number of LDS immigrants. The two Utah senators, Reed Smoot and George Sutherland, appealed to the commissioner of immigration and explained the Mormon policy of immigration and the rationale for gathering to Utah. Finally convinced of the errors of the stories they had heard, the commissioner promised that such detention incidents would not recur.

Why Not the Thistle? (1911)

Although Utah Saints had glorified the sego lily for a number of years, it was not until 1911 that the state legislature officially designated the sego as the state flower. Almost twice as many pioneer journal keepers mentioned the thistle as a source of food than they do the sego lily, however, perhaps because it had both edible roots and tops and was supposedly more tasty than the sego roots. Both plants have beautiful blossoms, so there was obviously a reason the sego won out in the legislature. Although the lily became a nuisance to ranchers, the Bible-savvy Saints were well aware of the part the thistle played in the curse that befell the earth in the story of Adam and Eve.

In the Footsteps of Judas (1911)

Most Saints familiar with their history are quick to recall the early days of the Church when even members of the Twelve were not immune to apostasy. Between 1839 and 1848 ten Apostles were either excommunicated or released from the Quorum. Since then, it becomes more difficult to name others who followed in the footsteps of Judas—unless we recall the year 1911 when John W. Taylor was excommunicated and Matthias Cowley was disfellowshipped. There have been others as well, including Amasa Lyman in 1870, Albert Carrington in 1885, Moses Thatcher in 1896, and Richard Lyman in 1943. Some of these sixteen Apostles were rebaptized and we can be consoled that there have been no such apostasies in the past sixty years.

"Stenographic Angels" (1911)

The end of the nineteenth century did not see the end of anti-Mormonism by any means. The Smoot hearings in Congress saw an avalanche of attacks by various popular periodicals. The epitome of ignorance of the Church was evident in a particularly negative series of articles appearing in *Cosmopolitan* during 1911. The first article in the series, entitled "The Viper on the Hearth," began with an illustration of a huge snake coiled around a defenseless family. The author, Alfred Lewis, although claiming to have spent time in Utah researching his article, asserted that Joseph Smith had devised his fraud with the help of two "stenographic angels, Thummim and Urim," who aided Smith in "convenient" trances to render "the [golden] plates into English."

A Temple Desecration (1911)

Even though many non-Mormons had seen the interior of the Salt Lake Temple during its open house several years previously, it was considered a desecration when Max Florence, a gentile Salt Lake City businessman, hired a disaffected member in 1911 to secretly photograph the interior. Florence then demanded the Church leadership buy the photos or he would sell them to the highest bidder. When the First Presidency refused to "deal with thieves or traffickers in stolen goods," Florence put them on the market. Although some were purchased and published, President Joseph F. Smith defused the embarrassing incident by commissioning James Talmage to write a book on the Temple, including pictures of the interior.

Predictions Fulfilled (1911)

The participation of the Tabernacle Choir at the Chicago World's Fair in 1893 was notable, but it was three years later that a tour made through twenty-five cities in the East fulfilled completely the predictions of Paderewski and John Phillip Sousa who had visited Salt Lake City shortly before and said the Mormon Church choir would be a sensation in the East. It was! During a ten-day stay at Madison Square Garden, they entertained nearly 250,000 guests. They received acclaim by sold-out crowds in Philadelphia, Topeka, St. Louis, and Detroit, and were praised by President Taft at a concert in the White House. The *New York Sun* reported that the crowd "nearly lifted the roof off the Hippodrome last night with a rebel yell for 'Dixie,'" the choir's own rendition of "Dixie" set in the Rocky Mountains.

The "Mormon Navy" (1911)

The Saints realized they had finally "arrived" in the eyes of the nation when they had a battleship named after the state of Utah. It happened on August 11, 1911, when the largest battleship afloat, launched two years previously, was commissioned the *Utah* in the Philadelphia Navy Yard. The Utah legislature had even appropriated a $10,000 silver service engraved with a picture of Brigham Young for use on the ship and the Tabernacle Choir was on hand at the launching to do the singing. Utah had reason to be especially proud of this honor, but there was to be a sad ending to the "Mormon Navy" thirty years later when the *Utah* was sunk by the Japanese at Pearl Harbor.

Knowing a Good Story (1912)

Latter-day Saints were not very familiar with Zane Grey before 1912, but when his book, *Riders of the Purple Sage*, appeared that year, they were convinced of his anti-Mormonism. Mormons appear as evil, detestable characters in many of his later western novels, but was he really anti-Mormon? His son, Romer, who traveled with his father throughout Utah and Arizona, denied that his father intended any ill will toward the Saints, saying only that Zane Grey "knew a good story when he saw it." As he traveled Utah in 1911 doing research for his seemingly most anti-Mormon novel, the author told his Mormon guide, "I see them as a wonderful people." Perhaps he did. He would later write an article for the *American Magazine* about one of his best friends, entitled "The Man Who Influenced Me Most." It was James Simpson Emmett, a Mormon cowboy.

More than Beautiful Scenery (1912)

It would be twenty-five years before Hollywood would make Kanab the movie town of Utah and teach the residents about the making of movies, but as early as 1912, the residents of Kanab could teach the world something about politics. In that year the small town became the first town in the country with an all-woman government. It started as a joke when the men challenged the women to do a better job in running the town than they had—and said they would support them. The sisters accepted the challenge and elected an all-woman town board with their own mayor, Mary Howard. In two years they cleaned up the town, literally, built bridges and a protective dam, prohibited gambling, restricted unlimited liquor sales, turned the Sabbath back into a day of quiet and rest, and so on. And then unlike male governmental bodies who do anything to be re-elected, they all refused to run again.

The Last Wife (1913)

When she died in Minersville, Utah, in 1913 at the age of ninety-five, Mary Rollins Lightner was the last of the Prophet Joseph's plural wives to pass on. Mary had garnered much attention in her long membership in the Church, beginning in 1833 when at the age of fifteen she and a friend saved a number of sheets of the Book of Commandments when the office of *The Evening and the Morning Star* was destroyed by a mob in Independence. She is also recognized with her husband Adam Lightner as being one of the two families offered to be spared by militia General Lucas before the anticipated attack and massacre of the Far West Mormons in 1838. Although not a member himself, Adam, along with his wife, refused the offer. It was because of Adam's non-membership that the Prophet Joseph was sealed to Mary in Nauvoo in 1842, an event Mary prized dearly the rest of her life.

Growing Fast! (1913)

When Maude Adams, the celebrated actress and "Audrey Hepburn" of her day, arrived in her native town of Salt Lake City to fill a theatrical engagement in April 1913, there were a number of Utahns who remembered her humorous stage beginning in their city. In 1873, according to Maude's mother, who was also an actress, they were performing a play called "The Lost Child," using a real baby. Maude herself, several months old at the time, had been brought to the theatre by the maid and was lying in a cradle. When the stage baby started crying so much that they could not continue, Maude's mother snatched Maude from the cradle and the manager was only too happy for the replacement. The much older child, now sitting up and cooing, vastly amused the audience.

Only a Sustaining Vote, Please! (1915)

When Angus M. Cannon died in 1915, he was remembered for not only his faithfulness in his callings but for his own confidence in his decisions. As President of the Salt Lake Stake, a position he held for twenty-eight years, he was once called on to release the bishop of the Herriman Ward. Upon doing this he presented the name of James S. Crane as the new bishop. Factions in the ward resulted in the majority voting against Brother Crane. President Cannon then disfellowshipped everyone who had so voted and set apart another man to act as presiding elder in placed of the rejected bishop until such time as the majority of the ward should repent. After three months the people repented and President Cannon returned. This time the ward sustained the new bishop. Years later ward members thought Bishop Crane was one of the best bishops who ever served in Herriman.

The "Temple Book" (1915)

On August 13, 1915, the First Presidency appeared to canonize a book other than the scriptures when they issued a statement urging all members to read *Jesus the Christ* by James Talmage. Because of continuing controversy over the LDS doctrine on the nature of Christ and the Godhead, the Presidency realized the need for an authoritative book on the subject and assigned Talmage the task. Because of the number of interruptions in his office and home he was directed to occupy a room in the temple where he would be free from such distraction. He later testified that completing the manuscript would not have been possible without the privilege of working in the temple where he also "felt the inspiration of the place."

A Cross for the Saints (1916)

It seems that most Latter-day Saints respond to charges of being un-Christian by trying to appear more traditionally "Christian." This seemed to be the case in May 1916 when the Presiding Bishop Charles W. Nibley petitioned the Salt Lake City commission to permit the placing of a huge concrete cross on Ensign Peak, large enough to be "seen from every part of the city." Immediately a tide of opposition arose from not only non-Christian groups but from those who sincerely opposed what they considered a violation of the First Amendment. The most influential opposition however, was from within the Church, whose members not only considered the cross a symbol of the death of Christ rather than His life but a traditional symbol of "Romanish superstition." Nibley and the Church quietly dropped the idea.

The Word of Wisdom's Influence (1916)

Prohibition was all the rage by 1916. Forty-three states had voted to go "dry"—but not Utah. Senator Smoot's Republican machine had been effective in blocking the necessary state legislation, but finally, noting the number of states that seemed to take a "word of wisdom" more seriously than the Saints in Utah, Smoot's machine decided to endorse it. Too late! Apparently, the embarrassed Saints didn't trust the machine and turned for the first time to a non-Mormon and a Democrat as their new governor. Simon Bamberger was a known "dry" and although it hurt many of the Saints to elect a gentile, he became the first non-Mormon governor since statehood.

Short-Lived Iosepa (1917)

The Church established the colony of Iosepa, made up primarily of Polynesian immigrants, in 1889 in Skull Valley, Tooele County. The colonists who consulted with the immigrants when it was apparent the immigrants did not fit easily into the Utah culture selected the 2000-acre tract. Contrary to the belief of many Saints, Iosepa was not named after Joseph the Prophet, but after Joseph Fielding Smith, who had served as a missionary in Hawaii. After the announcement of the building of a temple in Hawaii in 1915 and the change in the gathering policy of the Church, Iosepa's population started its decline. Although the colony reached its peak of 228 members in 1916, Joseph Fielding himself advised those reluctant to return to the Islands to do so since he would soon die and his successor might not care for them as he had. In 1917 Iosepa lay empty and the following year Joseph Fielding was dead.

Joseph's "Son" Becomes President (1918)

Latter-day Saints have lamented the fact that the Prophet Joseph's natural children did not remain in the Church or that his son Joseph III did not remain to become President of the Church of Jesus Christ of Latter-day Saints. However, in 1918, when Joseph F. Smith, a son of Hyrum, died, Joseph's "son" did become President. In Nauvoo Joseph had approached and been rebuffed by Rachel Ivins to be a plural wife, but later in Utah she had second thoughts and was sealed to the martyred prophet by proxy. She later married Jedediah Grant for this life only and thus when her son Heber J. Grant became President of the Church in 1918, under the celestial covenant, he was the "son" of Joseph Smith.

A More Rational Reason? (1918)

A common and comforting explanation for death is often given during Latter-day Saint funerals by saying the departed was needed for work on the other side. Several speakers at the funeral of Hyrum M. Smith, an Apostle, tried to comfort the family by offering that explanation. Charles W. Nibley offered a more rational reason, although it probably wasn't as comforting to the family. Nibley pointed out that Brother Smith would still have been alive if he had not refused medical attention. Hyrum's father, Joseph F. Smith, nodded agreement.

And No Funeral for the Prophet (1918)

The end of a successful war is normally a time to rejoice, but there was little rejoicing at the end of World War I. America and much of the world was in the midst of a great influenza epidemic in the fall of 1918—and it struck the Saints especially hard. Temples were closed, meetings were cancelled, the General Conference in the spring of 1919 had to be postponed, and when Joseph F. Smith died a week after the Armistice in November of 1918, there wasn't even a public funeral for him. Only a graveside service was held. More Americans died in the fall and winter of 1918 than American soldiers during the war. Over a thousand deaths occurred among the Latter-day Saints. If the same death ratio should occur among the Saints in an epidemic today, the Church would lose over 20,000 members.

Herbert Hoover's Gratitude (1918)

Beginning in the first years in the Salt Lake Valley, to meet recurring scarcity, President Young urged the Saints to adopt the policy of storing grain against a time of need. In 1880 the Relief Society assumed exclusive management of the project. Toward the end of World War I, when starvation was an imminent threat to millions in Europe, the Relief Society was in a position to offer over 12 million pounds of wheat to Herbert Hoover, administrator of the relief program. Although offered freely, the government insisted on paying, so the money received was invested as a trust fund en bloc, the interest being used for charitable purposes for other poor. On June 3, 1918, Mr. Hoover wrote a letter of gratitude to Utah's congressman, Milton Welling, who later read it to the applause of his colleagues.

Still the Question of Succession (1918)

When the sixth prophet of the Church, Joseph F. Smith, died in 1918, one would have thought the question of succession was settled—but it wasn't in the minds of some authorities. One of those authorities was the Presiding Patriarch of the Church, Hyrum G. Smith, who, like the Prophet Joseph's brother William, believed the office of Patriarch gave him the right to succeed the President. The Twelve disagreed, and to settle the question, they made public a letter President Woodruff had written in 1887 that ended up in Heber J. Grant's possession. It stated that until a revelation differed, he did not believe the day would come when the president of the Twelve would not become President of the Church.

Conscientious Objection (1919)

The question of conscientious objection and Mormonism did not become an issue until the beginning of World War I due to a misunderstanding as to where the Church stood on pacifism. There were a total of 3,700 conscientious objectors

(C.O.s) during that war, a number of them Latter-day Saints. Like others, the Saints were given an option of going to prison or performing "alternative service" such as firefighting or counseling mental patients in hospitals. The issue became predominant when Fort Douglas became a prison in 1919 for the C.O.s who refused the alternative service. The policy of the Church is still not totally understood in spite of its clarification that we believe in being subject to our secular governments but may choose C.O. status as a matter of personal belief.

Did Brother Young Ever Find Out? (1919)

When Heber J. Grant assumed the Presidency of the Church, it was his duty to present a name to fill a vacancy in the Quorum of the Twelve. After consulting with his counselors, he wrote the name Richard W. Young on a piece of paper and put it in his pocket. Brother Young had served as a general in the army, was a lawyer and a successful businessman, and had served as a stake president, but he was especially a close friend. When it was time to present Brother Young's name at the regular weekly meeting of the First Presidency and the Twelve in the temple, he pulled the slip of paper from his pocket. However, for a reason he was never able to explain outside of inspiration, he was not able to present Young's name. Instead, he presented the name of Melvin J. Ballard, president of the Northwestern States Mission, a man with whom he had had very little personal contact, and his friend Young never became a member of the Quorum.

Mormons and the League of Nations (1919)

As President Wilson worked desperately to encourage the United States to join the League of Nations in 1919, he found many Mormon Church leaders, including Utah Senator

Smoot, firmly opposed. The threat to American sovereignty was a general reason most opponents gave, but the LDS use of the Book of Mormon was a novel approach. As Smoot told a reporter in Washington, D.C., Mormon scripture shows that world peace is impossible, and this is evidence that the League of Nations will fail. Furthermore, he added, "I believe this land was held in reserve by God for ages, with a view of establishing upon it truth and liberty, and from this land truth and liberty would be carried to the farther ends of the world. . . . If this country enters the League of Nations, they will control and America will not be able to carry out its destiny."

Nothing New about Terrorism (1919)

After the Russian Revolution the Bolshevik threat became more pronounced in the United States and showed its strength primarily in labor organizations such as the Industrial Workers of the World (called Wobblies), who believed violence would have to overthrow capitalism to bring about a communistic paradise. On May Day 1919, thirty-six leading anti-labor leaders or prominent capitalists received mail bombs—three of them addressed to Utahns. One of these was an Apostle, Senator Reed Smoot, who was not known for anti-labor views. Other well-known recipients were John D. Rockefeller, J. P. Morgan, and Oliver Wendell Holmes, Jr. There were only two injuries, neither of them Smoot's, whose package bomb was returned to Gimbel's Store in New York from where it had been sent—for lack of postage. The terrorists were never found.

The "Manassa Mauler" (1919)

The 1920s were known as the "golden age of sports." Much of the reason professional sports became such a dominant theme in American culture was the beginning of commercial radio broadcasting in 1920. Equally important, however, was the triumph of the colorful heavyweight boxer, Jack Dempsey, nicknamed the "Manassa Mauler" after the small Mormon town in Colorado where the youthful Saint was born. His championship win over Jess Willard in 1919 captured the attention of a national audience, sickened by much of the corruption and greed in professional sports up to that time. His record-breaking fight with Gene Tunney before 120,000 people and a gate of nearly $2,000,000 brought the Church as much favorable publicity as the Tabernacle Choir.

No Encore! (1920)

When Joseph J. Daynes passed away in 1920, he had been the Tabernacle organist for over thirty years. He was chosen as organist when the famous organ was first installed, an organ that at first required four men to pump the bellows. When he announced he would play "Tannhauser" as an encore at one of his recitals, he found the organ without air. Going to the rear of the organ to discover the problem, he found the four pumpers sitting down, refusing to work the bellows until they received some of the credit that Daynes appeared to receive alone. Returning to the organ, Daynes had the four assistants named, one by one. The recital then continued.

Some Radical Legislation (1921)

Recent publicity and controversy surrounding smoking is certainly not new—at least not in Utah. An act of the 1921 Utah legislature dealt with that subject and was also controversial. It prohibited the advertising or sale of cigarettes to minors and smoking in enclosed public places. The *Salt Lake Tribune*, ever ready to denounce any legislation influenced by or favoring the Mormon Church, editorialized against the act, calling it a "monumental mistake" and saying it "marks the beginning of an anti-tobacco crusade in Utah." The *Tribune* seemed to be right—the nation made fun of such "radical legislation" and two years later the act was modified. Such laws don't seem quite as humorous today.

12
Acceptance at Last
(1922-1951)

The Sheik and the Mormon (1922)

He died prematurely from blood poisoning in 1926, but during his short movie screen life, Rudolph Valentino won the heart of thousands of women. One of those women was a Latter-day Saint, Winifred Shaughnessy, granddaughter of Heber C. Kimball, who had become stage-struck and taken the name Natacha Rambova. She became not only a member of the Imperial Russian Ballet but a writer, producer, costume designer, and director. Still she found time to be courted by Valentino with whom she eloped in 1922 and became his second wife. Most appropriately, as a Latter-day Saint, she was able to give the Utah Museum of Fine Arts several hundred Egyptian pre-dynastic artifacts and before her death in 1966, edited scholarly books on Egyptology.

Waiting for the Mike (1923)

Most Latter-day Saints associate broadcasts from the Tabernacle with the Tabernacle Choir that began in 1929. Actually, the first successful broadcast from that location occurred six years previously on the evening of June 26, 1923, when the President of the United States, Warren Harding, gave a live address from the Tabernacle over station KZN (later KSL). The primitive technology of the radio equipment of that time can be imagined when it is recorded that there was only one microphone and KZN had to go temporarily off the air while the mike was rushed from the station to the Tabernacle. The very first KZN broadcast was actually in May 1922, only eighteen months after the beginning of regular radio broadcasting in America by East Pittsburgh's Station DKDA with returns of the Harding-Cox election in November 1922.

Coca-Cola Complains (1924)

In October 1924 Coca-Cola representatives called on President Heber Grant to complain. They felt the state health director was using the Church, which was undoubtedly true, to discourage the drinking of Coke. Grant refused to interfere, saying that he himself had also discouraged the members, since Coke had four to five times as much caffeine as coffee. These figures came from the health director himself. The Coke representatives pointed out that the reverse was true, with coffee containing 1.7 grains of caffeine per cup as opposed to .43 grains for the same amount of Coke. After a second meeting Grant was apparently convinced and publicly stated that he no longer had "the slightest desire to recommend that the people leave Coca-Cola alone."

Still an Issue (1924)

By 1924, thirty-four years after the Manifesto of 1890, much of the anti-Mormonism as a result of polygamy was past—but not all of it. Reed Smoot, who had finally been seated in the Senate seventeen years earlier, sent a request to the State Department asking them to urge the proper authorities in several foreign countries to stop discriminating against the Saints by denying Mormon missionaries visas—specifically Denmark, Norway, Sweden, Switzerland, Holland, and South Africa: "There can be no possible reason for discriminating against this class of American citizens. . . . The recent and present policy has been very embarrassing and burdensome to the work of the church, and I ask you to endeavor to have it corrected."

"Do Not Violate History!" (1925)

In 1925 the Committee on Roads in the House of Representatives was holding hearings on naming the highway that followed the old Oregon Trail. E. O. Leatherwood, representative from Utah, testified and tried to correct an historical error by pointing out that the Oregon Trail followed the south side of the Platte whereas the road they were naming actually followed the north side of the river which was the location of the Mormon Trail: "If you want the name of the Oregon Trail where it belongs; if you want the name of the Mormon Trail where it belongs, and deem that you have power to name highways, do so, but do not violate history."

Temple Mercenaries (1926)

It was an innovation in April 1926 when the Church leadership announced that the names of faithful deceased members might be submitted to the temple in St. George where temple work could be done for them at the Church's expense if there were no relatives to do the work. It was the policy, unlike today, that temple work for the dead had to be done by family members although there were exceptions. Perhaps the most disturbing exception was the possibility of relatives hiring other temple recommend holders to do the work for them. It is a little more understandable when we discover that the length of the ceremony before its reduction in 1927 could be as long as six to nine hours.

By Word of Mouth (1927)

It had taken a few years but it was finally completed in 1927—a revision of the temple ceremonies and standardization of temple clothing. As late as 1923 parts of the ceremony had never been written down. When the St. George Temple opened in 1877, the ceremony was based on memory of the Nauvoo Temple ceremony over thirty years earlier. Since 1877 the ceremony was passed on by word of mouth and varied from temple to temple. In 1923 Stephen L. Richards received permission to write the ceremony down that a committee of the Twelve had been working on. Completed in 1927 the ordinances were adopted by the First Presidency and the entire Quorum. They were essentially as they are today and are consistent in all temples throughout the world.

The Jazz Singer in Utah (1927)

The first feature motion picture with synchronized speech, The Jazz Singer, appeared in 1927. It starred Al Jolson, the black-faced stage and screen star. It seems appropriate that as such actors moved from the stage to the screen, the glory days of the Salt Lake Theater would come to an end—which they did in 1928. Before the end, however, Al Jolson appeared on its stage. During his performance in a theater that many believed was haunted, a blood-curdling noise was heard off stage. Having heard of the many rappings and other noises associated with the spooks in the Old Playhouse, Jolson's stage companion looked at Al and asked in a terrified whisper, "What was that?" Just then the theater cat streaked across the stage. Grabbing his scared companion, Jolson said, "I dunno, ask that cat."

Out of Step? (1928)

Throughout the nineteenth century, anti-Mormons condemned not only the plural marriage doctrine of the Saints, but especially what they perceived as a monolithic organization with members in lock-step submission to church leaders. In 1928 this myth was shattered in an unusual way. Heber J. Grant announced the impending sale of the beloved Salt Lake Theater to a telephone company with plans for razing it. Widespread and popular opposition to this leadership decision reared its head. Such an act of "desecration" split the Mormon community. It was no longer Mormons versus anti-Mormons, but Mormons versus Mormons. And ever more telling, a number of faithful Saints questioned the decision of their revered "prophet, seer, and revelator." The first building placed on the site was a gas station built in the shape of a huge airplane.

But with Hats On (1928)

When the Salt Lake Theater closed in 1928, its sixty-six-year history had seen every notable visitor to Salt Lake pass through it doors during that time, and few were more impressed than the German travel writer who had attended a melodrama there only five years after its dedication. Theodor Kirchhoff, who was familiar with such theaters as the famous Berlin Opera House, wrote of his visit: "The actors, mostly Mormons, did credit to dramatic art. Some rose above the ordinary. . . . The sets were excellent; and costumes left nothing to be desired." He compared it favorably with the Metropolitan Theater in San Francisco and the Bowery in New York—but one thing shocked him. The orchestra members "kept their hats on when playing, a democratic custom I could not approve."

The Unknown Grave (1928)

The bodies of Joseph and Hyrum had originally been buried in unmarked graves to keep them safe from desecration by enemies, but as time went on their exact location was lost even to friends and family. They were aware that when James J. Strang established his apostate group on Beaver Island, he had offered William Smith the office of patriarch if he would join Strang and bring the bodies of his brothers to Michigan. He did not, but there were rumors the Utah Saints had exhumed and taken the bodies to Utah. Actually, the Saints in Utah enjoyed, as much as the Reorganized members, the song titled *The Unknown Grave*, written by Joseph's youngest son, David. Not until 1928, as the Mississippi waters rose as a result of the dam at Keokuk, did authorities make a serious search, discover the bodies, and move them to higher ground southwest of the homestead.

The Lost Gold Mine (1928)

A 1928 issue of the *Improvement Era* carried the story of a "lost" gold mine near Cedar City. A few years previously, a local sheep rancher had hired a young man to herd a flock of his sheep not far from Cedar City. When the young man showed up in the spring to collect his pay, he revealed he was going to look for work in Wyoming. Before leaving he gave his boss some interesting pieces of rock, saying only that he found them on one of the mountains during the winter. The sheep man forgot about them for several months and then one day looked more carefully at them, deciding to have them tested by an assayer. They proved to carry gold worth $65,000 per ton. Desperately, he tried to find the young man and the source of the rocks. He found neither.

Defeat Had Its Rewards (1930)

Certainly the "defeat" of the Saints in Ohio, Missouri, and Illinois had its rewards in establishing more firmly the Church in the sanctuary of the Rocky Mountains. But defeat also may work in the missionary program as it did in Germany at the end of World War I. The poverty-stricken condition of the Germans and a resulting humility seemed to make them more receptive to the gospel message. As missionaries streamed into Germany after the war, baptisms rose to uncharacteristic heights. Most Latter-day Saints are familiar with the success of the missionaries in the British Isles shortly after the Church was established, but in 1930, at the time of the centennial, there were over 11,000 Saints in Germany, more than in any other country outside the United States of America.

The Great Mexican Schism (1932)

The Mexican Revolution and the unsettling consequences that followed in the 1920s and 1930s resulted in the legal expulsion of all foreign clergy. The consequences of that action resulted in a growing feeling of independence among local LDS leaders. When their appeals to Salt Lake leaders for even more leadership were refused, they broke with the Church and became known as Conventionists because the dissatisfied leaders called their members together in a series of three Conventions. It was at the Third Convention in 1935, over which George Albert Smith was invited to preside, that the General Authorities made concessions (i.e., changing the excommunications of Convention leaders to disfellowships) and brought about a major reunification of approximately 1,200 Conventionists with the main LDS Church, the largest return ever of disaffected members.

Most American Thing in America (1932)

The "most American thing in America" died in 1932—or did it? The Chautauqua—this "thing"—reached its peak in 1924 when 30 million Americans attended these gatherings in tents across America to enjoy lectures, music, drama, and other cultural items designed to spread knowledge and entertainment. Such circuits had begun in Utah in 1915 but the last circuit ground to a halt in 1932, destroyed by the Model-A, radio, movies, and the Depression. But it didn't end among the Saints. Ten years earlier the first Leadership Week was held at BYU campus, modeled after the Chautauqua and this developed into the modern Education Week, held in a number of locations across the country. Thus, the Saints continue the "most American thing in America."

The Church and the Nazis (1933)

When the National Socialists, or Nazis, gained control of Germany in 1933, Church authorities were concerned over not just the future of missionary work in that country but possible persecution of native members. Although some small religious groups were banned, the Mormons were not. They were, however, persecuted. The Church was forced to drop the Scouting program because it conflicted with the Hitler Youth Movement. The book, *Articles of Faith*, was confiscated because of its references to Israel and Zion. In one place Church hymns that made references to these subjects were ripped from hymnbooks. Gestapo agents often observed meetings, and German police interrogated Church leaders about LDS doctrines and practices. And yet at the 1936 Berlin Olympics, Mormon missionaries were officially asked to referee basketball games.

A Little Bit of Irony! (1935)

In their desperation to make clear the disconnect between the Church of Jesus Christ of Latter-day Saints and the fundamentalists who continued to practice plural marriage, the predominantly Mormon legislature in 1935 passed an act "Making Unlawful Cohabitation a Felony, and Providing That All Persons Except the Defendant Must Testify in Proceedings Thereof." There was no way the Mormon members of that body didn't see the close resemblance between their act and the very same legislation they had denounced as unconstitutional when forced upon them by the U. S. Congress in the previous century—especially as it was later reported that the act was drafted by Hugh B. Brown, who would later become a member of the First Presidency.

Turning the Tide (1935)

Church leaders viewed with alarm the direction the New Deal seemed to be taking under FDR. A logical and simplistic approach that it took early in its Depression Era administration was the direct dole to the poor and unemployed, without a corresponding responsibility to work. Thus, in 1935 Harold B. Lee was called by the First Presidency to head up the Church's own welfare program, one that required work in return from those who were able. Although the economic welfare of its members was of prime importance, Elder Lee himself stated that one objective of the Church Welfare Program was to "turn the tide" against the dole. Shortly thereafter, Congress eliminated all direct relief in favor of work relief.

"A Bitter Tea to Swallow" (1936)

The Church Welfare Plan was not only successful in its application, but it generated badly needed favorable publicity, such as found in *The Catholic Worker* in 1936: "Mormons are personalities! Mormons have taken the lead from Catholics in caring for their needy. . . . [They] have set an example worthy of imitation by their fellow countrymen. . . . We suggest that our Catholic laymen cull a few pages from the record of the Church of Latter-day Saints. It is a bitter tea that we must swallow, and brewed by Mormon hands. It may be hard to take a lesson in Catholic charity and sociology from non-Catholics, but we trust that in the future we can afford to play 'hooky.'"

In Addition to Church Callings (1937)

One of the most dramatic features of the pageant, "America's Witness for Christ," which has been presented at Hill Cumorah in upstate New York nearly every summer since 1937, is the stereophonic sound system. This was one of the first applications of the invention by Harvey Fletcher, a graduate of BYU and Latter-day Saint director of the famous Bell Laboratories. But this was only one of the inventions he supervised. His research team also invented the transistor, the hearing aid, amplifiers, and loudspeakers. He also worked with Warner Brothers on the first sound film, The Jazz Singer, and made major improvements in the telephone to more accurately reproduce the human voice. All of this was in addition to a number of Church callings and the writing of Church lesson manuals.

The Bad Man of Brimstone (1937)

One of the most delightful small towns in Utah is Kanab, noted primarily for its connection to Hollywood. Numerous movies were filmed in that scenic red-rock country in extreme southwest Utah. The year was 1937 and a Hollywood motion picture company was making its first movie at Kanab, with such well-known film stars as Wallace Beery, Dennis O'Keefe, and Virginia Bruce. Beery was playing the title role in *The Bad Man of Brimstone*. This first Hollywood company brought over $50,000 into this Mormon community with a daily budget of $3,000 and remained for some three weeks. The beauty of the country and the hospitality of the Saints, however, brought a number of film companies after that and even today the town attracts tourists because of its Hollywood past.

Wearing the Union Jack (1938)

In April 1938, in the first international basketball match ever played in Great Britain, the British team beat Germany 40-35. Three weeks later the same team beat the French team 28-26 to win the International Basketball Tournament at Lille, France. This might not have been so unusual except the British team was made up of Mormon missionaries who had previously beaten the second-place British team to have the honor of wearing the Union Jack at the International Tournament. That second-place team was also made up of Mormon missionaries. Beating the Germans and the French was certainly satisfying to the British, but it is less likely that having Latter-day Saints represent them was comforting.

Men of Science (1938)

In a study done by Dr. E. L. Thorndike of Columbia University, he reported the number of scientists born in Utah per million population for the period 1890 to 1900, as listed in the 1938 edition of *American Men of Science*, represents a lead of 30% over the next highest state (Massachusetts) and was double the national average. Although some modern historians have dismissed the study because it failed to include women or races other than Caucasian, it is significant for a couple of reasons. First of all, since Utah had relatively few citizens who were not Caucasian, the study should compare comparable peoples— and it does. Second, the time period in which these men were born was an apex of persecution for Mormons (74% of Utahns).

"Best Book Not Written" (1938)

Bernard DeVoto, well-known Utah author of *Across the Wide Missouri* trilogy, whose mother was LDS, was a lifetime critic of Mormonism, although there were certain elements of Mormon history he came to admire. Like many literary people he was especially critical of the failure of Mormonism to make a name in the arts, but in this case he recognized his own failures. He began as a novelist, writing *The Life of Jonathan Dyer* and *Chariot of Fire*. As late as 1938, however, DeVoto predicted failure for anyone who tried "to compose fiction out of Joseph Smith and the Mormon people." He declared, "God, the best story-teller, has made a better story out of Joseph and the Mormon wandering than fiction will ever equal" and called his own Mormon novel "the best book I am never going to write."

It Took a Long Time (1939)

With the first foreign mission occurring in 1837, it is not surprising that the first translation of the entire Book of Mormon into a foreign language was made as early as 1851 when Peter O. Hansen translated it from English into Danish. What is surprising is that the Church did not employ a full-time translator for over 100 years. In 1939 Antoine R. Ivins wrote a letter to Brother Eduardo Balderas in El Paso, Texas, asking him to come to Salt Lake City to translate Church materials into Spanish. In addition to the numerous translations of Church magazines and manuals, the Book of Mormon is currently (2003) published in full in seventy-one languages and in selections in thirty-two languages.

A Turning Point in Hollywood (1940)

During Heber J. Grant's administration (1918-1945) no fewer than thirty anti-Mormon films were released to world audiences. Therefore, when Twentieth Century Fox contacted President Grant in 1938, requesting his cooperation in the making of another film on Mormon history, he was obviously skeptical. Nevertheless, the Prophet cooperated and the result was the 1940 film, *Brigham Young*, starring Dean Jagger, Linda Darnell, Vincent Price, and Tyrone Power. Although replete with historical inaccuracies, such as the burning of Nauvoo as the Saints left, it was nevertheless far more complimentary than previous Hollywood films and demonstrated the importance of religious toleration of a minority faith during a time of Jewish persecution in Europe. Hollywood had turned the corner.

Did Heber Agree? (1940)

The major criticism of Darryl Zanuck's film, *Brigham Young*, when it hit the theaters in 1940, was the portrayal of Brigham Young as a wavering, uncertain prophet of the Lord. When eighty-year-old George Pyper, Sunday School president and historical advisor on the set, objected to inaccuracies once too often, President Grant calmed movie executives saying, "Don't pay too much attention to that brother. We've got to have box office in this picture." Did this mean President Grant was willing to accept the film's inaccurate portrayal of Brigham? Heber accepted the inaccuracy because he wanted to insure the eventual success of *Brigham Young* in its positive portrayal of the Church. In achieving that it was a relieved Heber J. Grant who could state after the preview showing of *Brigham Young* in Salt Lake City, "This is one of the greatest days of my life."

Not the Results He Anticipated (1940)

Vardis Fisher, although raised as a Latter-day Saint, is remembered by most Latter-day Saints for not only his life-long rebellion against Mormonism but for authoring *Children of God*, for which he won the Harper prize in 1939. Although intended to be critical of the Church, it seemed to have the opposite effect. First of all, the 1940 film *Brigham Young*, which proved to be one of the first Hollywood films complimentary to the Saints, was based on it, and Fisher himself admitted he had received several letters from individuals who had read his critical book and converted. Reading the Reader's Digest condensation of part of the novel prompted a North Carolina woman's desire to learn more. The Latter-day Saint who responded to this desire happened to be Leonard Arrington, and their meeting eventually led to Grace Arrington's conversion and their marriage.

And Not By Plane (1941)

When Andrew Jenson died in 1941, he had set a record for Church service that would be matched by few non-Apostles. He traveled more than 300,000 miles in his lifetime—this by train, ship, wagon, and on foot. He circled the globe twice, crossed the Pacific Ocean four times, and the Atlantic Ocean thirteen times. He visited every Latter-day Saint mission except the one in South Africa, in addition to serving ten missions for the Church. Perhaps more importantly, at a time when Church history was not as much appreciated, he served forty-four years as assistant historian and compiled the immense chronological day-by-day account of the Church's history that became known as the *Journal History*.

"Even Hidden Treasures" (1942)

The 89th section of the Doctrine and Covenants promises that those who would keep this word of wisdom and walk in obedience to the commandments will receive "great treasures of knowledge, even hidden treasures." In the February, 1944 issue of *The Improvement Era* we find a graph showing the relative position of the states of the Union as to the number of scientists born in those states in proportion to population. The state of Massachusetts is next to the highest on the graph, but you have to go twenty percentage points higher up the graph to find Utah, the state that has produced more scientists born within its borders per capita than any other state in the nation. Latter-day Saints consider this a fulfillment of the promise of God as a result of observance of the Lord's commandments.

Illustrating the Dead (1942)

Most Relief Society sisters seldom give much thought to their monogrammed "RS," encircled by the quotation "Charity Never Faileth," the official seal that was designed for the 1942 centennial celebration. The winning design for the contest was submitted by Jack Sears, the well-known national illustrator, who started his career working for the *Deseret News*. One of his jobs for the newspaper was making chalk plate portraits of accident or foul-play victims in the city morgue when no photos were available. He accomplished this by having assistants prop up the corpse and hold the eyelids open while Jack chalked a life-like portrait.

Before the Blood Tribunal (1942)

Between 1933 and 1945 the Blood Tribunal in Nazi Germany (with judges dressed in blood-red robes) condemned 3,000 to be guillotined or hung for treason to Germany. The youngest was seventeen-year-old Helmut Huebner, an LDS deacon, who was beheaded in 1942 for distributing anti-Nazi propaganda. Two LDS friends who were tried and sentenced to prison were Rudi Wobbe and Karl-Heinz Schnibbe, who have since written books on this episode in Mormon history. This story is an excellent example of the moral conflict some Saints faced when required temporal loyalties conflict with religious doctrine. As an illustration, German Church officials quickly excommunicated Huebner, but the First Presidency reversed this excommunication in 1948.

Make Converts—Not War! (1944)

Perhaps during another time and place he would have been called a traitor. But in 1944, during the greatest war this nation has ever seen and after it had been attacked at Pearl Harbor, Brother Clark became a member of the board of directors of America's oldest pacifist organization and labored in it for the rest of his life. Throughout that war he encouraged young Latter-day Saints not to volunteer for the military but to go on missions instead. Such seemingly "anti-American" actions, if conducted by an ordinary member, would not have been that unique, but he was J. Reuben Clark, a counselor in the First Presidency who encouraged pacifism and aided conscientious objectors throughout his tenure.

No Conscientious Objection Here (1944)

Millions are familiar with the name Sullivan, the name of five brothers who died together on a ship in World War II. Few are familiar with the name Borgstrom, that of four Latter-day Saint brothers who died within months of each other in 1944. On June 26, 1948, the bodies of Clyde, LeRoy, Rolon, and Rulon (twins) were returned to their peaceful Bear River Valley in northern Utah, where a memorial service paid tribute to the four sons of Mr. and Mrs. Alben Borgstrom of Thatcher, Utah. Clyde fell with the Marines on Guadalcanal in 1944 and Elmer LeRoy was killed in Italy in June 1944. In August Rolon was killed on a bombing raid over Germany. Rulon, his twin, died of wounds seventeen days later in France. A fifth brother was released from service after his brothers' deaths.

Apostleship as Compensation (1945)

One of the few instances in Church history of an Apostle being dropped from the Quorum of the Twelve was that of Matthias Cowley who, because of a disagreement with the Church leadership over the issue of plural marriage, resigned from the Quorum in 1905. He was disfellowshipped in 1911, and although restored to full fellowship in 1936, he was never restored to the Quorum. George Albert Smith had felt that he should have been, so when Brother Smith became President of the Church in 1945, he presented the name of Matthew Cowley, Matthias's son, as an Apostle. The Prophet reportedly told Matthew's sister, "The mills of the gods grind slowly, but they grind exceeding fine."

The Opposer (1945)

Many Latter-day Saints who object to international organizations that are perceived as threats to American sovereignty often look to J. Reuben Clark as a spiritual and intellectual ally. There is no question that Clark was a great spiritual leader and a perceptive critic of social and political events. As a leading international lawyer, he was given important federal positions by seven American presidents as well as serving in the First Presidency of the Church for twenty-seven years. He was highly respected for his integrity and intelligence throughout the Church hierarchy in spite of his consistent opposition to what most Church leaders believed worthy of support—specifically the League of Nations, the New Deal, the United Nations, NATO, and support of conscientious objectors in war time.

Seventh on Execution List (1945)

Brother Vivian Meik's name on the list became only a footnote when World War II ended. As a world-traveling English war reporter, Brother Meik's war stories had prompted Mussolini to put a price on his head, and Hitler's propaganda chief, Joseph Goebbels, allegedly placed Meik seventh on the list of those to be executed after Hitler conquered Great Britain. At the time Meik worked for *London's People*, a newspaper with one of the largest circulations in the world. Meik's investigation of the LDS Church welfare system, in which he could find no fault, led him to investigate the Church for personal reasons and to join. He thereafter immigrated to Utah and joined the staff of the Church-owned newspaper, the *Deseret News*, in the summer of 1947.

Two Approaches to the Future (1945)

When World War II ended, George Albert Smith visited President Truman to enlist the government's cooperation in sending supplies to impoverished Europeans. When Truman asked how long it would take to get the supplies ready, Smith could not resist a political jab at the New Deal farm policy, but with a smile said, "When the United States Government was advising people to kill their pigs and refuse to plant grain we were building warehouses and granaries and root cellars, and during the war we have been filling these until we have plenty on hand." Truman smiled and offered the government's help in expediting the goods.

Denmark Was an Exception (1945)

When the war ended in Europe in 1945, its people, including thousands of Latter-day Saints, were impoverished. The outstanding exception was Denmark, where the people seemed to be well off with plenty to eat. In fact, the Danish Saints had even sent welfare packages to distressed Latter-day Saints in Holland and Norway. Even more amazing, membership had actually increased and tithing receipts in the Danish Mission had more than doubled. The Danish Saints considered their circumstances a direct fulfillment of a prophecy Elder Joseph Fielding Smith had made at the outbreak of the war—that "because Denmark had allowed missionaries being evacuated from Germany and Czechoslovakia to enter, its people would not suffer for lack of food during the war."

"They're Both Hot" (1945)

George Albert Smith is one of the lesser-known Church Presidents just as he was to many when he took office in 1945. His associates soon leaned, however, of not only his great love for his people but also of his sense of humor. Because of poor eyesight, Smith had his secretary Arthur Haycock open and read his mail to him. One letter especially caused his secretary to laugh. When questioned by the President, he quoted the author of the letter that asked, "What is the authoritative position of the Church in regard to cocoa and cremation." President Smith could not resist answering such a question: "Well, they're both hot."

"Baby of Promise" (1947)

When Bishop Sam Lee died in 1947, he had certainly fulfilled the family denomination of "baby of promise," not just by his exemplary life and faithful callings in the Church, but by his very survival that was important to the entire Church. He was born prematurely in 1875, the twelfth child born to his parents. The first eleven died at childbirth and Sam's mother died at his birth. The baby was so tiny that a finger ring could be slipped over his arm—but he lived. His great promise had yet to be fulfilled, and it was not jut that his father's posterity depended on Samuel. At the time of his passing, he had over twenty-five descendants, but even more important to Latter-day Saints, one of his sons was Harold B. Lee, a prophet of the Lord.

The "Last" Patriarch (1947)

At the time of the Prophet Joseph, the second most important office in the Church was Presiding Patriarch, the only inherited office. Holders of that office were sustained as "prophets, seers and revelators" along with the Apostles and members of the First Presidency. That office has now been vacant since the October Conference in 1979 when the First Presidency announced that "because of the large increase in the number of stake patriarchs and the availability of patriarchal service throughout the world, we now designate Elder Eldred G. Smith as a Patriarch Emeritus, which means that he is honorably relieved of all duties and responsibilities pertaining to the office of Patriarch to the Church."

Let's Not Be Technical! (1950)

Toward the end of his life, President George Albert Smith, who had suffered from a chronic illness for the last forty years, was losing his appetite for food. On a trip to Hawaii in 1950 for rest and recovery, his daughters tried to consider a meal that would appeal to their father. A suggestion was capon cooked in burgundy, to which he readily agreed. When Emily, mindful of her father's scrupulous adherence to the Word of Wisdom, reminded him that the capon was cooked in burgundy, he responded with a grin, "I don't care if it's cooked in Australia, I want some."

From Show Ranch to Church Farm (1950)

The Church of Jesus Christ of Latter-day Saints owns numerous properties throughout the world—some of them income producing and some for the Church Welfare System. A gem in the latter category is a farm in southern

California formerly owned by Louis B. Mayer, noted motion picture producer. Mayer spent at least 2.5 million dollars in developing the property into a famous racehorse-breeding farm before selling the property to the Statler Hotel interests from whom ten LDS stakes in southern California bought it as their welfare farm. This profitable farm that produces milk, beef, poultry, and hogs was referred to by Elder Henry D. Moyle of the Council of the Twelve as "far beyond the imagination of any of us in the welfare program."

"Most Difficult Mission Field" (1951)

There are still churches that refuse to recognize the Christianity of the restored Church or its increasing acceptance by society. A pamphlet published by the Presbyterians in Utah in the 1920s noted that in a state with 500,000 citizens, but only 10,000 "Christians," there was a pressing need for missionary work in "one of the most difficult mission fields in the United States." And in the 1940s the Catholic Church distributed a publication noting that in no other place in the United States was there such a need for expanded Catholic activity. But the optimism for eventual victory by such churches was still evident, although declining, when the Baptist Home Mission Society wrote in 1951, "We are not going to wipe out the Mormon empire within the foreseeable future."

"Today I Found One!" (1951)

David O. McKay, who became President of the Church in 1951, seemed to inspire respect by non-members in all walks of life. On his return from a trip to Europe, a *United Press* reporter and a photographer who was used to the harshest type of work in New York met him at the airport. Returning to his office, the photographer was chided by his boss for the huge number of photos he had taken and answered curtly that he (the photographer) would pay for them. When asked later what had happened, the photographer replied that as a child his mother had read to him stories of God's prophets and he had always wondered what a prophet of God must really look like. "Today I found one!" was his answer.

References

Adams, Charles P. and Gustive O. Larson. "A Study of the LDS Church Historian's Office, 1830-1900." *Utah Historical Quarterly*, Vol. 40, No. 4, Fall 1972.

Alexander, Thomas G. "Wilford Woodruff, Intellectual Progress, and the Growth of an Amateur Scientific and Technological Tradition in Early Territorial Utah." *Utah Historical Quarterly*, Vol. 59, No. 2, Spring 1991.

———. *Mormonism in Transition*. Urbana and Chicago: University of Illinois Press, 1996.

Allen, James B. "The Historians' Corner." BYU Studies, Vol. 15, No. 1, Fall 1974.

———. "Person Faith and Public Policy: Some Timely Observations on the League of Nations Controversy in Utah." BYU Studies, Vol. 14, No. 1, Autumn 1973.

Anderson, Edward H." The Bureau of Information." *Improvement Era*, Vol. Xxv, No. 2, December 1921.

Anderson, Nels. *Desert Saints: The Mormon Frontier in Utah*. Chicago: University of Chicago Press, 1966.

Arrington, J. Earl. "William Weeks, Architect of the Nauvoo Temple," *BYU Studies*, Vol. 19, No. 3.

Arrington, Leonard J., *Brigham Young: American Moses*. New York: Alfred A. Knopf, 1985.

———. *Great Basin Kingdom*. Lincoln, Nebraska: University of Nebraska Press, 1966.

———. "Persons for All Seasons: Women in Mormon History." BYU Studies, Vol. 20, No. 1.

———. "Willard Young: The Prophet's Son at West Point." Dialogue, Winter 1969, Vol. 4, No. 4.

Arrington, Leonard J. and Davis Bitton. *The Mormon Experience: A History of the Latter-day Saints*. New York: Alfred A. Knopf, 1979.

———. *Saints Without Halos*. Salt Lake City: Signature Books, 1981.

Arrington, Leonard J., Feramorz Fox, and Dean L. May. *Building the City of God*. Salt Lake City: Deseret Book Co., 1976.

Arrington, Leonard J. and Jon Haupt. "The Mormon Heritage of Vardis Fisher." BYU Studies, Vol. 18, No. 1, Fall 1977.

Arrington, Leonard J. and Susan Arrington Madsen. *Sunbonnet Sisters*. Salt Lake City: Bookcraft, 1984.

Ashton, Wendell J. *Theirs Is the Kingdom*. Salt Lake City: Bookcraft, 1945.

———. *Voice in the West: Biography of a Pioneer Newspaper.* New York: Duell, Sloan & Pearce, 1950.

As *Women of Faith: Talks Selected from the BYU Women's Conference.* Salt Lake City: Deseret Book Col, 1989.

Bailey, Paul. *Wakara, Hawk of the Mountains.* Los Angeles: Westernlore Press, 1954.

———. *Wovoka, The Indian Messiah.* Los Angeles: Westernlore Press, 1957.

Bancroft, Hubert Howe. *History of Utah.* San Francisco: The History Company, 1890.

Bashore, Melvin L. "The 1876 Arsenal Hill Explosion." *Utah Historical Quarterly,* Vol. 52, No. 3, 1984.

Barrett, Ivan J. *Heroic Mormon Women.* American Fork, Utah: Covenant Publications, 2000.

Bennett, Richard E. *We'll Find the Place: The Mormon Exodus 1846-1848.* Salt Lake City: Deseret Book Co., 1997.

Bennion, Kenneth S. "October in Southern Utah." *Improvement Era,* Vol. 31, No. 12, 1928.

Berrett, William E. *The Restored Church,* 7th ed. Salt Lake City: Deseret Book Co., 1953.

Berrett, William E. and Alma P. Burton. *Readings in L.D.S. Church History from Original Manuscripts.* (3 vols.) Salt Lake City: Deseret Book Co., 1955.

Betenson, Lulu Parker (as told to Dora Flack). *Butch Cassidy, My Brother.* Provo, Utah: B.Y.U. Press, 197.5.

Bigler, David L. and Will Bagley (eds.). *Army of Israel, Mormon Battalion Narratives.* Logan, Utah: Utah State University Press, 2000.

Birney, Hoffman. *Zealots of Zion.* Philadelphia, Pennsylvania: Penn Publishing Co., 1931.

Black, Susan Easton, *Who's Who in the Doctrine and Covenants,* Salt Lake City: Bookcraft, 1997.

Black, Susan Easton and Larry C. Porter (eds.). *Lion of the Lord.* Salt Lake City: Deseret Book Co.,1995.

Book Reviews. BYU Studies, Vol. 31, No. 1, Winter 1991.

Booth, Major C. C. "Lyman Wight, in Early Texas," *Improvement Era,* Vol. 57, No. 1.

Brewster, Hoyt W., Jr. *Martyrs of the Kingdom.* Salt Lake City: Bookcraft, 1990.

Britsch, R. Lanier *Unto the Islands of the Sea: A History of the Latter-day Saints in the Pacific.* Salt Lake City: Deseret Book Co., 1986.

Brooks, Juanita (ed.) .2 vols., *On The Mormon Frontier: The Diary of Hosea Stout*. Salt Lake City: University of Utah Press, 1964.

Brown, James S.,*Giant of the Lord: Life of a Pioneer*. Salt Lake City: Bookcraft, Inc., 1960.

Buchanan, Frederick S., "The Ebb and Flow of Mormonism in Scotland, 1840-1900." BYU Studies, Vol. 27, No. 2.

Bush, Lester E., Jr. *Health and Medicine Among the Latter-day Saints*. New York: Crossroad Publishing Co., 1993.

Bushman, Richard L. *Joseph Smith and the Beginnings of Mormonism*. Urbana, Illinois: University of Illinois Press, 1984.

Callis, Charles A. "Among the Catawbas," *Improvement Era*, Vol. Xxxix, No. 7, July 1936.

Cannon, Brian. "The Sego Lily, Utah's State Flower." *Utah Historical Quarterly*, Vol. 63, No. 1, Winter 1995.

Cannon, Donald Q. and Llyndon W. Cook (eds.). *Far West Record*. Salt Lake City: Deseret Book Co., 1983.

Cannon, Donald Q. and David J. Whittaker (eds.). *Supporting Saints: Life Stories of Nineteenth-Century Mormons*. Provo: BYU Religious Studies Center, 1985.

Carmack, Noel A. "Before the Flapper: The Utah Beginnings of John Held, Jr." *Utah Historical Quarterly*, Vol. 66, No. 4, Fall 1998.

Carroll, Elsie C. "The Family of Jonathan Heaton." *Improvement Era*, Vol. 32, No. 6, April 1929.

Carter, Kate B. (ed.). *An Enduring Legacy*. Salt Lake City: DUP, 1979.

———. *Heart Throbs of the West*. Salt Lake City: DUP, 1949.

———. *Our Pioneer Heritage*. Salt Lake City: DUP, 1958-75.

Chamberlain, Solomon. Autobiography, BYU Archives and Manuscripts, Writings of Early Latter-day Saints.

Cheney, Thomas E. (ed), *Mormon Songs from the Rocky Mountains*. Austin, Texas: University of Texas Press, 1968.

Christy, Howard A., " 'What Virtue there Is in Stone' and Other Pungent Talk on the Early Utah Frontier." *Utah Historical Quarterly*, Summer 1991.

———. "Weather, Disaster, and Responsibility: An Essay on the Willie and Martin Handcart Story." BYU Studies, Vol. 37, No. 1.

Church History in the Fulness of Times. The Church of Jesus Christ of Latter-day Saints, 1989.

"The Church Moves On," *Improvement Era*, 1941, Vol. 44, No. 2, February 1941.

Clark, James R. (ed.). *Messages of the First Presidency* (3 vols). Salt Lake City: Bookcraft Inc., 1966.

Coates, Lawrence C. "Brigham Young and Mormon Indian Policies:

The Formative Period, 1836-1851," BYU Studies, Spring 1978.

Compton, Todd. *In Sacred Loneliness: The Plural Wives of Joseph Smith*. Salt Lake City: Signature Books, 1997.

Conkling, J. Christopher. *A Joseph Smith Chronology*. Salt Lake City: Deseret Book Co., 1979.

Cooley, Everett L. *Utah Historical Quarterly*. Summer, 1970.

Cornwall, J. Spender. *Stories of Our Mormon Hymns*. Salt Lake City: Deseret Book, Co., 1975.

Cowan, Richard O. *The Church in the Twentieth Century*. Salt Lake City: Bookcraft, 1985.

Cowley, Matthias F. *Wilford Woodruff: History of His Life and Labors*. Salt Lake City: Bookcraft Incl., 1964.

Cracroft, Richard. "The Gentle Blasphemer: Mark Twain, Holy Scripture and the Book of Mormon." BYU Studies, Vol., 11, No. 1.

D'arc, James V. "Darryl F. Zanuck's Brigham Young: A Film in Context." BYU Studies, Vol. 29, 1989.

"David White Rogers of New York." BYU Studies, Vol. 35, No. 2.

Davidson, Alexander and Bernard A. Stuve. *A Complete History of Illinois from 1673 to 1873*. Springfield: Illinois Journal Company, 1874.

Dawson, Janice P. "Chautauqua and the Utah Performing Arts." *Utah Historical Quarterly*, Vol. 58, No. 2, Spring 1990.

Day, Robert B. *They Made Mormon History*. Salt Lake City: Deseret Book Co., 1973.

Derr, Jill Mulway, "The Significance of 'O My Father' in the Personal Journey of Eliza R. Snow," BYU Studies, Vol. 36, No. 1.

Devitry-Smith, John. "The Wreck of the Julia Ann," BYU Studies, Vol. 29, No. 1.

Doxey, Roy W. *Latter-day Prophets and the Doctrine and Covenants* (3 vols.)Salt Lake City: Deseret Book Co., 1978],

Dunn, Richard J. "Dickens and the Mormon." BYU Studies, Vol. 8, No. 3.

Ehat, Andrew F. and Lyndon W. Cook (eds.). *The Words of Joseph Smith*. Provo, Utah: BYU Religious Studies Center, 1980.

Elders' Journal (Southern States Mission). Chattanooga, Tennessee: Ben E. Rich, Publisher, 1906.

Ellsworth, Richard G. "The Dilemma of a Pernicious Zion." BYU Studies. Vol. 8, No. 4.

Evans, Richard L. *A Century of "Mormonism" in Great Britain*. Salt Lake City: Publishers Press, 1984.

"Events of the Month." *Improvement Era*, Vol. Vii, No. 11, September 1904.

Fales, Susan L. and Chad J. Flake. *Mormons and Mormonism in U. S. Government Documents*. Salt Lake City: University of Utah Press, 1989.

Fitzpatrick, Doyle C. *The King Strang Story: A Vindication of James J. Strang, the Beaver Island Mormon King*. Lansing, Mich.: National Heritage, 1970.

Flake, Lawrence R. *Prophets and Apostles of the Last Dispensation*. Provo, Utah: BYU Religious Studies Center, 2001.

———. "A Shaker View of a Mormon Mission." BYU Studies, Vol. 20, No. 1.

Galbraith, David B., D. Kelly Ogden, and Andrew C. Skinner. *Jerusalem: The Eternal City*, Salt Lake City: Deseret Book Co., 1996.

Garr, Arnold K. *Christopher Columbus: A Latter-day Saint Perspective*. Provo: BYU Religious Studies Center, 1992.

Garr, Arnold K., Donald O. Cannon, and Richard, O. Cowan. *Encyclopedia of Latter-day Saint History*. Salt Lake City: Deseret Book Co., 2000.

Gates, Susa Young. *The Life Story of Brigham Young*. New York: Macmillan, 1930.

Gentry, Leland H. "The Land Question at Adam-Ondi-Ahman," BYU Studies, Vol. 26, No. 2, Spring, 1986.

Gerlach, Larry R. "The Best in the West? Corinne, Utah's First Baseball Champions." *Utah Historical Quarterly*. Spring 1994.

Gibbons, Francis M. *John Taylor: Mormon Philosopher, Prophet of God*. Salt Lake City: Deseret Book Co., 1985.

Givens, George W. *In Old Nauvoo: Everyday Life in the City of Joseph*. Salt Lake City: Deseret Book Co., 1990.

Givens, Terryl L. *By the Hand of Mormon*. New York: Oxford University Press, 2002.

"Gladstone." *Improvement Era*. Vol. 1, No. 8, June 1898.

Godfrey, Kenneth W. "Charles W. Penrose and His Contributions to Utah Statehood." *Utah Historical Quarterly*, Vol. 64, No. 4, Fall 1990.

———. "Crime and Punishment in Mormon Nauvoo, 1839-1846." BYU Studies, Vol. 32, No. 1 & 2.

———. "A New Look at the Alleged Little Known Discourse by Joseph Smith." Fn, BYU Studies, Vol. 9, No. 1.

Grant, Heber J. Conference Report. April 1924.

Grant, Heber J. Conference Report. April 1926.

Greeley, Horace. *An Overland Journey from New York to San*

Francisco in the Summer of 1859. New York: Alfred A. Knopf, 1964.

Green, Doyle F. "Welfare Ranch." *Improvement Era*, Vol. 54, No. 8, August 1951.

Gregory, Thomas J. "Sidney Rigdon: Post Nauvoo." BYU Studies, Vol. 21, No. 1.

Gunn, Stanley R. *Oliver Cowdery: Second Elder and Scribe*. Salt Lake City: Bookcraft, 1962.

Gunnison, Lieut. J. W. *The Mormons or Latter-Saints*. Philadelphia: J.B.Lippincott and Co., 1856.

Halton, Harry J. "America's First Department Store." *Improvement Era*, Vol. 43, 1940.

Harmer, Mabel. *Our Utah Pioneers*. Salt Lake City: Deseret, 1966.

Heinerman, Joseph. "Reed Smoot's 'Secret Code.'" *Utah Historical Quarterly*, Vol. 57, No. 3, Summer 1989.

Hickman, Bill. *Brigham's Destroying Angel*. Salt Lake City: Shepherd Publishing Company, 1904.

Hicks, Michael. "Ministering Minstrels: Blackface Entertainment in Pioneer Utah," *Utah Historical Quarterly*. Vol., 58, No. 1., Winter 1990.

———. *Mormonism and Music: A History*. Urbana and Chicago: University of Illinois Press, 1989.

Hinckley, Bryant S. *Daniel Hanmer Wells*. Salt Lake City: Deseret News Press, 1942.

Hinckley, Gordon B. *What of the Mormons?* Salt Lake City: Deseret Book Co., 1947.

"The Historian's Corner," BYU Studies, Vol. 23 (1983), No. 1.

Holzapfel, Richard Neitzel. *Every Stone a Sermon*. Salt Lake City: Bookcraft: Bookcraft, 1992], 101.

Holzapfel, Richard Neitzel and T. Jeffery Cottle. *Old Mormon Palmyra and New England*. Santa Ana, California: Fieldbrook Productions, Inc., 1991.

Hunt, Andrew. "Beyond the Spotlight: The Red Scare in Utah." *Utah Historical Quarterly*, Vol. 61, No. 4, Fall 1993.

Hunter, Milton R. *Archaeology and the Book of Mormon*. Salt Lake City: Deseret Book Co., 1956.

Iverson, Joan H. "The Tabernacle Choir." *Improvement Era*, Vol. 58, No. 8, 1955.

Jenson, Andrew. *Church Chronology: A Record of Important Events Pertaining to the History of The Church of Jesus Christ of Latter-day Saints*. Salt Lake City: Deseret News, 1914.

———. *Encyclopedic History of the Church of Jesus Christ of Latter-*

day Saints. Salt Lake City: Deseret News Pub. Co., 1941.

——— (ed.). *The Historical Record, a Monthly Periodical* (vol. 5, 7 and 8). Salt Lake City: Pub. By Andrew Jenson, 1888.

———. *Latter-day Saint Biographical Encyclopedia* (4 vols.) Salt Lake City: Western Epics, 1971.

Jessee, Dean C.(ed.). *Letters of Brigham Young to His Sons*. Salt Lake City: Deseret Book Co., 1974.

———. John Taylor. *Nauvoo Journal*. Provo, Utah: Grandin Book Company, 1996.

———."Joseph Knight's Recollection of Early Mormon History," BYU Studies, vol. 17, No. 1, Autumn 1976.

———. "The Writing of Joseph Smith's History." BYU Studies, Vol. 11, No. 4, Summer 1971.

Journal of Discourses (JD) (26 vols.). Liverpool: Pub. By John Henry Smith, 1884, Reprint, BYU Library (ed. & compiled—1959).

Journal of Mormon History. Vol. 29, No. 1, Spring 2003.

"Journal of Thomas Bullock (1816-1885)." BYU Studies, Vol, 31, 31 August 1845 to 5 July 1846.

Kane, Elizabeth Wood. *Twelve Mormon Homes*. Salt Lake City: University of Utah Library, 1974.

Kimball, Stanley B. *Heber C. Kimball, Mormon Patriarch and Pioneer*. Urbana,Illinois: University of Illinois Press, 1981.

Langley, Harold D. (ed.). *To Utah With the Dragoons and Glimpses of Life in Arizona and California 1858-1859*. Salt Lake City: University of Utah Press, 1974.

Larson, Gustive O. *The "Americanization" of Utah for Statehood*. San Marino, California: Huntington Library, 1971.

———. *Prelude to the Kingdom*. Francestown, N. H.: Marshall Jones Company, 1947.

Launius, Roger D. "Crossroads of the West: Aviation Comes to Utah, 1910-1940." *Utah Historical Quarterly*, Vol., 58, No. 2, Spring 1990.

"Life and Character Sketch of Lorenzo Snow." *Improvement Era*, Vol. Ii, No. 7, May 1899.

Lindsay, John S. *The Mormons and the Theatre*. Salt Lake City: n.p., 1905.

Littlefield, Lyman Omer. *Reminiscences of Latter-day Saints*. Logan, Utah: 1888, (fr. GospeLink 2001)

Ludlow, Daniel H. (ed.). *Encyclopedia of Mormonism,* 4 vols., New York: Macmillan, 1992.

Lundwall, N. B. (comp). *Temples of the Most High*. Salt Lake City: Bookcraft, 1993.

Madsen, Brigham D. *The Shoshoni Frontier and the Bear River Massacre.* Salt Lake City: University of Utah Press, 1985.

Madsen, Carol Cornwall. *Journey to Zion: Voices from the Mormon Trail.* Salt Lake City: Deseret Book Co., 1997.

———. "The Nineteenth Century Church." *Sunstone.* Vol. 6, No. 6.

———. "Sisters at the Bar: Utah Women in Law." *Utah Historical Quarterly, Summer* 1993, Vol. 61, No. 3.

Madsen, Truman G. *Defender of the Faith: The B. H. Roberts Story.* Salt Lake City: Bookcraft, 1980.

Mann, Mary. "Hollywood Comes to Zion." *Improvement Era*, Vol. 11, No. 10, October 1937.

Marquardt, Michael. "An Appraisal of Manchester as Location for the Organization of the Church," *Sunstone*, 16 (February 1992).

McClintock, James H. *Mormon Settlement in Arizona.* Phoenix: Manufacturing Stationers Inc., 1921.

McConkie, Bruce R. *Mormon Doctrine.* Salt Lake City: Bookcraft, 1966.

McCusker, John J. "How Much Is That in Real Money?" *McCusker's Composite Consumer Price Index.* Proceedings of the American Antiquarian Society, October, 1991.

McGavin, E. Cecil. *Nauvoo the Beautiful.*Salt Lake City: Bookcraft, 1972.

McKiernan, F. Mark, Alma R. Blair, and Paul M. Edwards. *The Restoration Movement: Essays in Mormon History.* Lawrence, Kansas: Coronado Press, 1973.

McKiernan, F. Mark and Roger D. Launius (eds.). *An Early Latter Day Saint History: the Book of John Whitmer.* Independence, Missouri: Herald Publishing House, 1980.

Metcalf, Warren. "A Precarious Balance: The Northern Utes and the Black Hawk War." *Utah Historical Quarterly.* Winter 1989, Vol. 57, No. 1.

Mill, John Stuart. *On Liberty and Other Essays.* New York: Oxford University Press, 1991.

"Monument at Pioneer View." *Improvement Era*, Vol. Xxiv, No. 11. September 1921.

Mooney, James. "The Ghost Dance Religion and the Sioux Outbreak of 1890," Annual Report of the Bureau of American Ethnology 14 (1892-1893).

Morgan, Dale L. *The Great Salt Lake.* Indianapolis and New York: Bobbs-Merrill Company, 1947.

Morton, Sunny McClelland. "The Forgotten Daughter: Julia Murdock Smith." *Mormon Historical Studies.* Vol. 3, No. 1.

Newell, Linda King and Valeen Tippetts Avery. *Mormon Enigma: Emma Hale Smith*. Champaign, Illinois: University of Illinois Press, 1994.

Nibley, Hugh. *Tinkling Cymbals and Sounding Brass: The Art of Telling Tales About Joseph Smith and Brigham Young*. Salt Lake City and Provo: Deseret Book Co., Foundation for Ancient Research and Mormon Studies, 1991.

———. *Brigham Young: The Man and His Work*. Salt Lake City: Deseret Book Co., 1970.

Oaks, Dallin H. and Marvin S. Hill. *Carthage Conspiracy: The Trial of the Accused Assassins of Joseph Smith*. Urban, Illinois: Univ. of Illinois Press, 1980.

Oviatt, Joan. *Amazing But True Mormon Stories*. Bountiful, Utah: Horizon Pub., 1994.

Panek, Tracey E. "Life at Iosepa, Utah's Polynesian Colony." *Utah Historical Quarterly*, Vol. 60, No. 2, Winter 1992.

Patton, Annaleone D. *California Mormons by Sail and Trail*. Salt Lake City: Deseret Book Company, 1961.

Peterson, Janet and LeRene Gaunt. *Elect Ladies*. Salt Lake City: Deseret Book Co., 1990.

Peterson, Paul H. *The Mormon Reformation*. A Dissertation Presented to the Department of History, BYU, Published by the Joseph Fielding Smith Institute, Provo, Utah: 2002.

Poll, Richard D., Thomas G. Alexander, Eugene E. Campbell, and David E. Miller. *Utah's History*. Logan, Utah: Utah State University Press, 1989.

Pratt, Parley P.(ed.). *Autobiography of Parley P. Pratt*. Salt Lake City: Deseret Book Company, 1973.

Proctor, Scot Facer and Maurine Jensen Proctor (eds.). *The Revised and Enhanced History of Joseph Smith by His Mother*. Salt Lake City: Bookcraft, 1996.

Pusey, Merlo J. *Builders of the Kingdom*. Provo, Utah: BYU Press, 1981.

Pyper, George D. *The Romance of the Old Playhouse*. Salt Lake City: Deseret New Press, 1937.

Quinn, D. Michael. "The Mormon Succession Crisis of 1844." BYU Studies, Vol. 16, No. 1, Autumn 1975.

———. "Conscientious Objectors or Christian Soldiers?" *Sunstone*, Vol. 10, No. 2, March 1985.

Reeve, W. Paul. "A Little Oasis in the Deseret: Community Building in Hurricane, Utah, 1860-1920." *Utah Historical Quarterly*, Vol. 62, No. 3, Summer 1994.

Reinwand, Louis. "Andrew Jenson, Latter-day Saint Historian." BYU Studies, Vol. 14, No. 1, Fall 1973.

Reynolds, Noel B. (ed.) *Book of Mormon Authorship Revisited.* Provo, Utah: F.A.R.M.S., 1997.

Rich, Ben. E. *Scrap Book of Mormon Literature* (2 vols.) Chicago: Henry C. Etten & Co., n.d.

Rich, Russell R. *Ensign to the Nations.* Provo, Utah: BYU Pub., 1972.

Richards, Paul C. "The Salt Lake Temple Infrastructure: Studying It Out in Their Minds." BYU Studies, Vol., 36, No. 2, 1996-1997.

Roberts, B. H. *A Comprehensive History of the Church* (6 vols.) Provo: B.Y.U. Press, 1965.

———. *The Missouri Persecutions.* Salt Lake City: Bookcraft, 1965.

Robinson, Phil. *Sinners and Saints.* Boston: Roberts Brothers, 1883.

Robison, Elvin C. *The First Mormon Temple.* Provo, Utah: Brigham Young University Press, 1997.

Romney, Thomas Cottam. *The Mormon Colonies in Mexico.* Salt Lake City: Deseret Book Co., 1938.

"Sail and Rail Pioneers Before 1869," BYU Studies. Vol, 35, No. 2, 1995.

Schindler, Harold. "Frederick Benteen and the Fort Damn Shame." *Utah Historical Quarterly*, Vol. 66, No. 3, Summer 1998.

Seifrit, William C. "The Prison Experience of Abraham H. Cannon." *Utah Historical Quarterly*, Summer 1985.

Sharp, James P. and Glynn Bennion. "One Indian's Vengeance." *Improvement Era.* February 1936, Vol. 39, No. 2.

Shipp, Richard Cottam (ed.). *Champions of Light.* Orem, Utah: Randall Book Co., 1983.

Smith, George Albert. Conference Report, October 1945. First Day— Morning Meeting.

Smith, George D. (ed.). *An Intimate Chronicle: The Journals of William Clayton.* Salt Lake City: Signature Books, 1995.

Smith, Joseph Fielding. *Answers to Gospel Questions*, 5 vols. Salt Lake City: Deseret Book Co., 1957-1966.

———. *Church History and Modern Revelation*, 4 vols. Salt Lake City: The Church of Jesus Christ of Latter-day Saints, 1946-1949.

———. *Doctrines of Salvation*, 3 vols., Salt Lake City: Bookcraft, 1954-1956.

Snow, Eliza R. *Biography and Family Record of Lorenzo Snow.* Salt Lake City: Deseret News, 1884l.

Sonne, Conway B. *Saints on the Seas: A Maritime History of Mormon Migration.* Salt Lake City: University Of Utah Press, 1983.

Sorenson, Victor. "The Wasters and Destroyers: Community-sponsored Predator Control in Early Utah Territory," *Utah Historical Quarterly*, Winter 1994, Vol. 62, No. 1.

Spencer, Clarissa Young and Mabel Harmer. *Brigham Young at Home*. Salt Lake City: Deseret News Press, 1947.

Sperry Symposium on the Doctrine and Covenants and Church History, *The Heavens Are Open*. Salt Lake City: Deseret Book Co., 1993.

Stanley, Reva. *The Archer of Paradise*. Caldwell, Idaho: Caxton Printers, Ltd., 937.

Stout, Wayne. *The History of Utah* (2 vols). Salt Lake City: n.p., 1967.

Stuy, Brian H. (ed.). *Collected Discourses* (5 vols.) Burbank, California and Woodland Hills, Utah: B.H.S. Publishing, 1987-1992.

Talmage, Dr. James E., "Were They Crickets or Locusts, and When Did They Come?" *Improvement Era*, December 1909.

Taylor, P.A.M. *Expectations Westward: The Mormons and the Emigration of Their British Converts in the Nineteenth Century*. Ithaca, New York: Cornell University Press, 1966.

Taylor, Samuel W. *The Kingdom or Nothing: The Life of John Taylor, Militant Mormon*. New York: Macmillan Pub. Co., 1976.

Taylor, Troy. *Down in the Darkness*. Alton, Illinois: Whitechapel Productions, 2003.

Tobler, Douglas F. and Nelson B. Wadsworth. *The History of the Mormons*. New York: St. Martin's Press, 1989.

Topping, Gary. "Zane Grey in Zion: An Examination of His Supposed Anti-Mormonism." BYU Studies, Vol, 18, No. 4.

Trautmann, Frederic (ed.). "Salt Lake City through a German's Eyes: A Visit by Theodor Kirchhoff, in 1867." *Utah Historical Quarterly*, Vol. 51, No. 1, Winter 1983.

Tuckett, Madge Harris and Belle Harris Wilson, *The Martin Harris Story*. Provo, Utah: Vintage Books, 1983.

Tullidge, Edward W. *Life of Brigham Young or Utah and Her Founders*, 1876.

Tullis, F. LaMond. "A Shepherd to Mexico's Saints: Arwell L. Pierce and the Third Convention." BYU Studies, Vol. 37, No. 1.

Turley, Richard E., Jr. *Victims: The LDS Church and the Mark Hofmann Case*. Urbana and Chicago: University of Illinois Press, 1992.

Tyler, Sergeant Daniel. *A Concise History of the Mormon Battalion in the Mexican War*. Waynesboro, Virginia: M & R Books, 1064.

Utley, Robert M. *Frontiersmen in Blue: The United States Army and the Indian 1848-1865*. New York: Macmillan Publishing Co., 1967.

Van Noord, Roger. *King of Beaver Island: The Life and Assassination of James Jesse Strang*. Urbana: University of Illinois Press, 1988.

Van Wagoner, Richard S. *Mormon Polygamy: a History*. Salt Lake City: Signature Books, 1986.

Van Wagoner, Richard S. and Steven C. Walker. *A Book of Mormons*. Salt Lake City: Signature Books, 1982.

Walker, Ronald W. "A Gauge of the Times: Ensign Peak in the Twentieth Century," *Utah Historical Quarterly*, Vol. 62, No. 1, Winter 1994.

———. "Growing Up in Early Utah." The Wasatch Literary Association, 1874-1878." *Sunstone*, Vol. 6, No. 6.

———. "Young Heber J. Grant's Years of Passage." BYU Studies, Vol. 24, No. 1.

Walker, Ronald W. and Alexander M. Starr. "Shattering the Vase: The Razing of the Old Salt Lake Theater." *Utah Historical Quarterly*, Vol. 57, No. 1, Winter 1989.

Watt, Ronald G. "Sailing 'The Old Ship Zion': The Life of George D. Watt." BYU Studies, Vol. 18, No. 1.

Webster, Noah. *An American Dictionary of the English Language*. New Haven: S. Converse, 1828.

"When the Mormon Battalion Came to Tucson," *Improvement Era*,Vol. Xlix, No. 12, December 1946.

White, Jean Bickmore, "Gentle Persuaders: Utah's First Women Legislators." *Utah Historical Quarterly*, Vol. 38, No. 1, Winter 1970.

Whitney, Helen Mar. *A Woman's View: Helen Mar Whitney's Reminiscences Of Early Church History*. Provo, Utah: BYU Religious Studies Center, 1999.

Widstoe, John A. "Joseph Smith as Philosopher." *Improvement Era*, Vol. Ix, No. 2, December 1905.

Wilcox, Pearl. *The Latter Day Saints on the Missouri Frontier*. Independence, Missouri: n. p., 1972.

Woods, Fred E. *Gathering to Nauvoo*. American Fork, Utah: Covenant Communications, Inc., 2001.

Woodward, Arthur. *Feud On The Colorado*. Los Angeles: Westernlore Press, 1955.

Young, Biloine Whiting. *Obscure Believers: The Mormon Schism of Alpheus Cutler*. St. Paul, Minnesota: Pogo Press, 2002.

2004 Church Almanac. Salt Lake City: Deseret News, 2004.

Index

About the Author

George W. Givens
1932-2004

George W. Givens spent twenty years teaching American History in schools in upstate New York, Arizona, and Virginia before opening what became the largest family-owned bookstore in Virginia. George joined the LDS Church while living in Tucson, Arizona, in 1964. He and his wife Sylvia spent several summers in Nauvoo, Illinois, as in-house historians. They are the parents of eight children.

George developed an avid interest in LDS Church history upon learning of ancestors who joined the Church in upstate New York in 1830. His other published titles include *In Old Nauvoo, The Nauvoo Fact Book, Language of the Mormon Pioneers, The Hired Man's Christmas*, and *500 Little-known Facts in Mormon History*.

George passed away peacefully on June 5, 2004, after a 10-month battle with cancer. He was surrounded by friends and family while listening to "A Poor Wayfaring Man of Grief"—his favorite hymn.

NOTES

NOTES

NOTES

NOTES

NOTES